URDU LANGUAGE AND LITERATURE
Critical Perspectives

URDU LANGUAGE AND LITERATURE
Critical Perspectives

Gopi Chand Narang
Professor of Urdu
University of Delhi
National Fellow, U.G.C.

STERLING PUBLISHERS PRIVATE LIMITED

STERLING PUBLISHERS PRIVATE LIMITED
L-10, Green Park Extension, New Delhi-110016
G-2, Cunningham Apartments, Cunningham Road, Bangalore-560052
Mishradeep, Patliputra Path, Rajendra Nagar, Patna-800016

Urdu Language and Literature: Critical Perspectives
© 1991, Gopi Chand Narang

PRINTED IN INDIA

Published by S.K. Ghai, Managing Director, Sterling Publishers Pvt. Ltd., L-10, Green Park Extension, New Delhi-110016, Laserset at Laser Print, C-10, South Extension Part–II, New Delhi-110049. Printed at Crescent Printing Press, Connaught Circus, New Delhi-110001.

To

My Parents

دفترِ ہستی میں تھی زریں ورق تیری حیات
تھی سراپا دین و دنیا کا سبق تیری حیات
زندگانی تھی تری مہتاب سے تابندہ تر
خوب تر تھا صبح کے تارے سے بھی تیرا سفر
یاد سے تیری دلِ درد آشنا معمور ہے
جیسے کعبے میں دعاؤں سے فضا معمور ہے

Iqbal, 'Wālidah Marhūma kī Yād men'

Preface

THE present volume is a cross-section of the work I have been doing for the last many years. The Urdu language and literature have been a passion with me, not because they are part of my career, but because I have believed that Urdu has certain features and a sense of destiny ordinarily not enjoyed by other languages. From the choice of my subjects, it should be apparent that I started writing in a rather difficult period. At the crack of freedom on a bleak wintry night, my mother with eight children landed in the tumult of Delhi looking for shelter and refuge, where I had sneaked in a year before from the rugged terrains of Baluchistan searching for means to continue my education. The Delhi College was my goal, but in fact, it took me six years to get there. The climate was still charged and discouraging for the studying of Urdu, and it was in this atmosphere of uncertainty and doubt that I started my work. For years I was the only Urdu student at the University of Delhi pursuing graduate studies. The things somewhat changed in the sixties but the difficulties remained, and throughout I had to work against heavy odds. That explains an undercurrent in my work of a search for the Indian roots of Urdu, its indigenous base and the syncretic qualities which have rendered it unique. This search has been a mission with me and I have a conviction that in spite of the brunt Urdu has borne, and the turn of events, and the communalisation of language and politics, Urdu along with Hindi is destined to play a syncretizing role in a pluralistic, secular and democratic India. This is the thrust of most of the studies included here.

The book is divided into four sections, the first dealing with the classical period of Urdu literature, the second with the modern poetry, the third with the modern fiction, and the fourth with the problems of Urdu language and orthography. The intrepid reader of Urdu linguistics may refer to the following two studies done jointly by the author and Prof. Donald A. Becker published elsewhere, and available on microfiche from the sources indicated:

(i)   "Aspiration and Nasalization in the Generative Phonology of Hindi-Urdu", *Language*, New York, Vol. 47, No. 3, September 1971, pp. 646-667.

(ii) "Generative Phonology and the Retroflex Flaps of Hindi-Urdu", *General Linguistics*, Pennsylvania State University Press, University Park, and London, Vol. 14, No. 3 (1974), pp. 129-155.

Since some of the studies appeared in journals and periodicals, of varying kinds both in India and abroad including U.S.A., Canada, U.K. and Czechoslovakia at different times, there is some variance in the transliteration of Urdu words. A consistency has been attempted in vocalics indicating the lengths as evenly as possible, but the consonantals have been left as they are following the general practice. Any inconvenience to the readers on this account is regretted.

I am indebted to Dr. Leslie Flemming for her help with the translation of the sections on Ghalib, and the Modern Urdu Poetry, and to Jai Ratan for Bedi, and the New Urdu Short Story. Translations of Urdu verses in the article on Firaq are by the author and Prof. Richard H. Robinson, and in the article on Faiz by V.G. Kiernan.

I owe a debt of gratitude to Shri Balu Rao, formerly Editor, *Indian Literature*, Sahitya Akademi, for kindly going through the press-copy and making valuable suggestions. I am also grateful to Prof. M. Hanif Kaifi of the Jamia Millia Islamia from whose comments I have benefited. My thanks are also due to the discerning readers whose observations have contributed to the improvement of the studies included in the book, and to Shri O.P Ghai and Shri S.K. Ghai of Sterling Publishers but for whose interest the book would not have appeared in the present form.

Gopi Chand Narang

Acknowledgements

GRATEFUL acknowledgements are made to the editors and publishers of the journals and books in which some of the articles first appeared. They are :

"Ghalib and the Rebellion of 1857", *Indian Literature*, New Delhi, July-August 1972; "The Impact of Islamic Mysticism on Urdu Literature", *Indian Literature*, New Delhi, March-April, 1989; "The Princeton Manuscript of Kulliyat-e-Sauda", *Journal of the American Oriental Society*, Vol. 93, No. 4 (1973); "Some Social and Cultural Aspects of Urdu Masnawiis", *Mahfil*, Chicago, Vol. III, Nos. 2-3 (1964); "The Indian Freedom Struggle and Urdu Poetry", *Indian Literature*, New Delhi, July-August 1986.

"The Sound Structure of Iqbal's Urdu Poetry", *Iqbal Commemorative Volume*, ed., Ali Sardar Jafri and K.S. Duggal, New Delhi 1977, and *The Hindustan Times*, 6 Nov. 1977; "Tradition and Innovation: Firaq Gorakhpuri", *Poetry and Renaissance, Kumaran Asan Birth Centenary Volume*, ed., M.Govindan, Madras 1974, and *New Orient*, Vol. 5, No. 2, Prague 1966; "Tradition and Innovation: Faiz Ahmad Faiz", *Indian Literature,* New Delhi, March-April 1985; "Modern Urdu Poetry: the Indian Panorama", *Indian Poetry Today,* Vol. 4, Indian Council for Cultural Relations, New Delhi 1981.

"Major Trends in the Urdu Short Story", *Indian Literature,* New Delhi, June 1975; "Rajinder Singh Bedi's Art and Style: Metaphorical and Mythical Roots", *Urdu Canada,* Ottawa, Vol. 2, No. 1 (1988); "Krishan Chander: an Impression", *Krishan Chander: Selected Short Stories,* New Delhi 1990.

"The Three Language Formula and Urdu", *Seminar,* New Delhi No. 332, April 1987; "Development and Use of Writing System Across Cultures: The Case of Arabo-Persian Urdu Orthographical Model", *Journal of South Asian and Middle Eastern Studies,* Villanova, Pa., Vol. X, No. 2, Winter 1986.

Contents

1

Ghalib and the Rebellion of 1857

MIRZA GHALIB remained in Delhi throughout the uprising of 1857. He recorded the events of this period, particularly those from 11 May, 1857[1] to 31 July 1858,[2] in his Persian diary, *Dastambū*. His thoughts and feelings about his experiences during the 'Mutiny', however, can be found not only in *Dastambū*, but also in his letters which were written with comparatively greater freedom and boldness.

During the days of the uprising, Ghalib stayed at home with his family.[3] In a letter he wrote: 'Here in this city with my wife and sons, I am swimming in a sea of blood. I haven't stepped over my threshold. Neither have I been caught, thrown out, imprisoned, nor killed.'[4] After the British re-occupied Delhi, however, he began to encounter various difficulties. He was then living in the house of Hakim Mahmood Hasan Khan in the Ballimaran section, and for two days after the capture of the city, neither food nor water was available.[5] On the third day, however, soldiers arrived, sent by the Maharaja of Patiala to protect Hakim Mahmood Khan's property. Through them Ghalib also saved his own house from being looted,[6] but he lost to the victorious army whatever valuables and jewelry his wife had put for safekeeping in Miyan Kale Sahab's cellar.[7] Next, Ghalib was arrested in his home by a few British soldiers and brought before Colonel Burn,[8] who was staying at that time near the house of Haji Qutb ud-Din. He was questioned,[9] but fortunately was released.[10]

On or about the 31st of September, the house of Ghalib's brother, Mirza Yusuf, was looted by British soldiers. On October 19, Mirza Yusuf's old servant informed Ghalib that after five days of fever his brother had died the night before. With neither a shroud, nor a person to bathe the corpse, nor a grave-digger to be had during these days, Mirza Yusuf's funeral and burial were taken care of by Ghalib's neighbours. They, out of concern for his dire situation, arranged the burial with the help of one of Patiala's soldiers.[11]

During the time of the 'Mutiny', many of Ghalib's friends, relatives and students were either murdered, reprimanded by the British, or they had left Delhi after the ruin of their families. For example, both Imam Bukhsh Sahbai and Muhammad Husain Azad's father, Muhammad Baqar, were shot. Maulvi Fazl-e-Haq Khairabadi was sentenced to life imprisonment in the Andaman Islands, and Shaifta to seven years. After the British capture of Delhi, Nawab Zia-ud-Din and Nawab Amin-ud-Din left for Loharu, but had only reached Mehroli when they were robbed.[12] Meanwhile, looters also ransacked their house in Delhi, including a library valued at about Rs. 20,000. In their collection were many of Ghalib's Persian and Urdu works, which were also lost.[13] Muzaffar-ud-Din Haider Khan and Zulfiqar-ud-Din Haider Khan (Husain Mirza) suffered even worse: not only was their house looted, but the curtains and shades were also set on fire and the entire house was razed.[14] In a letter to Yusuf Mirza, Ghalib describes these tragedies:

Only my Lord and Master knows what is really happening to me. People go mad from great sorrow . . . Would it be surprising if I should lose my mind from this onslaught of grief? . . . What grief haven't I suffered: grief in death, in separation, in loss of income, and in honour. Besides the tragic events at the Red Fort, I know so many of my Delhi friends who have been killed: Muzaffar-ud-Daula, Mir Nasar ud-Din, my nephew Mirza Ashur Beg, his twenty-one year old son, Ahmed Mirza, Mustafa Khan ibn-e-Azam-ud-Daula, his two sons, Irtiza Khan and Murtaza Khan; Qazi Faiz Ullah. I feel as if they were members of my own family! And how can I forget Hakim Razi-ud-Din Khan and Mir Ahmad Husain Maikash? Allah! Allah! How can I ever bring them back![15]

He writes in another letter:

Don't think that my grief is only for myself. Of many British whom these filthy natives have murdered, some were my benefactors, some my patrons, others my close comrades, and still others my students. Even among Indians I have lost relatives, friends, students and lovers. Now every one of them is gone. It is so terribly difficult to mourn for a single relative or friend. Think of me who has to mourn for so many. My God! So many of my friends and relatives have died that if now I were to die, not a single soul would be left to mourn for me.[16]

And, finally, Ghalib writes in *Dastambū*:

May the sockets of my eyes be filled with dust if during this tragic time I have seen anything but weeping . . . My sorrows are incurable and my wounds will never heal: I should feel as if I am already dead.[17]

Because of these great personal tragedies, and for other reasons as well, Ghalib has used the harshest of terms in his description of the 'Mutiny'. In *Dastambū* particularly, he denounces the rebellion and, drawing out a chronogram, calls it,

rastakhez-e-be-jā,[18] ('the untimely resurrection'). Eloquently
'memorializing' in *Dastambū* those of his countrymen who
fought against the British, he calls them 'traitors', 'filthy
vagabonds', 'undisciplined people', 'black-faced thieves', and
'black-faced fighters'.[19] He describes the army of Meerut: 'Some
wretched, undisciplined soldiers entered the City (Delhi); they
were extremely cruel and destructive, and, traitors, they were
thirsty for the blood of the British.'[20] In another place, he says:
'How I wish that God would crush their hearts and make their
hands powerless.'[21]

These quotations, however, show only one side. In *Dastambū*
not only did Ghalib deride the 'Mutiny' and denounce the
mutineers, he also lavishly praised the British. Eulogizing them,
he used such terms as 'upright rulers', 'the shining stars in the
sky of leadership', 'lion-hearted conquerors', 'knowledge and
wisdom incarnate,' and 'rulers famous for their virtue and fine
character.'[22]

Having left the protection of just rulers (the British),
Indians are now caught in the traps of beastly men.[23]

Truly we cannot hope for justice under any other
government but that of the British.[24]

Whoever disobeys the orders of the rulers deserves to be
beaten with shoes . . . . It is altogether fitting that we Indians
should bow in front of those blessed by God with good
fortune; obedience to the orders of the rulers is obedience
to God.[25]

After the 'Mutiny', the British put up gallows all over Delhi
and began to hang suspected citizens.[26] Under such conditions,
Ghalib could hardly be expected to have supported the
rebellion and opposed the British; yet, his praise of the British
is astonishingly lavish. What, then, was it that forced Ghalib to
offer so much praise? In answering this question, a study of the
following events should be of interest.

In 1855, Ghalib had sent to England via Lord Canning a Persian *qasīdah* he had written in praise of Queen Victoria. Attached to it was a statement to the effect that as the courts of Turkey and Iran had greatly honoured poets, if the Queen of England would likewise honour him with a title, robe of honour and pension, he would be very grateful. In January, 1856, London replied that his request was being looked into and that he would be informed of the decision.[27] Three months after Ghalib received this reply and began dreaming about being Poet Laureate, the 'Mutiny' broke out.

During the 'Mutiny', a spy by the name of Gauri Shankar secretly informed the British that Ghalib had attended the court held by Bahadur Shah on 18 July 1857 and had recited a *sikkah* (a chronogram commemorating coronation).[28] Thus, after the establishment of peace, when Ghalib began moving to have his pension restored and his place in the *darbār*, he was clearly told by the British that he had maintained relations with the mutineers during the rebellion,[29] and that consequently his pension and *darbār* were suspended. To Abdul Ghafoor he wrote about this: 'The charge of a *sikkah* has hit me like a bullet or a cannon-ball; whom should I speak to, who can testify for me?'[30] Believing that the *sikkah* ascribed to him had actually been presented by Zauq at the coronation of Bahadur Shah in 1837,[31] Ghalib asked his friends for newspapers of 1837, and particularly for a copy of the *Urdū Akhbār*,[32] a newspaper which belonged to Muhammad Husain Azad's father, Maulvi Muhammad Baqar, with whom Zauq had close relations. Feeling that the newspaper would certainly have published the *sikkah* presented by Zauq, Ghalib wrote to Yusuf Mirza:

> If a copy of that issue of the Delhi *Urdū Akhbār* could be found it would certainly be very useful, but actually there isn't any danger. The high authorities will not take this very seriously. I didn't compose the *sikkah,* and if I had, it would have been to save my name and honour. Surely this isn't a crime, and even if it is, is it so great that it can't be erased by a proclamation of clemency? Good God! They

pardon gunpowder-makers, gunners and bank robbers, but they can't even pardon a poet for two lines of poetry![33]

Unfortunately, however, the particular issue of the *Urdū Akhbār* was not found, and Ghalib could not get himself cleared of the charge. Not only had he lost his salary from the Red Fort, but also his pension and *darbār*, and, on top of that, his hope of being named Poet Laureate had vanished as well. Consequently, during this period, Ghalib's financial condition deteriorated. Describing it in *Dastambū*, he wrote: 'I now see no way of getting back the pension I once had from the British. I'm carrying on by selling my bedding and clothing: other people eat bread, I eat clothing.'[34]

At this time what Ghalib needed above all was the renewal of his pension, and this was impossible until the British were convinced of his loyalty. Consequently, after the British recapture of Delhi, Ghalib wrote a Persian *qasīdah* praising Queen Victoria and congratulating the British for their victory. After sending it to the high authorities, he received the reply that it was to be sent through the Chief Commissioner, and, having done this, he was then told that there was no need to send a letter that only contained greetings.[35] This answer deeply depressed Ghalib; consequently he attempted to achieve through *Dastambū* what could not be done by the *qasīdahs*. To Har Gopal Taftah, who was supervising the publication of *Dastambū*, Ghalib wrote:

When you see this manuscript (*Dastambū*) you will understand . . . I shall present one copy to the Governor General of India and through him one copy to her Royal Highness the Queen of England. Now you can guess what the style of the writing is going to be.[36]

Here we clearly see that *Dastambū* was published largely for the sake of expedience. In addition, Ghalib described the occupation of Delhi by the mutineers in only five or six pages, though they remained in control of Delhi for over four months; most scholars maintain that while in the beginning Ghalib described events in detail, after the victory over Delhi it would not have been appropriate to publish the original manuscript. In fact, *Dastambū* was brought out almost solely for the purpose of being presented to the British. As Ghalib puts it, 'The applicant reminds the Overseas Department (Board of Directors) of the East India Company of his rights and desires recognition from the Government.'[37] Ghalib also included in *Dastambū* the Persian *qasīdah* for Queen Victoria, *shumār yāft, rozgār yāft,* and in the end he again clearly stated his intention: 'Would that my three wishes, namely for a title, a robe of honour and a pension be granted by the Blessed Emerald Empress . . . . My eyes and my heart look towards her . . .'[38]

It is also important to note that though Ghalib had been Bahadur Shah's salaried courtier and teacher, in *Dastambū* he has not mentioned him at all, and even the princes are mentioned only in passing.[39] In addition, Ghalib does not mention his two formerly close friends, Fazl-e-Haq Khairabadi and Sadr-ud-Din Azardah (who had signed the proclamation of the 'Holy War' against the British, in punishment for which Fazl-e-Haq Khairabadi was imprisoned for life in the Andaman islands and Azardah's employment was terminated and his property confiscated). The only name Ghalib mentioned was Hakim Ahsan Ullah Khan's who was an accomplice of the British and whose name was highest on the list of traitors![40]

Furthermore, in *Dastambū* Ghalib put all the responsibility for the 'Mutiny' on the 'faithless' sepoys and the 'evil and lawless' soldiers, although he knew full well that in an effort to save their crumbling empires it was actually the Indian ruling classes who had staked everything they had. In some detail Ghalib has described the valiant efforts of the fighters of not only the seven princely states surrounding Delhi, but also of those of Lucknow, Bareilly, Moradabad, Gwalior and Farukhabad.[41] Because he himself was related to the nobility, however, he was loath to throw the entire responsibility for the 'Mutiny' on the ruling groups or on the nobility.

Although Dr. Muhammad Ashraf, in his paper, 'Ghalib and

the Revolt of 1857',[42] has carefully established the historical importance of *Dastambū*, in view of *Dastambū's* demonstrated limitations, we shall not emphasize any further that as far as historical accuracy is concerned, it is not a very important work.

The question remains as to Ghalib's real attitude towards the 'Mutiny'. Did he really consider British Government a blessing or was he sympathetic to the efforts of the Indians who risked their lives for the sake of their country?

In order to answer this question it seems most important to focus on Ghalib's own character. Ghalib, according to Muhammad Ikram, 'was like a true Mughal, who is a leader of the caravan in comfortable times but shrinks back from being a martyr'.[43] In almost every aspect of his life he was a pragmatist rather than an idealist. This fact is further established when we take into account his heritage, his environment, his life-style, and his Urdu and Persian works.

Ghalib was of Turkish descent, and the same blood flowed in his veins as in those of the Mughal kings. Almost from early boyhood, he appreciated the value of grandeur, dignity, position and wealth, and although Providence seldom favoured him, throughout his life he made every effort to fulfil his desires for them. Deeply convinced of the importance of high position and personal respectability, he undertook travels, suffered hardships, and even fought lawsuits. He was extremely ambitious and his keen desire for good life lasted as long as he lived. As he himself said, one must not be a 'fly of honey' (which easily gets stuck), but rather a 'fly of crystal-candy' (which enjoys it and comfortably gets away).[44]

Undoubtedly Ghalib admired British learning and constitutional law, but perhaps more important to him was his own future. His *Jagīr* had been a grant from the British government. On the one hand, he had no deep attachment to Bahadur Shah and the court of the Red Fort, which he likened to a 'morning lamp' soon to be put out.[45] On the other hand, he maintained close relations with several English officers, such as Sterling, Major John Cobe, Sir John McLeod, Metcalf and

Thomas. In some respects he preferred the British law to the Mughal administrative system. Thus, when Sir Sayyid Ahmad Khan sought Ghalib's opinion of his edition of the *Aain-e-Akbari*, the *maṣnawī* that he wrote was critical of the old order rather than laudatory, and consequently was not published with the book. In addition, Ghalib began to align his future with the British during the year preceding the 'Mutiny', when the decision was made to dissolve the Mughal court after the death of Bahadur Shah. We have already spoken, in this connection, of the Persian *qasīdah* in praise of Queen Victoria which he had sent through Lord Canning.

Shortly before the 'Mutiny', Ghalib was not unaware of the growing hatred and unrest towards the British among the people. In this connection we must mention the letters Ghalib wrote to Yusuf Ali Khan, the Nawab of Rampur, which were destroyed on Ghalib's request. *Makātīb-e-Ghālib* contains the letter of 15 February 1857, but about the letter of 8 March 1857, Imtiyaz Ali Arshi says, 'Only the envelope of this letter exists in the file and on the back of it is written: "Letter destroyed by the order (of the Nawab)".' [46] Arshi further states: "Ghalib wrote another letter on 1st April, 1857; again in the file we have only the envelope of this letter, on the back of which is written: "Letter destroyed by the hand (of the Nawab)".' [47] Finally, in the notes to *Makātīb-e-Ghālib,* Arshi has reproduced the letter of the Nawab of Rampur of 23 March 1857, to Ghalib in which he assured Ghalib that, as requested by him, his letter was destroyed:

> Your gratifying letter . . . was received and the contents thereof thoroughly perused. The letter was destroyed . . . Your wishes concerning such letters will continue to be respected in future as well.[48]

Clearly this correspondence was of a confidential nature and it was destroyed at Ghalib's request. What might have been the reason for such a request? It is Arshi's opinion that 'We cannot see any other reason for this request than that these letters had to do with current politics.' [49]

When the 'Mutiny' broke out, Ghalib's correspondence with the Nawab of Rampur was perhaps still going on. As practicality demanded, he continued to maintain relations with the Red Fort as well. Ghalib's statement, however, that he never visited the court during the 'Mutiny' and that he never even left his house[50] seems to be rather inaccurate. To begin with, we have evidence from the Agra newspaper, *Āftāb-e-'Ālamtāb,* that Ghalib continued to maintain relations with Bahadur Shah during the 'Mutiny'. Furthermore, Jivan Lal writing in his diary about the *darbār* of 13 July 1857, states that Mirza Naushah (Ghalib) and Mukarram Ali Khan recited *qasīdahs* in praise of the early victories over the British. Although Ghalib was being charged with a *sikkah* which was not his own, still, we have Jivan Lal's clear evidence that Ghalib actually did compose a *sikkah*, which Khwaja Ahmad Faruqi has now found in the manuscript of Jivan Lal's diary.[51] Thus, Ghalib not only composed a *sikkah,* but also attended the court in the Red Fort regularly. After the British had re-occupied Delhi and things had calmed down, that he would then attach himself to the victorious party is hardly surprising. Furthermore, only a few months before the 'Mutiny', Ghalib had been associated with the Rampur government which had aided the British against the mutineers during the fighting. Since there was a danger that even the slightest doubt of Ghalib's sincerity might result in his relations with Rampur being severed, after the 'Mutiny' he emphasized most strongly that he had remained isolated during the uprising and that he had sincerely wished the British well.[52]

For reasons explained, Ghalib's harsh descriptions of the 'Mutiny' stem particularly from the fact that it destroyed his plans for the future. It does not follow, however, that he was oblivious to the troubles of his countrymen. In his inimitable way, he says at only one place in *Dastambū:*

> The heart is not a piece of iron or stone; how can it not be full? The eyes are not holes in a stone wall that do not shed tears. One must grieve over the deaths of rulers, and weep for the destruction of India.[53]

For Ghalib's real feelings about the 'Mutiny' and the British we must turn to his private letters to friends, which, freed from the need for expedience, display more forcefully his deepest feelings. A few months prior to the 'Mutiny', he wrote, speaking of the annexation of Oudh:

> Think about these evil times we are fated to live in . . . It's true that I am not personally affected, yet, I am saddened by the destruction of Oudh. Surely an Indian who doesn't feel its effect is totally without a sense of justice.[54]

When he later learned that Maharaja of Alwar was being reinstated with full powers, Ghalib who believed in determinism rather than in free will, wrote sarcastically:

> Now we are all in the same boat. I hear that in November the Maharaja is being restored his powers. You may be sure that it is only those powers which Almighty God has conferred on us. For, truly, He can do whatever He pleases, but we are the ones who get blamed. . . . .[55]

Ghalib felt very deeply the terrible cruelties imposed on Indians by the British after the 'Mutiny', and his descriptions of the ruin, both of his class and of the city, are very painful. While he did not, like some other Delhi poets, compose any *shahrāshob* on the city's troubles, still, his letters have such detailed descriptions of the destruction of Delhi and her people that no historian of the period can ignore them. After the reoccupation of Delhi, no one could of course speak out against the British, yet Ghalib (in his letters) points very strongly to their excesses and cruelties. And though he wrote very circumspectly,[56] much of what the conditions must have been in Delhi comes through. A few quotations will suffice:

> You must have heard of the conditions here. If we are still alive and can meet again, the story will be told. Otherwise the story is over. I am afraid to write.[57]

In a letter of 26 December 1857, he wrote to Hakim Ghulam Najaf Khan:

> Think of my situation. I am writing, but what can I write? Can I really write anything, and is it proper to write? This much is true: You and I are still alive. Neither of us should say any more than that.[58]

To Mir Mehdi Majruh, he wrote:

> If we are alive, then we will meet again and the story will be told.[59]

> The city I am in is still called Delhi and this section still called Ballimaran, yet, of all my former friends, I can't find anyone. I'm not exaggerating when I say that rich and poor, all have left, and those that remained have been driven away . . . . Many houses are without lamps.[60]

In another letter Ghalib clearly describes what difficulties the people of Delhi had to endure, and in one part, in which he speaks of the cruelties of the British, we see clearly the intensity and boldness with which he describes the realities of the situation:

> This city has sustained five attacks. The first was that of the army of native sepoys, who robbed the confidence of the people of the city. The second was that of the army of the British who destroyed life, wealth, honour, property, indeed, all the signs of our life.[61]

To Mir Mehdi Majruh, he wrote again:

> Brother, what are you asking? What can I write? Life in Delhi depended on five things: the Red Fort, Chandni Chowk, the daily assembly at the Jama Masjid, the weekly stroll along the Jamna bridge, and the annual gathering of the flower-sellers. No longer are these things to be seen in Delhi . . . Tell me how can there be a Delhi without

them . . . Yes, once in India there used to be a city called Delhi.[62]

And to Ala-ud-Din Ahmad Khan he wrote:

> O God! This is not the Delhi where you were born . . . This is a camp . . . The male members of the royal household whom the sword spared are now each getting Rs. 5 a month as pension. Of the women, the older ones have become madams, and the young ones are prostitutes.[63]

After the 'Mutiny', the British demolished the houses of many of the noblemen. Explaining this as 'the excesses of a monkey with the heart of a lion and the body of an elephant', Ghalib wrote: 'Well done, O Monkey, this violence inside the city.'[64] Ghalib's calling the British 'monkey' is not without amusement.

After the 'Mutiny', particularly severe pressure was put on Muslims.[65] Although the order was given for Hindus to live in Delhi as early as January 1858, Muslims were not permitted to return to the city until much later. Then it was ordered that those Muslims who paid a fine and obtained a permit could, with the approval of the government, enter the city. We may see how forcefully Ghalib ridiculed this unjust action of the British:

> Whether a Muslim can come back to the city depends on how much of the fee he can pay. The government of course decides on how much you will have to pay. They ruin you but they say you are settled again.[66]

In this context, we should especially note the *qat'ah* which Ghalib wrote in a letter to Nawab Ala-ud-Din Ahmad Khan Alai, in which he describes the ruin of Delhi, and in particular, the helpless condition of the Muslims:

> Surely today every English tommy is Almighty God. Now every man going from his house to the *Bazaar* is panic-stricken. The market-place has become a slaughter-house, and the house looks like a prison. The very particles of dust in Delhi thirst for the blood of Muslims.[67]

In short, if we wish to know Ghalib's real attitude towards the 'Mutiny', *Dastambū* is not enough; we must also take his letters into account. At the most, we may take *Dastambū* as Ghalib's 'well-prepared defence', though unfortunately it did not further the cause for which it was written. However, three years later, in May 1860, through the efforts of the Nawab of Rampur,[68] Ghalib's pension was restored, but his dream of being named Poet Laureate never became a reality.

Notes

1. *Dastambū*, p. 9.
2. *Ibid.*, p. 76.
3. *Ibid.*, pp. 11, 26, 27, 34.
4. To Abdul Ghafoor Suroor, *Urdū-e-Mualla*, p. 104.
5. *Dastambū*, p. 32.
6. *Ibid.*, p. 33.
7. *Ibid.*, pp. 73-74.
8. Colonel Burn, Henry Pelham, the Military Governor of Delhi.
9. *Dastambū*, p. 45.
10. Ghalib has mentioned this episode in that selection of his prose and poetry which he presented to Sir John McLeod. He says that while being taken by the British soldiers, a sergeant joined them on the way. Looking at the unusual dress of Ghalib, the sergeant asked, 'Say, are you a Muslim?'
    Ghalib replied, 'Half Muslim.'
    The sergeant asked, 'Oh? What do you mean by "half-Muslim"?'
    Ghalib replied, 'I drink, but I don't eat pork.'
    Later, having been brought before Colonel Burn, Ghalib showed him his correspondence with Queen Victoria and assured him of his loyalty. Then the Colonel asked, 'During the fighting, why didn't you come to the Ridge (an area outside the Kashmiri Gate in Delhi) where the British armies and their allies were gathered?'
    Ghalib replied, 'The rebels weren't allowing anyone out of the city; how could I have come? And had I made an attempt to sneak out and go to the Ridge, the British sentry would have shot me. Even if I had escaped and the sentry hadn't shot me, of

what use could I have been to you ? . . . I'm old, weak and deaf.
I'm fit neither for fighting nor for advising. Of course, I would
have prayed, but I was already doing that right in the city.'
Colonel Burn, hearing this, smiled and released Ghalib.
Inshā-e-Ghālib (MS.), pp. 25-26.
While Hali, in *Yādgār-e-Ghālib* (p. 36), has described this
incident in the same way, Nawab Ghulam Husain describes it
somewhat differently; it appears from his account that Ghalib
was released on the recommendation of a friend. Nawab
Ghulam Husain, who was the brother-in-law of Ghalib and the
father of Arif, kept a diary in Persian during the 'Mutiny', which
has been translated into Urdu by Khwaja Hasan Nizami and
published under the name of *Ghadr kā Natīja*.
In this, the following reference is made to Ghalib's capture: 'A
few British sepoys entered Ghalib's house and arrested him. He
was taken to Colonel Burn. Fortunately, one of his friends
happened to be there, and on his recommendation Ghalib was
released.'

11. *Dastambū*, pp. 48-49.
12. *Ibid.*, p. 51.
13. *Urdū-e-Mualla*, pp. 151, 153, 193, 243.
14. *Dastambū*, p. 54.
15. *Urdū-e-Mualla*, p. 255.
16. To Har Gopal Tafta, *Urdū-e-Mualla*, p. 91.
17. *Dastambū*, pp. 46-47.
18. *Ibid.*, p. 9. According to the rules of *Abjad*, the numerical value
     of the phrase *rastakhez-e-be-jā* comes to the 1273 Hijra (1857
     A.D.).
19. *Dastambū*, pp. 13, 27, 14, 21, 30, 15, 58 respectively.
20. *Ibid.*, p. 9.
21. *Ibid.*, p. 45.
22. *Ibid.*, pp. 66, 58, 27, 11 respectively.
23. *Ibid.*, p. 6.
24. *Ibid.*
25. *Ibid.*, p. 63.
26. 'It is generally estimated that 27,000 persons were hanged or
     shot in the city of Delhi alone.' Ashraf, note 4.
27. *Zikr-e-Ghālib*, p. 92.
28. *Ibid.*, p. 80.
29. *Urdū-e-Mualla*, p. 211.
30. *Ibid.*, p. 102.
31. *Zikr-e-Ghālib*, p. 81
32. *Urdū-e-Mualla*, p. 99; *Ūd-e-Hindī*, p. 19.

33.   *Urdū-e-Mualla*, p. 249.
34.   *Dastambū*, p. 74.
35.   *Ibid.*, p. 62.
36.   *Urdū-e-Mualla*, p. 41.
37.   To Ghulam Ghaus Be-Khabar, *Ūd-e-Hindī*, p. 114.
38.   *Dastambū*, p. 76.
39.   *Ibid.*, p. 55.
40.   *Ibid.*, p. 21.
41.   *Ibid.*, pp. 53, 24 and 58, 23 and 65, 66, 67, 22 respectively.
42.   See 'Works Cited'.
43.   *Āsār-e-Ghālib*, p. 377.
44.   *Khutūt-e-Ghālib*, vol. I, p. 247.
45.   'The Mughal princes gather in the Red Fort and recite their
      ghazals . . . . This assembly is for a few days only. How can it be
      permanent? Who knows if they'll meet tomorrow, and if they do,
      whether or not they'll meet after that.' To Qazi Abdul Jamil
      Junun, *Ūd-e-Hindī*, p. 154.
46   *Makātīb-e-Ghālib*, text, p. 6.
47.   Ibid.
48.   Ibid., notes, p. 121.
49.   Ibid., introduction, p. 80.
50.   *Khutūt-e-Ghālib*, vol. 2, p. 199; *Dastambū*, p. 46.
51.   That *sikkah* is the following:
      'bar   zar-e-āftāb-o-nuqrah-e-māh
      sikka zad dar jahān Bahādur Shāh.'
      (The MS of the original diary of Jivan Lal, fol. 38b, vide K.A.
      Faruqi, *'Ghālib ka Sikka-e-She'r,'* *Muārif*, Nov. 1958, pp. 388-
      394.) The *sikkah* ascribed to Ghalib by Gauri Shankar is the
      following:
       'ba-zar zad sikka-e-kishwar-sitānī
       Sirāj-ud-Dīn Bahādur Shāh Sānī.'

      Malik Ram has found the above *sikkah* appearing under the
      name of Hafiz Ghulam Rasul Vīrān, a student of Zauq, in the 6
      July, 1857 issue of *Sādiq-ul-Akhbār*. (Malik Ram, *'Ghālib par
      Sikke kā Ilzam,'* *Muārif*, Feb. 1959, pp. 141-150.) It has thus
      finally been proved that the *Sikkah* reported by Gauri Shankar
      was not Ghalib's. It is ironical that, although the *Sādiq-ul-
      Akhbār* was published from the Red Fort in Delhi, Ghalib was
      totally unaware of the appearance in it of that *sikkah* .
52.   *Makātīb-e-Ghālib*, preface, p. I and text, p. 8.
53.   *Dastambū*, p. 14.
54.   To Ghulam Hussain Qadr Bilgirami, *Urdū-e-Mualla*, p. 403.

55. *Ūd-e-Hindī*, p. 93. (To Majruh)
56. 'I am afraid to write in detail. The servants of the court are being questioned and imprisoned and are being subjected to great cruelty.' To Har Gopal Tafta, *Urdū-e-Mualla*, p. 58.
57. To Shahab-ud-Din, *Urdū-e-Mualla*, p. 217.
58. *Khutūt-e-Ghālib*, vol. 2, p. 67.
59. *Ibid.,* vol. I, p. 296.
60. *Urdū-e-Mualla*, p. 58.
61. To Anwar-ud-Daulla Saad-ud-Din Shafaq, *Urdū-e-Mualla*, p. 226; *Ūd-e-Hindī*, p. 52.
62. *Urdū-e-Mualla*, p. 136.
63. *Ibid.,* p. 318.
64. *Ibid.,* p. 228.
65. *Ibid.,* pp. 58, 61, 136, 144; *Dastambū,* pp. 56, 60.
66. To Majruh, *Urdū-e-Mualla*, p. 145.
67. *Urdū-e-Mualla*, p. 303.
68. *Zikr-e-Ghālib*, p. 85.

Works Cited

1. Arshi, Imtiyaz Ali, ed. *Makātīb-e-Ghālib*. Rampur, 1949.
2. Ashraf, K.M., 'Ghalib and the Revolt of 1857,' in *Rebellion 1857.* ed. P.C. Joshi, Delhi. 1957, pp. 245-256.
3. Faruqi, K.A., 'Ghālib kā Sikka-e-She'r'. *Muārif,* Nov., 1958, pp. 388-394.
4. Ghalib, Mirza, *Urdū-e-Mualla* (collection of letters). Lahore, 1922.
5. Ghalib, Mirza, *Ūd-e-Hindī* (collection of letters). Lahore, 1922.
6. Ghalib, Mirza, *Dastambū.* Agra, 1858.
7. Ghalib, Mirza, *Insh ā-e-Ghālib* (Manuscript). Microfilm owned by Malik Ram.
8. Hali, Altaf Husain, *Yādgār-e-Ghālib.* Lahore, 1919.
9. Hasan Nizami, Tran., *Ghadr kā Natīja* (*Nusrat Nāma-e-Government*). Delhi, 1930.
10. Ikram, Mohammad, *Āsār-e-Ghālib.* Lucknow, 1950.
11. Mehr, Ghulam Rasul, *Ghālib.* Lahore, 1936.
12. Mehr, Ghulam Rasul. *Khutūt-e-Ghālib,* vol. 1 and 2. Lahore, 1949.
13. Malik Ram, *Zikr-e-Ghālib.* Delhi, 1950.
14. Malik Ram, 'Ghālib par Sikke kā Ilzām' *Muārif,* February 1959, pp. 141-150.

The Impact of Islamic Mysticism on Urdu Poetry

THE Urdu language is a unique linguistic phenomenon which occurred during the medieval ages in the Indian sub-continent as a result of the interaction of the Islamic and Indo-Aryan traditions. One may not like to differ with Rashid Ahmad Siddiqui's aphoristic saying that the three greatest legacies of the Mughals to India were the Taj Mahal, the poetry of Ghalib and the Urdu language, but as a matter of fact, the Urdu language had come into existence long before the advent of the Mughals, and it had started to be used in musical compositions, as its earliest name *Rekhtah*, "mixture or mixed language", indicates, though at that stage it lacked the polish and perfection it later achieved. Islam reached the Indian sub-continent in the eighth century but it had to wait till the eleventh century when under the Ghaznavis a regular process of interaction between the two great cultures started. The Indo-Aryan speeches spread all over north India, from Punjabi and Sindhi to Bengali, Oriya and Assamese, had already crossed two stages of their linguistic development, i.e., the Old Indo-Aryan, comprising the Indic used in the times of the Vedas, and the refined Sanskrit, in which the Upanishads, Puranas, Shastras, the epics, and all other religious, philosophical, and scholastic literature of ancient India was written; and second, the Middle Indo-Aryan, i.e., the

Prakrits and Pali which served as the vehicle of the two great reformist movements of Jainism and Buddhism in the 6th and 5th century before Christ. It was around the end of the tenth century A.D. when the Prakrits had already started yielding to Apabhramshas, i.e., the deformed speeches, as part of the natural processes of linguistic simplification, and they were at the threshold of the modern stage in their development when they were flooded with Arab-Persian influences. The Middle Indo-Aryan speeches would have yielded to the Modern Indo-Aryan speeches anyway, but as put by Suniti Kumar Chatterji, the advent of Islam accelerated the process, and deeply influenced the formation of the modern Indian languages. The Islam influenced almost all the languages in the North, and some in the South, but it was the Urdu language which was influenced the most. It superbly absorbed both the traditions, linguistically as well as culturally, and in the course of centuries came to represent the true blossoming of the linguistic as well as aesthetic synthesis of the Indian and the Islamic cultures on this sub-continent, and which, because of its sheer beauty, charm and elegance, could be truly compared to the artistic excellence of the Taj Mahal.

It took the Urdu language five to six centuries to reach its level of perfection and poetic excellence. Though the first compositions are ascribed to Masud Sa'ad Salman, a court poet of Mahmood Ghaznavi at Lahore, nothing is extant and it is only with Amir Khusrau (died 1325) in the 14th century that we have a clear evidence that the new Indo-Aryan language had already come into vogue. The great genius, as Amir Khusrau was, composed verses in *Rekhtah* or Hindavi, or Zaban-e-Delhi as Urdu was called in those times, though just for fun, or for the pleasure of his friends as stated by him in the preface to his third Persian Diwan, *Ghurratul-Kamaal*. Amir Khusrau in the third Chapter of his famous Masnawi, *Nuh-Sipihr*, where he had sung sensuous praises of India, its flora and fauna, learning and culture, and the beauty of its people, has given full details of the Indian languages prevalent at that time. The Hindavi or Zaban-e-Delhi that he mentions was, in fact, the forerunner of

Urdu. The word Urdu, Turkish in origin, which means, camp or army, must have been used later for this language because of this newly formed language's association with the army camps and bazars where firstly it must have served as the common language between the incoming foreigners and the local inhabitants. In spite of its dominating position, the Urdu language for three centuries did not receive the patronage of the royal court in the North. But the patronage of the people speaking this language was never lacking, and it was because of the pressure of social forces that this Urdu or Hindi (or Gujri, or Deccani, as it was variously called) became the lingua franca of the sub-continent. Persian was the language of administration, and also of the elitist class, whereas Urdu was the language of the people. It was because of this situation that the Muslim State of Bahmanis when it broke off from the North during the reign of the Tughlaqs, provided a natural breeding ground for this language, and later under the Qutb Shahis and the Adil Shahis, Urdu actually blossomed into a literary language during the 15th and the 16th centuries.

The religious fervour and the simple social structure of Islam by this time had already stirred the inertia of the Indian masses, and a new wave of spiritual awakening and enthusiasm resulting in the birth of the two great religious movements, the Bhakti Movement and the Movement of the Islamic Mystics, permeating the whole medieval age, had already begun. The imagination of poets and writers all over India was fired by these spiritual movements, but Urdu being the common core language, and being the most convenient vehicle for addressing the masses, was recipient of the deepest impact of Islamic Mysticism. Be it Nizami, Mohd. Quli Qutb Shah, Wajhi, Ghawwasi, Nusrati, Muqeemi, Ibn-e-Nishati, Wali or Siraj in the Deccan, or Mazhar Jan-e-Janan, Hatim, Mir, Sauda, Qaim, Yaqeen, Taban, Bedar, Asar, Dard, Mushafi, Aatish, Ghalib, Zauq, Momin or Shaifta in the North, the imagination of all the classical poets of Urdu, bears a clear mark of Islamic Mysticism, and their radicalism and humanism are deeply inspired by the spiritual world-view generated by the Islamic Mysticism.

Having originated in Arabia, the Islamic Mysticism spread to all the countries wherever the Muslims went, but perhaps nowhere did it make such profound impact, and was received with such openness of mind and heart, as in India. The reasons could be many, but the most important single factor which contributed to the acceptance of the Islamic mystical ideas was perhaps the transcendental quality of the Indian mind. The advent of the Islamic Mysticism in India could be compared to the meeting of the two parallel streams of thought heading towards the same destination. The Islamic Mysticism became popular in India mainly because it was not alien to India's own genius. The history books and *Tazkirahs* are full of the accounts of the Muslim saints and sufis who followed the Muslim settlements, or wherever the Muslim traders went. It is said that Mansur al Hallaj made a voyage to India in the tenth century and left behind many followers. Among other saints or scholars who visited India, or came to reside here were Ali bin Usman Al Hujwiri, the author of *Kashful Mahjūb*, who died in Lahore in 1072 or 1076, Shaikh Ismail Bokhari, Fariduddin Attar, the celebrated author of *Mantiqut Tair*, and the most celebrated Khwajah Moi'nuddin Chishti who settled in Ajmer in 1197, and died there in 1234. It was the Chishtia *Silsilah* started by Khwajah Moi'nuddin Chishti that flourished in India later, and produced great mystic luminaries like Khwajah Fariduddin Ganj-e-Shakar, Khwajah Nizamuddin Aulia, Shaikh Nasiruddin Chiragh-e-Delhi and Khwajah Banda Nawaz Gesudaraz. Similarly, the visits or settlements of Shaikh Jalaluddin Tabrizi, Jalaluddin Bokhari, Abdul Karim al Jili, Syed Shah Mir, Qutbuddin Bakhtiyar Kaki, Bahauddin Zakaria and dervishes like Shah Madar and Sakhi Sarwar also contributed immensely to the spread of Islamic mystical ideas in India.

The Islamic Mysticism could be compared to a stream gathering volume by the joining of tributaries from many lands. Of course, its original source was the Quran and the life of the Prophet, but many other transcendental thoughts had swelled it by the time it reached India. As noted by Dr. Tara Chand,

Hinduism and Buddhism may also have supplied a number of ideas. India and the Persian Gulf during those times had a close commercial interaction. As detailed by Dr. Tara Chand, "With trade, undoubtedly, ideas were exchanged. The eastern dominions of the empire, that is, Khorasan, Afghanistan, Sistan and Baluchistan were Buddhist or Hindu before they were converted. Balkh had a large monastery *(vihara)* whose superintendent was known as the Baramak. His descendants bacame the famous Barmakide Vizirs of the Abbaside Caliphs. The Arabs familiarised themselves from early times with Indian literature and sciences. They translated Buddhist works in the second century of the Hijra, for instance, *Kitābal-Bud* and *Bilawhar wa Budasif;* treatises on astronomy and medicine called *Sindhind (Siddhānta)* and *Shushrud (Susruta)* and *Sirak (Charaka);* story books like *Kalīlah Damnah (Panchatantra)* and *Kitāb Sindbād;* ethical books of *Shanaq (Chānakya)* and *Bidpā (Hitopadesa);* and treatises on logic and military science. The legend of the Buddha entered into Muslim literature as the type of a saintly man, and Muslim theologians assimilated the stories of Ibn Adham to the Buddhist legend. What wonder then that the conception of *Nirvāna,* the discipline of the eightfold path, the practice of *Yoga* and the acquaintance of miraculous power were appropriated in Islam under the names of *Fanā, Tarīqah* or *Sulūk, Murāqabah* and *Karāmat* or *Mu'jiza.*"[1]

The Islamic Mysticism, by the time it reached India, growing from the 'monotheistic quietism' of the first two centuries, had blossomed into a full-fledged 'pantheistic mysticism.'[2] The Urdu ghazal poets of the medieval times fall into many categories, either owing allegiance to a common sufi saint leader, or scaling the interior landscape in the light of their own intuitive experiences. It would be wrong to assume that all the classical poets of Urdu were practising mystics. They were not. As a matter of fact, the pantheistic view of mysticism was so lyrical and poetical in its very nature that in course of time blending harmoniously with the creative flights of the poets' fancy and imagination, it became the hallmark of medieval poetry. Needless to say the Urdu poets, in their thinking and expression, were influenced by the Persian masters also, both Iranian and Indian, such as Hafiz, Saadi, Khusrau, Faizi, Urfi, Talib, Naziri, Zahoori, Bedil and others, but their spiritual thoughts are not mere echoes of their Persian predecessors. Although during the medieval ages it was commonly held that Mysticism, *Tasavvuf*, was most convenient for poetical exercise *(barāe she'r guftan khūb ast)*, still with genuine poets, the portrayal of a mystical idea was the expression of a deeply realised truth. Undoubtedly, Urdu poets like Siraj Aurangabadi, Khwajah Mir Dard Dehlavi and Shah Niaz Bareilavi, to name a few, were practising mystics, but the majority of the poets were believers, in the sense that they held to the truth of the day, and perceived the Ultimate Reality and its relation to the human soul and the universe in terms of the commonly held view of mysticism.

Poets are universally known for the poetic licence they can take with any precise idea or thought. The same is true of the mystical utterances of the classical Urdu poets also. The suggestive and symbolic nature of the genre of ghazal further complicates matters. The Urdu ghazal like its Persian counterpart is governed by a set of conventions, and each word used has its own train of linguistic and semantic connotations and denotations. Still, generalisations are not impossible, and could be attempted. It is in this light that the examples quoted here may be viewed.

For Urdu poets, God is the Ultimate Reality, and everything in the universe has emanated from Him. The human soul is the dwelling place of the Ultimate Reality, the seat of Love. God is illuminated by Love, and from this illumination comes the multiplicity of His attributes and names. The attributes and names are not the real thing. The real thing is God. Like Mansur, the Urdu poets conceive their relation with God as the infusion of the Divine into the human soul. They echo the famous pronouncement:

I become that which I love and that which I love becomes

mine. We are two spirits, infused in one body. To see me is to see Him, to see Him is to see us.[3]

In the Urdu ghazal, again and again, one comes across the various renderings of Mansur's declaration, "I am God" (*an-al-Haqq*). Though for some poets there is some difference of level or potential between the Absolute Reality and His image, yet for many the relationship is the complete fusion with the Absolute (*fanā fillah*).

It is in this context that song and dance have verily been in vogue in different sufi orders. Though there has been much dispute among theologians as to the lawfulness of music as religious exercise yet because of the sanction of great scholars like Ghazali, and distinguished saints like Jalaluddin Rumi, and also because of the practice of Persian ghazal, the Urdu ghazal with an optional touch of Braj or Awadhi, had been used for centuries in musical sessions of mystical assemblies, called *Sama'*. Gradually, a new style of group singing marked by joyous rapture and ecstasy known as *qawwāli* singing, developed in India, and in the course of time, passing from mysticism and gaining in popularity like its indigenous counterparts such as the Hindu *kirtan* or *bhajan* (religious singing), and outgrowing its religious connotations, the *qawwāli* entrenched itself as a full-fledged style of popular love lyric singing, and became an integral part of the secular North Indian music. The mystic poets were, in fact, deeply infused with the music, inner as well as oral, which stirred up in them greater love towards God, and often obtained spiritual visions, *irfaan*, and ecstasies, *haal*, which, as they believed, could never be attained by any amount of mere outward austerities.

The greatest emphasis has been on the unity of creation, and the absolute oneness of the Creator and the created. The later school of mystic thought originating with the teachings of the great saint, Mujaddid-e-Alf-e-Sani crystallized into the philosophy of *wahdat ushshuhood*, i.e., *hamah az oost*, as compared to the earlier school of thought known as *wahdat ulwujood*, i.e., *hamah oost*, maintained that though God manifested Himself in every particle of creation, the created could never be one with the Creator. The idea of the complete fusion to them was a mere illusion and simply a stage in the realisation of the Absolute. Though the Urdu poets have been echoing both the sentiments, still, because of the imprecise nature of the poetical rendering, it is rather difficult to pinpoint the exact shade of thought. However, it could be said that the general trend has been in favour of the idea of *wahdat ulwujood* or *hamah oost*:

WALI:

> '*iyān hai har taraf 'ālam men husn-e behijāb uskā*
> *baghair az dīda-e-hairān nahin jag men niqāb us kā*

His uncovered beauty is in evidence everywhere in
this universe,
There is no cover except the bewildered eye itself.

SHAH ALAM AFTAB:

> *vāhid hai lā-sharīk tū sānī tirā kahān*
> *'ālim hai sab ke hāl ka tū zāhir-o-nihān*
> *zāhir men tū agar ce nazar ātā hai nahīn*
> *dekhā jo main ne ghaur se tū hai jahān tahan*

You are One, there is no second,
You know everything about what is seen and what is not seen,
The eyes cannot see You,
But if one concentrates intently You are everywhere.

SAUDA:

> *is qadar sāda-o-purkār kahīn dekhā hai*
> *be namūd itnā namūdār kahīn dekhā hai*

Have you seen anyone so simple yet so skilful,
He is not obvious, but is present everywhere.

MIR:

gul-o-rang-o-bahār parde hain
har 'iyān men hai vo nihān ṭuk soć

The colourful rose bud and the dancing spring are mere covers,
If one cares to behold, He is manifest in all the things He is hidden.

ānkhen jo hon to 'ain hai maqsūd har jagah
biz-zaat hai jahān men vo maujūd har jagah

If one has the sight the Essence could be beheld everywhere,
He Himself is present in this universe everywhere.

DARD:

jag men ā kar idhar udhar dekhā
tū hī āyā nazar jidhar dekhā

Having come to this world I have seen here and there, everywhere,
Whatever meets the eyes is nothing but You.

hai ghalat gar gumān men kuch hai
tujh sivā bhī jahān men kuch hai?

It is wrong if anyone has doubts about the reality,
There is nothing in this universe but You.

GHALIB:

> *dahr juz jalvah-e-yaktā'ī-e-m'asūq nahīn*
> *ham kahān hote agar husn na hotā khud-bin*

The world is nothing
but the splendour of the uniqueness of the Beloved,
How could we be, were the Beauty not fond of the manifestation of Her own glory.

> *asl-e-šahūd-o-šāhid-o-mašhūd ek hain*
> *hairān hūn phir musāhada hai kis hisāb men*

If the essence of the viewer, the viewed, and the view is the
same,
Then I wonder what's all this viewing about?

The core of the mystical influences is the emphasis on the
idea of *'ishq*, love. *'Ishq* is the pivot around which everything
else revolves. *'Ishq* is not taken in a narrow physical sense,
rather, it is an all-pervasive energy, the drawing force of the
universe, centre of creativity, and the very being of reality. The
suffering of *'ishq* perfects the soul. It is the fire that consumes all
impurities, and it is the force that binds the physical with the
spiritual, *al-majaaz qantratul haqīqah*, 'physical (love) is a
step towards the spiritual.' In Urdu poetry, as in the Persian, the
term , *'ishq* has many connotations, sacred as well as profane,
physical as well as spiritual. The seeker must fully appreciate the
implications of *'ishq*, and take its sufferings as true joys before
he embarks on his journey.

MIR TAQI MIR:

> *mauj zanī hai mīr falak tak har lujjah hai tūfān zā*
> *sar-tā sar hai talātum jis kā vo 'āzam daryā hai 'išq*

The tides, O Mir, are skyhigh, waves are truly turbulent,
Love is like a stormy sea, rocking both heavens and earth.

'išq hī 'išq hai jahān dekho
sare 'ālam men bhar rahā hai 'išq
kaun manzil ko 'išq bin pahunčā
ārzū 'išq mudda'ā hai 'išq

Whatever you see is permeated with Love
The whole universe is filled with Love
No one ever reached his goal without Love
The desire is Love, the object also is Love.

'išq se nazm-e-kul hai yānī 'išq ko'ī nāzim hai khūb
har šai yān jo paidā hu'ī hai mauzūn kar lāyā hai išq

All organisation is because of Love,
Love is the great organiser,
All that is created here,
has been shaped by Love.

Once inspired by *'ishq*, love, the seeker must not be dependent on the exterior of reality, but should start looking *within* for light. Contemplation and introspection are strongly emphasised. The exterior, *khārij*, induces involvement and sin, whereas attunement to the interior, *bātin*, leads to detachment and self-realization. For this, one must concentrate on the *qalb*, *dil*, i.e. the heart, because *qalb* is the seat of all truth and knowledge.

MIR:

dair-o-haram ko dekhā allāh re fuzūlī
yeh kyā zarūr thā jab dil sā makān banāyā?

I saw the temple and the sanctuary, O God, What a waste!
Were they really needed,
When You had an abode like the heart to live in?

DARD:

ghāfil tu kidhar bahke hai tuk dil kī khabar le
šīšah jo baghal men hai usī men to parī hai

O you ignorant, you know nothing,
Just think of your own heart,
The flask that contains the true wine, it is within.
(The mirror that reflects the true beauty, it is within).

The pantheistic idea of the Absolute permeating the whole of
the universe paved the way for socio-religious tolerance in
medieval Indian society. In fact, it provided the basis for
humanism which inspired the whole of Bhakti Movement from
the 14th to the 18th centuries and great saints, such as
Ramananda, Kabir, Guru Nanak, Dadu, Dhanna, Namdev, Tuka
Ram, and millions of their followers throughout the length and
breadth of India. The Urdu poets like the Sufi saints and the
Bhakti poets emphasized the idea that in fact all beliefs were
concepts about the same reality, and all modes of worship were
expressive of some aspect or the other of the same reality. The
differences of caste, creed and religion, they say, are due to the
variety of names of attributes, and all put together they lead to
the perfection of the whole. The aim of the human soul is
complete union (*fanā*) with the Divinity (*Haqīqat*), the
transformation of man, his will (*irādah*), intellect ('*aql*) and
emotion (*jazbah*) and the attainment of the unitive state
(*baqā*). They say that when the ultimate goal is the same there
may be many paths leading to the same goal. In such poetry
both the sanctuary (*haram*) and the temple (*dair*) attain
symbolic significance. They are manifestations of the orthodox
ritualism of the priestly class, against which the seeker (*sālik*)
must rise in rebellion. The humanism of the Urdu poets borders
on radicalism in the sense that they are against all religious and
social taboos. They expose the priestly class for its exploitation
of the people. They denounce strongly all differences based on
caste or because of class structure, and they advocate that all

men are born equal and should be treated equal. They make a mockery of the so-called piety, righteousness and honesty of the ruling class and the priestly class and deeply satirise their hypocrisy, conceit, and ungodly manners of luxurious living. The Urdu ghazal poets, all through the medieval ages, have been echoing these sentiments protesting against the priestly class and rising against the differences created by orthodoxy:

MOHD. QULI QUTB SHAH:

main na jānūn   ka'ba-o-butkhāna o maikhāna kūn
dekhyā hūn har kahān distā hai tujh mukh kā safā

I don't know much about the Kaba,
or the temple or tavern,
I look for You everywhere,
and I see the radiance of Your face everywhere.

SHAH HATIM:

ye kis mazhab men aur maśrab men hai hindu mausalmāno
khudā ko chor dil men ulfat-e-dair o haram rakhnā

O Ye Hindus and Muslims,
tell me in which religion or creed it is allowed
to ignore God,
and to adorn the temple or the sanctuary.

SAUDA:

bahke gā tū sun ke śukhan-e-śaikh-o-brahman
rahtā hai ko'ī dair men aur ko'ī haram men

You will be misled if you pay heed to Sheikh and Brahman.

The one is confined to the temple, the other to the
sa

MIR:

> mujh mast ko kyā nisbat ai mīr masā'il se
> munh śaikh kā masjid men main rakh ke masal dālā

What do I care, O Mir, about religious rituals and
polemics
I have already crushed and mutilated
the face of the Sheikh in the mosque behind.

> gośko hoś ke ṭuk khol ke sun śor-e-jahān
> sab kī āvāz ke parde men sukhan-sāz hai ek

Open thy ears, and listen carefully to the music of the
universe,
the inner note of all the sounds comes just from a single
source.

> ham na kahte the ke mat dair-o-haram kī rāh čal
> ab ye jhagrā haśr tak śaikh-o-brahman men rahā

Didn't I warn not to tread
the path of the temple and the sanctuary,
now the Sheikh and the Brahman will keep
fighting about it till the end of the world.

GHALIB:

> ham muwahhid hain hamārā keś hai tark-e-rusūm
> millaten jab miṭ ga'īn ajzā-e-īmān ho ga'īn

I am a monotheist, my religion is to reject all externals.
When the creeds were ground down, they became
elements of the Faith.

PYARE LAL ASHOB:

> *apnā to sar jhuke hai donon taraf ke us kī*
> *tasvīr but-kade men aur hai haram men khākā*

My head bows in reverence on both sides, because
the temple has His picture, and the sanctuary His concept.

MADHO RAM JAUHAR:

> *dair-o-masjid pe nahīn mauqūf kuch ai ghāfilo*
> *yār ko sijde se matlab hai kahīn sijdah kiyā*

Why only in a temple or a mosque?
If the aim is to worship the beloved, this can be done
anywhere.

Since the Urdu poet believes in the human soul striving for
living in essential unity with God, and progress towards *ma'rifat*
(realisation of reality), he considers a true seeker to be above
both *īmaan* (belief) and *kufr* (non-belief). For him the outward
illusion of subject and object does not matter much. He believes
in the submission and annihilation of the self, or individual ego
(*anā*), and wants the limited self to become one with the spirit
of the universe, just as a drop (*qatrah*) merges with a river
(*daryā*) as Ghalib puts it '*ishrat-e-qatra hai daryā men fanā
ho janā* (the absolute joy of the drop is to be one with the
river), or a particle (*juzv*) enjoys its entity as part of the whole
(*kul*). This complete surrender is not a negative aspect of the
cosmic consciousness, but has positive connotation, because it
was this feeling of the pervasiveness of the Absolute and its
basic unity with the individual soul that gave millions an
assimilative spiritual outlook about life and paved the way for an
affectionate living together of peoples belonging to different
faiths and communities in a country which has been marked
with all sorts of diversities. Here we quote a superb ghazal by

Siraj Aurangabadi, a Deccani poet of the late 18th century, which amply illustrates the points made above:

> <u>kh</u>abar-e-tahaiyyur-e-'i<u>s</u>q sun na junūn rahā na parī rahī
>
> na to tū rahā na to main rahā jo rahī so be<u>kh</u>abarī rahī
>
> šah-e-be<u>kh</u>udī ne atā kiyā mujhe ab libās-e-barahnagī
>
> na <u>kh</u>irad kī ba<u>kh</u>yagirī rahī na junūn kī parda-darī rahī
>
> ćalī samt-e-<u>gh</u>aib sen kyā havā ke ćaman zuhūr kā jal gayā
>
> magar ek šā<u>kh</u>-e-nihāl-i <u>gh</u>am jise dil kaho so harī rahī
>
> vo 'ajab ghaṛī thī main jis ghaṛī liyā dars nus<u>kh</u>a-e-'i<u>s</u>q kā
>
> ke kitāb 'aql kī tāq men jūn dharī thī tyūn hī dharī rahī
>
> kiyā <u>kh</u>āk ātiš-i-'i<u>s</u>q ne dil-e-benawā-e-sirāj kūn
>
> na <u>kh</u>atar rahā na hazar rahā magar ek be-<u>kh</u>atarī rahī

When I heard the news of the wonder of love, neither frenzy remained nor the sweetheart. I and You were no more. All that remained was oblivion.

Now the Lord of Ecstasy has bestowed on me the clothes of nakedness. The stitching of wisdom and the exposure of the secret of madness have no longer remained.

What was it that came from the direction of the Invisible that the garden of the Visible was burnt up? But one branch of the sapling of grief, which they call the heart, remained green.

It was a strange hour when I studied the manuscript of love. For the book of intelligence was put on the shelf and has remained closed ever since.

The fire of love turned the poor heart of Siraj to ashes. There was no more fear, no more caution, but what remained was a (sense of) freedom from danger.[4]

Here are some more couplets by two major poets:

MIR:

> *galī men us kī gayā so gayā na bolā phir*
> *main mīr mīr kar usko bahut pukār rahā*

> I entered the lane, was lost, didn't utter a word,
> I called Mir, again and again, in vain.

> *bekhudī le ga'ī kahān ham ko*
> *der se intizār hai apnā*

> Where my frenzy of love has taken me to,
> as if for long I were waiting for myself.

GHALIB:

> *ham vahān hain jahān se ham ko bhī*
> *kuch hamārī khabar nahīn ātī*

> I am at a place where I myself,
> do not know anything about my own self.

The impact of Islamic Mysticism on the Urdu poetry is so deep and pervasive, and the mystical ideas expressed by the Urdu poets, over the centuries, are so rich and varied that a brief study could only present a cursory account of the actual reality. In conclusion, one may say that the medieval Urdu poetry's whole scheme of reality, its appreciation of the relationship of man and universe with the Absolute, its moral code (*akhlāq*), sense of good and evil (*haq-o-bātil*), virtue and sin, (_khair-o-shar_), its idea of the progression or perfection of the human soul, or the understanding of the spiritual, intuitive and creative faculties of the human mind, or its concept of reason ('_aql_), frenzied love ('_ishq_), bordering on insanity (_diwāngi_, profound thinking (_fikr_), intuition (_wijdān_), and realisation (_ma'rifat_), are, in fact, all derived from Islamic Mysticism, or are dependent on the synthesis of the Islamic and the Indian mystical thought. This confluence of ideas, undoubtedly, not only provided a meeting ground for major religions in India, but also paved the way for an emotional, spiritual and aesthetic _modus vivendi_ which sustained the Indian society throughout the medieval times, and different faiths flourished and coexisted in harmony and peace.

Notes

1. _Influence of Islam on Indian Culture_, Allahabad 1946, pp.65-67.
2. _Ibid._, p.69.
3. _Ibid._, p.71.
4. Translation: Matthews and Shackle, _An Anthology of Classical Urdu Love Lyrics_, Oxford 1972, pp.36-38.

3

The Princeton Manuscript of Kulliyāt-e-Saudā

MIRZĀ MUḤAMMAD RAFĪʻ (died A.D.1781), who wrote under the pseudonym of Saudā, is universally considered as one of the great Urdu poets of India. Saudā's ancestors came from Kabul, Afghanistan, and were soldiers by profession. His father, Mirzā Muḥammad Shafīʻ, left his native home to settle as a merchant at Delhi during the reign of Aurangzeb (A.D.1658-1707). It was here that Muḥammad Rafīʻ was born. His date of birth is not known, but from accounts of his later life it appears that he was born in the first or second decade of the eighteenth century.[1] Following his ancestors, he began his career in the military and went to Deccan for a short time. Returning to Delhi, he became an *aide-de-camp* of a Mughal noble, Basant Khān, and was later dependent on the patronage of Sādāt Khān and ʻImād-al-Mulk. Gifted with a poetic genius, Saudā's creative faculties blossomed under the guidance of Sulaimān Qulī Khān ʻWidād' and afterwards, that of Shāh Ḥātim. He soon became immensely popular and was awarded the title of *Malik-al-Shuʻarā*, 'poet-laureate', by the Mughal king of Delhi. In his later years, compelled by the highly unstable political conditions prevailing at Delhi, he moved to the neighbouring state of Farrukhabad, stayed there for a few years, then moved to Faizabad, where he enjoyed the patronage of Nawab Shujā'-al-Daulah (A.D. 1753-1775). Saudā eventually settled at Lucknow with Nawāb Āṣaf-al-Daulah (A.D. 1775-1797), where he died in A.H.1195 (A.D. 1781). His death is recorded in many chronograms composed by his friends and disciples. One of them, by Nāsikh, reads *saudā jauhar-e-fazl*, "Saudā the essence of learning."[2]

Saudā's services to Urdu poetry and to the technique of versification are unique. He was adept in all kinds of poetical composition, and he remains unsurpassed in the *qaṣīdah*, or laudatory ode, and in the *hajv*, the satire. Indeed, he is regarded as the originator of the *hajv* in Urdu poetry which he made a weapon of great strength and power. As a man of fiery temper, he was quick with the satirical retort. However, though many of his satires are directed against individuals, his best are those in which he lashes out at the degenerating social and political order and exposes the incompetence of the kings and the selfishness of the nobles. He lived in an age when Delhi, once the powerful centre of the Mughal Empire, was being repeatedly overrun by invaders. On the one hand, the British were establishing their rule in Bengal, and on the other hand local nobles and lords were defecting to the Afghans and the Mahrattas, who repeatedly attacked and plundered Delhi. Kings were enthroned and dethroned like puppets, and anarchy flourished. Saudā, because of his associations with nobility, was pained at Delhi's degeneration and debasement. Though dependent on the aid of the nobles, he was not prevented from ridiculing their hypocrisy and false standards. Through his verse, he laid bare the debased and intrigue-prone nature of the ruling class. His satires thus make an interesting and sensitive account of life under the later Mughals. Because of his vital nature and buoyancy of spirit, he reacted strongly to his environment and fully used his gifts as a poet to speak indignantly and vehemently against the all-pervading rottenness. Still, Ralph Russell, comparing Saudā to Rabelais, rightly points out that, "the mainspring of Saudā's satire, as of all truly great satire, is a deep compassion for humanity and a keenly felt sorrow and anger at the conditions of an age which deform and degrade man from his true greatness."[3]

In A.D. 1803, the poems of Saudā were first arranged and compiled with an introduction by Ḥakīm Sayyid Iṣlāḥ-al-Dīn Khān, of Calcutta. A volume of selections was published in 1810 under the editorship of *Munshīs* of the College of Fort William, and a revised edition with additional poems was issued at Culcutta in 1847 by Maulawī Ghulām Haider, Hindi *Sarishtedār* of the College. The first lithographed edition of the *Kulliyāt* (in which the poems are arranged in seven *Dīwāns*) was published at Delhi by Mir 'Abd-al-Raḥmān Āhi· This was followed by a few editions of selected poems published at Agra, Lucknow, and Calcutta. Another complete edition was published in 1821, by Nawal Kishore at Kanpur, and was reprinted several times. Major Henry Court published his English translation of the *Mathnawīs* of Saudā at Simla in 1872, and a revised edition was prepared by Captain H.S. Jarrett and printed in Calcutta in 1875. The available Urdu *Kulliyāt*, in two volumes, was compiled by Āsī and published by Nawal Kishore in 1932. Although considered the most complete of all the editions published so far, this edition is quite unreliable, containing, as it does, verses of some of Saudā's contemporaries, wrongly attributed to Saudā by scribes, and omitting some of Saudā's own poems found in the manuscripts which were discovered later.

Outside India, the manuscripts of the poetical works of Saudā are widely scattered. The India Office has ten,[4] the British Museum, six,[5] the Asiatic Society, London, one, and the Bodleian, two.[6] The India Office Ms. include the *Kulliyāt*, presumed to have been presented by the poet himself to Richard Johnson, the then Resident of Lucknow. The only known copy of the *Kulliyāt* in the United States is preserved in the Garrett Collection of the Princeton University Library, described in H.I. Poleman's *A Census of Indic Manuscripts in the United States and Canada*.[7] This manuscript, presumably one of the most prized possessions of its owner, who commissioned it, apparently became lost during the political convulsions of the nineteenth century, when, among other things, many imperial

and private collections were destroyed and the fragments of
their acquisitions scattered over the world. The manuscript
eventually turned up in London and was purchased from
Quaritch in 1900 for £ 4.4 by Robert Garrett.[8] The manuscript,
on glazed oriental paper and bound in leather, consists of 455
folios, 8.5" x 14.5," with 13 lines to a page.

Beginning:

huā jab kufr thābit hāi woh tamghā-e-musalmānī

End:

angusht men pahnāwe jis tarah kōī challā

The *Kulliyāt* is divided into six[9] sections: fols. 1-105: panegyric
Qaṣīdahs; fols. 106-178: satires and elegies on the death of Imām
Ḥusain; fols. 179-195: Persian *Ghazals*; fols. 196-361: Urdu
Ghazals; fols. 362-416: *Mukhammas*, satires; fols. 417-455:
Mathnawīs, most of which are satires.

The Garrett manuscript is written in a neat and clear hand in
Nasta'līq style. There is no colophon, and the name of the
scribe is not mentioned. However, the beginning of each *Dīwān*
and the end of the *Kulliyāt* is marked by a seal, *Mahtāb-al
Dāulah, Kaukab-al Mulk, Sayyid 'Alī Khān Bahādur,
Darakhshān Sitārah-e-Jang, 1269*. This indicates that this copy
was specially prepared for a noble, Sayyid 'Alī Khān, in A.H.
1269 (A.D. 1852-53). As it is a fairly late copy, it is for obvious
reasons more complete than many earlier versions. The work of
systematic re-editing of the *Kulliyāt* is being carried on at Delhi
and Patna, where this newly discovered copy will doubtless be
invaluable.

Besides its historical and literary value, the Princeton
manuscript is a good example of Mughal miniature painting and
of the art of illumination of books, for in the manuscript the
beginning of each Dīwān is fully illuminated. The upper part of
the page is divided into triangles with mounting curves and

arches harmonized by an inlaid rich floral design. The prominent colour is gold, and the bordering lines are done in blue. The outer border, the central margin, and the space between the verses are also illuminated and filled with gold.

The copy is further decorated by ten coloured miniature paintings. Though the art of calligraphy and miniature painting went hand in hand, the number of manuscripts adorned with miniatures is much smaller than those in which the beginnings are illuminated. Excepting the India Office Ms. which has only one miniature, no other manuscript of the *Kullīyāt* is so fully decorated. The India Office Miniature, somewhat damaged by dampness, shows a scribe seated on a carpet smoking a *ḥuqqah*, an attendent standing behind him. As this copy is said to have been presented by the poet to Richard Johnson, Resident of Lucknow at that time, it is presumed that the "miniature [is] probably intended for the poet."[10] The Princeton copy, however, has three such miniatures. Sheikh Chānd suspected that the India Office Miniature might be that of Johnson himself and not of the poet. Unless more evidence is discovered, it is difficult to decide whether it really is an authentic portrait of the poet. However, the Princeton copy was prepared seventy-four years after Saudā's death, and it is highly improbable that the artist had seen Saudā. In view of this, these three miniatures are either later copies of originals which have disappeared, or else they are simply imaginative portraits.

One common feature of these three miniatures is the appearance of an angel in the sky, depicted as shedding light over the head of the person seated below, a light which may be interpreted in terms of heavenly blessings or of divine inspiration. The appearance of angels is nothing new in Persian and Mughal miniatures, but they are met with only in miniatures either intended for the Prophet or for persons of great historical or religious importance.[11] Saudā was devoted to the *Shī'a* sect, and two of the three miniatures occur with odes in praise of Ḥaẓarat 'Alī (A.D. 599-661). Furthermore, the praying posture of the figures, their green robes and the holding of rosaries, all lend credence to the view that the miniatures were intended for religious personages, perhaps Ḥaẓarat ʿAlī, Imām Ḥusain, or someone of that stature.

Miniatures four and five are of Nawāb Shujāʿ-al-Daulah and Āṣaf-al-Daulah, the two famous Nawābs of Oudh, both patrons of Saudā. Their miniatures appear along with odes composed in their praise. Shujāʿ-al-Daulah (1753-1775)[12] played an important role in the early history of British India. He was present in the 1761 battle between Aḥmad Shāh Abdālī and the Mahrattas; he was appointed *wazīr* to the Emperor Shāh ʿAlam and was later defeated by the English in the famous battle of Buxar in 1764, which hastened the progress of the British into North Central India. After Shujāʿ-al-Daulah's death, his son Āṣaf-al-Daulah (1775-1797)[13] succeeded him. Known for his love of art and poetry, he was very friendly toward Saudā, composed verses under the pseudonym of Āṣaf, and was the author of a *Dīwān* in Urdu and Persian. Despite the mystery surrounding their artist, both the miniatures seem to have been done with great care and accuracy. A golden halo appears around the heads, the robes appear of fine silk and muslin, and the turban is studded with rubies and pearls. There are two attendants standing on each side of the Nawābs.

The remaining five miniatures simply illustrate moods or situations described in the poems. Of these, the most interesting is a caricature of a horse, a caricature illustrating a sharp satire where Saudā ridicules a Mughal soldier and his battle horse. It presents a vivid picture of the poverty of the age and the fallen splendour of the great Mughal power, and reads as follows:

The times have changed. The lords who in their stables had once Arabian horses of the finest breed have now become penniless, and are not in a position to pay for the mending of their shoes. I know a person who is employed in the Mughal army and has a horse. But as he can't afford to feed it well, it has withered to a mere skeleton and looks as if it were dying. Whenever its master rides through the *bāzār*, the butcher and the tanner say, 'When will you call us for your horse, sir?' The horse is so emaciated that it can no longer neigh, and when it meets a mare, it simply starts releasing wind. It appears as if it has neither bones nor flesh in its body, and when breathing looks like the bellows of a blacksmith.

One day it so happened that I had to go somewhere and asked my friend if I might borrow his horse. With all humility he said, 'The horse is at your disposal. But, believe me, you will do better if you ride a donkey. Recently a young friend of mine took it for his marriage procession; it moved so slowly that by the time he reached his bride's home, he had grown old. I recall riding on it when the Mahratta army invaded Delhi. I was ordered to take part in the combat, but in spite of all the whipping and spurring, the horse wouldn't move. The people in the streets jeered and taunted, 'Why don't you fix wheels or tie sails to it so that it moves?' Nevertheless, I arrived at the battlefield, but on discovering that it was a real battle where I had to fight, I simply took to my heels and returned home. If you still insist upon riding this horse, I will indeed have no objection.'[14]

The miniature shows the horse and the rider, the rider conversing with a person standing nearby. The representation of horses is common in Mughal miniatures but caricatures of them are quite rare. One good example is where Mullā Dō Piyāzah, the famous buffoon of Akbar's court, is shown riding a horse.[15] In the present miniature the figure is more realistic and convincing.

Another imaginative miniature is that of a young man talking to a beautiful lady in a garden where flowers are blooming and, in the foreground, fountains are running.

Most impressive in all these miniatures is their simplicity of design and microscopic exactness. The colouring is harmonious and the perspective fairly good. The delicacy with which the hair is drawn displays mastery with a single hairbrush. The microscopic rendering of the costume is delightful as much as it is never obtrusive. Very often slight shading is used, giving the figures an effect of roundness. The stiff formalism of the early

Mughal period is absent, and men and women appear in natural attitudes. In view of their artistic and historic value, these miniatures deserve the attention of scholars of Mughal art.

Notes

1   Sheikh Chānd, *Saudā, Life and Works* (Aurangabad, 1936), p. 35. James Fuller Blumhardt, in the *Catalogue of the Hindustani Manuscripts in the Library of India Office* (London, 1926), pp. 146-155; and Mohamad E. Moghadam, Yahya Armajani and Philip K. Hitti, in *The Descriptive Catalogue of the Garrett Collection of Persian, Turkish and Indic Manuscripts in the Princeton University Library* (Princeton, 1936), p.83, quote, A.H. 1125 (A.D 1713) after Muhammad Husain Azad's *Āb-e-Ḥayāt*, which however, was not accepted as correct by Shiekh Chānd, Saudā's biographer.

2   For details see: Sheikh Chānd, op. cit.; Charles Stewart, *Catalogue of the Oriental Library of the Late Tipoo Sultan of Mysore* (Cambridge, 1809), p. 181; A. Sprenger, *Catalogue of the Arabic, Persian and Hindustany Manuscripts of the Libraries of the Kings of Oudh* (Calcutta, 1854), pp. 285 and 636; Garcin de Tassy, *Histoire de la Littérature Hindoue et Hindoustanie* (Paris, 1870), vol. III, pp. 66-85; Blumhardt, op.cit.; pp. 146-155.

3. Ralph Russell, "An Eighteenth Century Urdu Satirist, Saudā," *Indian Literature,* October 1958 and March 1959, pp.36-43.

4. Blumhardt, *loc. cit.*

5. Idem, *Catalogue of Hindi, Punjabi and Hindustani Manuscripts in the Library of British Museum* (London, 1899), pp. 28-31.

6. Hermann Ethe, *Catalogue of Persian, Turkish, Hindustani and Pashtu Manuscripts in the Bodleian Library* (Oxford, 1930), part II, nos.2323-2324.

7. The American Oriental Society, 1938, p. 325, no. 6195a.

8. Robert Garrett (1875-1961) was a member of the Board of Trustees of the Princeton University.

9. Not "five" as mentioned by Moghadam, Armajani and Hitti , op.cit., p.83.

10. Blumhardt, *India Office Catalogue,* p.147.

11. *Jāmi'-al-Tawārikh*(A.D. 1314), University of Edinburgh. The angel Gabriel shown with the Prophet vide F.R.Martin, *Miniature Paintings and Painters of Persia, India and Turkey* (London,1912), fig. 13, p. 24; *Album of Mughal Miniatures*, G 102, Princeton University, fol.45B, angels attending on King Solomon; ibid., fol.33 B, an angel descending from the clouds with a crown for King Shahjahan.

12. Thomas William Beale, *Oriental Biographical Dictionary* (Calcutta, 1881), p.259; Ashirbadi Lal Srivastava, *Shuja-uddaula* (Lahore, 1945).

13. Beale, op. cit.,p. 55; Abu Talib, *History of Asaf-ud-daulah*, tr. by W. Hoey (Allahabad,1885).

14. For Urdu text, see Āsī, *Kulliyāt-e-Saudā*(Lucknow, 1932) pp. 371-375.

15. Free Library of Philadelphia, miniature numbers M141 and M213; *Album of Mughal Miniatures*, 102G, Princeton University Library, fol.45 A.

4

Some Social and Cultural Aspects of Urdu Maṣnawiis

URDU has been profoudly influenced by Persian literature and is rich in Iranian and Islamic traditions. But this does not mean that Urdu is devoid of Indian cultural influences. In fact, Urdu is an Indo-Aryan language and its literature, in spite of foreign influences, has roots deep in Indian soil. It has met the demands of history and portrays very faithfully medieval Indian life from the sixteenth to the nineteenth century. Like other forms of Urdu poetry, the masnawii has also been affected by the process of cultural assimiliation inherent in a mixed society. Maṣnawii, meaning literally 'paired, wedded or double-rhymed', is one of the most developed forms of Urdu poetry and is generally composed in seven meters. A maṣnawii can be of as few as ten to twelve or as many as five thousand to seven thousand verses. In Urdu it is usually used for ballads, romances, epics and versified stories. The Urdu maṣnawii writers have drawn not only on Islamic sources but also made use of Indian myths and legends, tales and traditions.

The tradition of Urdu maṣnawii goes back to the early fifteenth century. The first Urdu maṣnawii was written by Nizaamii of Deccan during the reign of Aḥmad Shaah Bahmanii (1422-1435). It is based on the Indian folk tale *Kadam Raao Padam Raao*. Urdu gained in popularity during the reign of the

Qutb Shaahii (1518-1687) and 'Aadil Shaahii (1490-1673) kings. Scores of Urdu poets devoted to the masnawii tradition thrived under their patronage. Wajhii versified the love affairs of Sultaan Muḥammad Qulii Qutb Shaah (1580-1611) in his masnawii *Qutb Mushtarii* (1609). Ġawwaasii on one hand wrote the masnawii *Saif-ul-Muluuk-o-Badii'-ul-Jamaal* based on the Arabian Nights and on the other hand versified two Indian tales, the *Tuutii Naamah* (The Parrot's Tale) and *Miinaa-o-Satwantii*. Nuṣratii composed a masnawii based on the Indian folk tale of Manohar and Madhumaaltii. During the same period Ibn-e-Nishaatii wrote his famous masnawii *Phuulban* (1655), which describes the adventures of an Egyptian prince who comes to India and settles down here.

Many poets in North India also based their masnawiis on Indian tales and legends. These masnawiis form a treasure house for scholars studying medieval Indian society and culture. For detailed study, these can be divided into the following five classes.[1]

1. Religious Masnawiis

The famous Indian epic *Raamaayana* was versified by Jagan Nath Khushtar and Shankar Dayaal Farḥat. Khushtar also composed a masnawii based on another epic, the *Mahaabhaarata*. Other religious masnawiis include the *Mahaabhaarata* by Totaa Raam Shaayaan; *Giitaa Mahattam* and *Bishan Liilaa* by Raam Sahaae Tamannaa; and *Brij Chab* by Banwaarii Laal Sholah.

2. Historical Masnawiis

These include '*Alii Naamah* (dealing with 'Aadil Shaahii kings) by Nuṣratii; *Mezbaanii Namah* and *Zafar Naamah-e-Nizaam Shaah* by Shauqii; *Taariikh-e-Salaatiin-e-Bahmaniyah* (history of Bahman kings) by Suhail; *Phuul Naamah* (history of Jind state) by Raae Braj Naaraain Varmaa

Naazim; and *Taariikh-e-Badii'* (history of Rampur State) by Amiirullah Tasliim Lakhnawii.

3. Patriotic Masnawiis

These usually convey the patriotic feelings of the poet for either his own region or for the country. Some are in praise of the seasons, fruits and produce of India. A few were chiefly written to inspire the Indian people against the British during the great uprising of 1857. Shaah Muraad, Walii, Hidaayat, Sa'aadat Yaar Khaan Rangiin and Muhammad Bakhsh Shahid composed poems dealing with Lahore, Surat, Banaras, Delhi, and Lucknow. King Waajid 'Ali Shaah wrote the masnawii *Huzn-e-Akhtar* (Akhtar's Sorrow) narrating the events of the annexation of Oudh and his deposition. Momin Dehlavii wrote the *Masnawii-e-Jihaadiyah* urging the people to rise in arms against the English. When the British forces were being held at the outskirts of Delhi, a short Urdu masnawii composed by Maulwii Liyaaqat 'Alii, a rebel leader, was distributed to the masses.

4. Social Masnawiis

These include the works which directly or indirectly throw light on different aspects of Indian social life. Many Urdu poets described the feasts, festivals and ceremonials of India in their poems. Haatim (d. 1781), Miir (d.1810), Raagib, Faa'iz, Qaaim and Afsoos composed poems on Holii and Diwaalii. Haatim was attracted by the delicacies of *huqqah* smoking, whereas Miir in one of his masnawiis appears to be critical of cock-fighting. Miir Hasan (d. 1786) surpassed all his predecessors in describing the splendour of the processions and gatherings of Lucknow and Faizabad. The masnawiis of Nusratii, Miir, Miir Hasan and Nawaab Baadshaah Mahal present authoritative accounts of contemporary marriage ceremonies.

5. Cultural Maṣnawiis

These include maṣnawiis derived from Indian myths and legends. They in fact form the core of the maṣnawii literature in Urdu and are so varied in nature that a proper study of them necessitates their sub-division into the following four categories.

5.1. Maṣnawiis derived from Puranic tales. They deal with the legends of Nal and Damayantii, Dushyant and Shakuntlaa and Satyawaan and Saawitrii. First among the translators of Nal and Damayantii is Ilaahii Bakhsh Shauq, who completed his poem in 1802 under the auspices of the Fort William College of Calcutta. A copy of the manuscript is preserved in the British Museum, London. Five other poets of the nineteenth century, Aḥmad Saraavii, Niyaaz 'Alii Nikhat Dehlavii, Akbar 'Alii Akbar, Bholaa Naath Faraag and Bhagwant Raae Raahat Kaakorwii, also versified this story. Raahat's poem became very popular and was reprinted more than twenty times. The well-known tale of Shakuntalaa was first adapted into Urdu by Kaazim 'Alii Jawaan and Lalluu Laal, again for the Fort William College in 1801. This early translation was followed by three other translations in verse, *Rashke-e-Gulzaar* (Garden's Envy) by Sayyid Moḥammad Taqii, *Gaazah-e-Ta'ashshuq* (The Cosmetic of Love) By ʿInaayat Singh, and *Nairang-e-Saḥar* (Morning's Glory) by Iqbaal Varmaa. The legend of Satyawaan and Saawitrii, in which the piety and truthfulness of a married lady are described, was introduced to the Urdu readers through the efforts of Jigar Barelvii in this century.

5.2. Maṣnawiis derived from Indian folk tales. The source material for maṣnawiis under this category was largely taken from the *Panchatantra, Shuka-Saptatii, Baitaal Pachiisii, Kathaa Sarit Saagara* and *Jataka Tales*. The seventy tales of the parrot were named *Ṭuuṭii Naamah* or *Tootaa Kahaanii* in Urdu. Their original can be traced back to the earliest Indian sources. For instance, a few episodes are derived from the *Panchatantra*, and the basic connecting tale is the same as is found in the "Raadhaa Jataka", 145 and 198. Besides these, a few tales of the *Ṭuuṭii Namah* also resemble certain stories in the *Baitaal Pachiisii* and *Hitopdesha*. These tales are so popular that even outside India they were translated into 37 different languages. In Urdu they have been translated by eight different authors; of these Ġawwasii's and Nuṣratii's maṣnawiis are considered to be works of high literary merit.

Manohar Madhumaaltii is another well-known Indian tale. The Hindi version of Manjhan became so popular that it was translated seven times into Persian. The successful adaptation into Urdu is by Nuṣratii.

The folk tale of Kaamruup and Kaamlataa is somewhat similar to the story of Sindbad the Sailor in the *Arabian Nights*. In Urdu it was versified by Taḥsiin-uddiin , who was followed by Kamaal Khaan and four others. The renowned orientalist Garcin de Tassy loved this book. He not only published the Urdu text from Paris, but also translated it into French. The first French edition appeared in 1834 and the second in 1859. It was translated into English and German as well. Goethe liked the German translation of Tahsiin's maṣnawii so much that he is said to have used the word *unschätzbar*, 'priceless,' for it.

5.3. Semi-historical maṣnawiis. The tales narrated in these masnawiis are said to be based on historical events. They are popularly regarded as historical but are not entirely verifiable, and hence the term semi-historical. Of these maṣnawiis, *Hiir Rāājhaa, Sassii Punnūū, Padmaawat* and *Chandarbadan-o-Mahayaar* deserve special mention. *Hiir Rāājhaa* is a tragic tale of two lovers of the Punjab. Rāājhaa is a poor boy; Hiir is the daughter of his master. They love each other, but because of their different social levels, they cannot marry. Hiir is eventually married to a rich man in a far off village. Rāājhaa follows her and there serves her husband as a cowherd. The lovers keep on meeting stealthily under the cover of darkness and one night try to flee unsuccessfully. Hiir's parents, frightened by further reproach, mix poison in their daughter's food, and so Hiir dies. Rāājhaa, struck with grief, also dies. The tale was originally written by Waaris Shaah in Punjabi and is very popular in that language. In Urdu we have nine recensions of this tale, five of which are in the form of masnawiis, written by Najiib-uddiin, Muul Chand Munshii, Karam Ilaahii, Abdul Gafuur and Miir Fazl-e-'Alii.

Another famous tale is *Sassii Punnūū*. The locale is in Sindh, but the story is quite popular in the whole of the North-western Indian sub-continent. This tale again is a tragedy. Punnūū, a gypsy trader, falls in love with a pretty girl called Sassii during one of his trips; he settles down in her village, forgetting about his home. His parents send his brothers to persuade him to return. On reaching the village, they play a trick on Punnūū, drugging him, and while Sassii is asleep, carry him away on their camels. Sassii cannot bear the separation and runs after the camels, following their trail into the desert. She runs for hours, crying "Punnūū, Punnūū." The day is very hot, and finally she dies of thirst and exhaustion. Punnūū, when he regains consciousness, rebukes his brothers and returns, only to see the dead body of Sassii lying in the desert. Struck with grief he also dies. In Urdu this tale was versified by five different poets. The poems of Muhabbat Khaan Muhabbat and Jiyaa Laal Khastah are the best known.

Padmaawat is a tale of North Eastern and Central India. Originally it was composed by Malik Muhammad Jaaisii in the Awadhii language in the sixteenth century. In Urdu six different authors have versified this tale; of them Gulaam 'Alii 'Ibrat and 'Ishrat, and Qaasim 'Alli have been quite successful.

5.4. Indo-Iranian masnawiis. Besides the above-cited masnawiis, there are many others, which the poets in the opening lines claim to be set in far-off lands, Arabia, Iran or China. But the social behaviour, food, dress, customs, feasts, festivals and ceremonies are Indian. Since the poet's imagination was conditioned by his environment, even when he claimed to be narrating a non-Indian tale, he unconsciously presented it in an Indian social setting. Such masnawiis are far too numerous to be mentioned here. They form the core of the maṣnawii lite:ature in Urdu and can be of valuable help in presenting a true picture of medieval Indian society. It would not be an overstatement to point out that Urdu has so well developed an expression of the composite culture of India that it is impossible to construct a complete history of medieval Indian society without the help of Urdu sources. In this connection maṣnawiis *Seḥr-ul-Bayaan* (The Magic of Rhetoric) and *Gulzaar-e-Nasiim* (The Garden of Naseem) deserve special mention. They are considered to be the best maṣnawiis of Urdu and in the following discussion we shall be quoting freely from the former.

First, let us take up the Indian festivals. Holii and Diwaalii are the two most important festivals of North India. Diwaalii (festival of lights) is celebrated when the rainy season is over. Houses are cleaned and whitewashed, new utensils and household articles are purchased. At night the buildings, streets and roads are illuminated, and the approaching winter is welcomed. The festival, in fact, symbolizes the ultimate victory of good over evil, of happiness over misery, and of light over darkness. There are quite a few maṣnawiis on Diwaalii in Urdu. Through these poems we learn that the Mughal kings of India used to patronize this festival. On the eve of Diwaalii, the king was weighed against gold and silver and the money was distributed among the poor. In the Red Fort at Delhi, the goddess of wealth and fortune, Lakṣhmii, was worshipped on *Amaavas*, 'the last day of the dark fortnight.' Ladies of the royal family used to adorn themselves with the proverbial *Solah Singhaar*, 'the sixteen articles of decoration,' and dress in their best. The turrets, terraces, and the parapet walls of the Red Fort were lit with thousands of lamps, and fireworks were displayed throughout the night. Sayyid Aḥmad Dehlavii writes that the Muslims of Delhi considered Diwaalii as one of their festivals like Ramaẓaan and 'Iid and exchanged gifts on this occasion. In medieval times, the mixed society had reached a degree of cohesion under the influence of India's assimilating genius and Diwaalii was not celebrated as merely a religious festival. The people, irrespective of religion and creed, participated in the festivities and rejoicings. An

eighteenth-century poet of Delhi, Shaah Ḥaatim (d.1781),
describes Diwaalii in these words, rendered by us into English
prose.

> The tiny lamps of Diwaalii are twinkling in small rows.
> They look as beautiful as the gleaming golden marginal
> lines of a book. The tiny flames are shining like golden
> tassels. On doors, walls, balconies, courtyards and gardens
> the lamps have turned night into day.

Holii is celebrated when the winter is over, usually in the
month of March. This, along with Basant, is a festival of Spring,
lasting for fifteen days, the last three days of which mark its
climax. People spray colour on one another and indulge in
various sorts of revelries. Splashing of colour is symbolic of
happiness and merriment. Holii provides an opportunity for the
free play of repressed emotions. Many social restrictions are set
aside; young and old, male and female, servants and masters, all
feel free and participate in this game of colour. Saffron and
gulaal, a red powder, are smeared on the face; drums are beaten
and processions are taken out. The Urdu poets Faa'iz, Miir,
Ḥaatim and Qaa'im have written masnawiis about Holii, showing
that the Muslims also enjoyed this festival. Two of the Mughal
kings of India, Shaah 'Alam II, Aaftaab (1759-1806) and Bahaadur
Shaah Ẓafar (deposed,1857) were fond of composing short
musical poems called *Holiyāā*, which are popular and are sung
in India even now. These few lines from Ḥaatim, depicting the
romantic aspect of Holii, are interesting.

> They have filled their bags with red powder, *gulaal*, mixed
> with mica, and are shouting: 'Come on! It is Holii today.'
> There is colour everywhere and they are splashing it all
> about with syringes. Beautiful maidens are playing the
> sport of colour. Some are fair, some are dark, and some
> are of the color of sandalwood. One of them is very
> young. Her complexion is white like a *champaa* flower.
> Another is creamy like a peeled almond, and yet another

is red like a blooming rose. One is running with a syringe in her hand. Another has drenched her dress. One has bared her chest; another is smilingly chewing betel leaves. One is preoccupied with her make-up; another is proud of her tight gown with open strings. One is throwing balls of flowers; another is dressing her injuries. One is squeezing her clothes, and another is gesturing mischievously with her eyes. The strips of tinsel and pieces of mica strewn in their loosened tresses are shining like stars. There is fun and frolic all around and everyone is playing the game of love.

After discussing the festivals, a reference to the marriage ceremonies is not out of place. Here again we see the process of cultural synthesis at work. Though the marriage ceremonies of Hindus and Muslims are different from each other, the basic pattern is the same. Urdu masnawiis profusely illustrate that, apart from several religious rites, the ceremonies are performed more or less along the same lines. There is a marriage procession, called *baaraat*, in each one. The *baaraat* starts at the groom's house and proceeds to the bride's home. The final uniting ceremony is always performed by a *pandit* or a *qaazii* at the bride's home and the bride leaves fully covered and veiled in a palanquin. Several days before the marriage she is ceremoniously seated on a bed, and is unveiled by the ladies. These ceremonies are called *māājhe biṭhanaa* and *ruup darshan*. On this occasion, in some of the Muslim families, the relations apply a fragrant paste to each other, which is known as *ubṭan khelnaa*. These are all typically Indian ceremonies. In both the Hindu and Muslim ceremonies, the girls sing nuptial songs called *ghoṛiyāā*. The bride, on the night of marriage, is dressed in her best. Usually she wears a red or pink robe. Vermilion is applied for the first time on the parting line of her hair. Many types of cosmetics are used. They are called *suhaag puṛaa*. The nuptial mark *ṭiikaa* is made on her forehead. Miir Ḥasan tells us that even the Muslims adopted this as early as the eighteenth century.

Her hair was braided in so charming a manner that the discerning onlookers lost their hearts. The nuptial mark, *ṭikaa,* on her forehead made even the moon feel envious of her. The bell-shaped pendants of her earrings seemed more beautiful than the Pleiades. The gold ring in her nose enhanced the glow of her complexion and her fair face was gleaming under the veil. She looked very youthful with a mole made of lampblack, on her chin. There were diamond bracelets around her arms and golden anklets on her ankles. She indeed was tastefully bedecked with gold, and looked wonderful.

The *baaraat* is generally headed by the bridegroom, riding a horse. Money is lavishly spent on the arrangements for the marriage procession. Drums are beaten and *shahnaaii,* the Indian clarion, is played. The *shahnaaii,* an important part of the orchestra, is considered auspicious. Here are a few lines from a masnawii by Miir Taqii Miir (d. 1810) describing the marriage of Nawaab Aaṣaf-uddaulah of Lucknow:

The main attraction of the procession is the royal elephant, which is moving gracefully like a spring cloud. The macebearer walking in front of the elephant appears like a moving mountain of shining gold. The elephants are moving in the back and step like intoxicated youths. The battalions of soldiers move swiftly like the eyelashes of the beloved. The beat of the drum is alluring and the roads are strewn with roses.

The bride leaves her father's house in the morning after the marriage. The ceremony is quite touching. The ladies of the house and the bride's girl friends sing the parting song, *manḍhaa,* full of pathos. Every heart is moved and tears stream from the eyes. Miir Ḥasan writes:

At dawn the rites were performed and all was in readiness for the heart-rending farewell. The relatives were standing quietly. O God, what a world! Even dear ones must part one day. The sobbing bride embraced all her relatives one by one. She parted from her parents with tearful eyes. The dowry was brought out of the house like the tears that roll forth from an eye. Then the palanquin of the bride was carried by the servants and gold was showered from all sides. But the friends standing nearby with tearful eyes quietly presented the pearls of their tears.

This touching finale is a common sight in India. A few other cermonies such as *sehraa bandii* 'garlanding,' *saṭhne* 'polite abuses,' *neg jog* 'customary presents', and *salaamii* and *ruu-numaaii'* money given to a bride for a showing of face, are common to Hindus and Muslims. This shows that in course of time the Muslims and Hindus adopted each other's practices and prepared to find a *modus vivendi* as neighbours. Gradually, through the process of mutual exchange, a common order emerged. This social synthesis was also marked in food and dress and jewellery.

Urdu maṣnawiis are very rich in descriptions of the ladies of eighteenth and nineteenth centuries. With the help of these writings, we can easily reconstruct the dress, hair styles, jewellery and cosmetics then in vogue. The maṣnawiis of Muḥammad Qulii Qutb Shaah (1580-1611), Miir Taqii Miir, Miir Aṣar, Miir Ḥasan, Daya Shankar Nasiim (d. 1843) and Mirzaa Shauq Lakhnawii are very important in this respect. They abound in pen portraits of queens and princesses, and women from upper and middle-class families. Even the gypsy girls, dancing girls, maids and female devotees did not escape the notice of these Urdu poets.

The heroine of the maṣnawii, *Zahr-e-'Ishq*, is from a middle-class family. She is described masterly by Mirzaa Shauq in the following manner:

The beauty of her face is as dazzling to me as was the proverbial flame on Mount Sinai to Moses. May God preserve her eyes from evil glances; they are sparkling like pearls. Her tresses move gently across her face. Her petal-like lips are red from chewing betel leaves. There is an ornamental speck on one side of her nose. She is very young and appears pert and playful. She wears a bodice with tight sleeves, and has an air of sauciness about her youthful figure. She is tall and looks engaging. There is a thread around her fair neck in token of the vows once made to God. Her flexibile waist is as thin as the vein of a flower, and when she walks, her ankle-length hair swings.

Other aspects of the contemporary social life portrayed through Urdu masnawiis include scenes from North Indian streets and bazaars, and details of household articles. In the following verses Miir Hasan presents a pen-picture of a bazaar in Faizabad, also mentioning several Indian dishes and popular sweetmeats:

There are jewellers and cloth-merchants on one side of the bazaar, the goldsmiths and gilders on the other. The watermelons and muskmelons are lying in heaps. The female gardeners are standing nearby selling flower necklaces and wreaths. One peddler is hawking his sugarcanes, while another shouts that his are better. At the sweetmeat seller's, the rice dishes of *fiirnii* and *faaluudah* are like moons and stars. The gram-seller smilingly says, 'Parched crackling grams mixed with lime juice'. On one side there are shops of roasted meats, and on the other side they sell *shiir-maal* (bread kneaded with milk) and *naan* (plain bread).

Similar descriptions of the markets of Lucknow were written by Channuu Laal Tarab and Baadshaah Husain in their masnawiis.

Here is clear evidence that Urdu poets addressed their creations to the society around them. And their images are those held out to them by their environment. Thus, their poems provide very useful information to scholars of Indian social life. They show that in spite of the political degeneration in the eighteenth and nineteenth centuries, the social ties of mutual love and regard were quite strong. The Hindus and Muslims participated in one another's festivals and evolved common practices. No doubt the *pandit* and the *maulvii* always remained separated by the gulf of religion, but at the level of the masses both communities came closer to each other. Their behaviour was marked by mutual respect and tolerance. India has always been a meeting place of different religions, creeds and communities, that constantly strive to attain a degree of unity amidst diversity. It is to this process of integration and assimilation that Urdu maṣnawiis bear indirect testimony, while providing valuable information about medieval Indian society.

Note

1. For references and other information regarding the Maṣnawiis and authors quoted in this paper, please refer to the author's book, *Hindustaanii Qissō se Maa khuuz Urduu Maṣnawiyāā* (Urdu Maṣnawiis Based on Indian Tales), Maktabah-e-Jaamiah, Delhi 1962. Most of the Maṣnawiis mentioned here are still unpublished, and are preserved in the India Office and the British Museum, London, and in university libraries and private collections in India and Pakistan.

5

The Indian Freedom Struggle and Urdu Poetry

A POET is an artist first and last. An artist's responsibility in any period is that he has to prove true to his art. It is difficult to say which of the fine arts is pure art, but it is admitted universally that poetry is the supreme form of literature. So are music, dance, painting and sculpture in their own realms. We always expect of a musician to sing well, and of a dancer to dance well. We do not make any demand other than excellence in their respective art forms from these artists, but coming to literature, aren't all sorts of demands made of the poet? This is a unique situation. Nonetheless, the answer is not far to seek. The medium of poetry is language whose main function through the arbitrary system of phonological and orthographical symbols is to convey meanings. These meanings primarily function for communication. But mundane language which is generally used for day-to-day interaction and communication, when used emotively or creatively by a poet, achieves the level variously referred to as literariness or poeticality. Thus while primarily playing its role as an inexhaustible source of aesthetic pleasure, poetry conveys meanings at the same time, which too are part of the aesthetic pleasure. It is here that the social or the patriotic role of literature comes in. During all periods of history we have poets who have sung praises of their country to which they belong, or join a crusade for social change, or herald a revolution for the good of a particular people or country. But what is the worth of such poetry if it does not break the barriers of region, language, or country? Can such poetry claim an element of universality or durability? Normally it is seen that whenever a nation is in a turmoil or passing through a period of historical crisis, or rising against an alien domination or subjugation, or fighting for its survival, there is a lot of activity on the literary front, and heaps of poetry are produced which pass under the general label of patriotic poetry. But soon after the period of turmoil is over, a major part of such poetry is forgotten, and only those very few pieces which shine forth literarily survive. Here we have no intention to enter into the elements of good or bad poetry, or poetry or non-poetry, but it may be admitted that all that passes in the name of patriotic poetry is not poetry. The difficult question, therefore, in literature is whether the element of survival is related to the patriotic and nationalistic feeling, or to the poeticality of the muse? We may argue any amount on either side, still this much is obvious that even a patriotic poem has to be a poem in the first place, otherwise howsoever much it may carry the patriotic message, if it is not endowed with the qualities of poetry and the use of the medium is not artistic enough, the poem may not survive for too long, and perish when a particular historical phase is over. Therefore, only that poetry which has withstood the test of time and has survived will be taken up and discussed in this article.

Nationalism as a state of mind indicative of the loyalty of the individual to a nation-state is a nineteenth century phenomenon in India, but its process had started earlier in the eighteenth century with the gradual strengthening of the British colonial hold over India. The Urdu language, which had originated as a linguistic by-product of the cultural synthesis of the Hindus and Muslims in the medieval times, patronized by both the courts and courtiers, sufis and saints, and common people, had, by the eighteenth century, been perfected as a medium of poetry by scores of masters. The eighteenth century

Urdu poetry, which reflects the contemplative, transcendental mood of the Indian mind, refuses the oppressive influence of the religious dogma, and emphasising the unity of man and humanism, is permeated with sentiments of attachment to the Indian soil, and its syncretic cultural tradition. But as the spectre of the British colonialism grows from Bengal to Oudh and Delhi and to vast areas in South India, the sentiments of patriotism give place to feelings of nationalism in Urdu poetry. The earliest expressions are found in the stray couplets of the Ghazal poetry, which over the ages has been by far the most common genre of Urdu. Usually these are veiled in the romantic metaphors of established usage, but because of the system of conventions operative in the Ghazal, and because of the denotations and connotations of certain words, these couplets lend themselves to deeper political interpretations conveying a whole range of meanings reflective of the distress and agony of the Indian people during those times.

The battle of Plassey in 1757 was a turning point in the history of India, and according to chroniclers, struck by the tragic death of the heroic Nawab Sirajud Daula at the hands of the British, one of the contemporary poets, Raja Ram Narain Mauzun, is said to have composed the following verse:

Ghazālān tum to wāqif ho kaho Majnoon ke marne kī,
Diwāna mar gayā aakhir ko virāne pe kyā guzrī.

O gazelle, you are a witness to the death of Majnoon,
The mad (*patriot*) is no more, what now will be the fate of the desert (*country ruined by the alien rule*).

Time and again sentiments like these couched in the romantic imagery of the Ghazal were expressed, either obliquely or directly, by the eighteenth century Urdu poets, and we come across classical masters like Mir Taqi Mir and Hatim, grieving over the rot that had set into the Mughal administration, and the tragic downfall of the great empire, as well as the heart-rending sites of the ravaged cities of India. Mushafi and Jurat were direct witnesses to the thumping advance of the British colonialism into Oudh and Delhi:

Dillī men aaj bhīk bhī miltī nahīn unhen,
Thā kal talak dimāgh jinhen takht-o-tāj kā.

Today in Delhi even alms are not available to those who till yesterday adorned the royal throne.

—Mir

Kaurī kaurī bikte hain gul kishwar-e-dillī ke bīch,
Husn ke mālik jo the woh aise arzān ho gae.

The roses (*royal princesses*) are sold for a pittance in Delhi,
Alas, those who personified beauty have become so cheap today.

—Mushafi

Hindostān kī daulat-o-hashmat jo kuch ke thī,
Kāfir farangiyon ne ba-tadbīr khench lī.

Whatever wealth and riches India had,
The Kafir Farangis (*British*) have by their tactics usurped.

—Mushafi

Kahiye na inhen amīr ab aur na wazīr,
Angrezon ke haath qafas men hain asīr,
Jo kuch wo paṛhāyen so ye monh se bolen,
Bengāle kī mainā hain ye pūrab ke amīr.

Now they do not deserve to be called nobles and nabobs.
They are stooges in the hands of the British,
They say only whatever they are tutored,
They are like the puppets of Bengal in the hands of the British.

—Jurat

The annexation of the State of Oudh by the British in the middle of the nineteenth century was a personal tragedy for many poets of Urdu. Commenting on this, Abdul Halim Sharar, a noted cultural historian of Lucknow writes that the news of the deposition of Nawab Wajid Ali Shah was so shocking that many

lost their minds, and many their patronage, and had nowhere to
go. Fat-hud-Daula Barq, who was one of the companions of the
king from his boyhood, accompanied the king in his exile, and
stayed in Matiya Burj in Calcutta's Fort William with him to his
last day. Mir Anees, the doyen of Urdu *marsiyah* (elegy),
expressed his grief in the following quatrain:

> Kyon-kar na dil-e-gham zadah faryād kare,
> Jab mulk ko yon ghanīm barbād kare,
> Mango ye duaa ke phir khudāwand-e-karim,
> Ujri hui saltanat ko aabaad kare.

Why shouldn't my heart grieve
When my country is plundered so badly by the enemy?
Pray that God may have mercy
And the Sultanate be set up again.

These events were followed by the great Rebellion of 1857,
which by many is termed as the First War of Indian
Independence. The Urdu poets fanned the fires of revolt, and
many died fighting the British. Imam Bakhsh Sahbai, a close
friend of Ghalib and a renowned scholar and poet, was brutally
slaughtered along with the members of his family; Mufti Sadrud
Din Azarda, another contemporary of Ghalib, who at that time
was the Mufti of Delhi, was charged with siding with the revolting
armies, and of signing the Declaration of Holy War (*Fatwā-e-
Jihādiyah*) against the British. He was dismissed from service,
and his property was confiscated. He spent the remaining years
of his life in ignominy. Ghalib, the greatest of Urdu poets, stayed
in Delhi throughout this period, and recorded the events of the
war in his Persian diary, *Dastambū*, as explained in chapter 1.
Nevertheless, we may recapitulate some of its highlights here.
Ghalib's thoughts and feelings and his experiences during the
rebellion can also be found in his private letters to friends and
disciples, which were written with comparatively greater freedom
and boldness. During the uprising, many of Ghalib's friends,
relatives, and patrons were either murdered, reprimanded by the

British, or they fled from Delhi after the ruin of the city. Because of these and other reasons, Ghalib writes in *Dastambū*:

> May the sockets of my eyes be filled with dust if during this tragic time I have seen anything but weeping. My sorrows are incurable and my wounds will never heal. I feel as if I am already dead.

During the rebellion, Ghalib attended the court of the Mughal king Bahadur Shah Zafar, and also composed a *sikka-e-sher*, a verse chronogram commemorating the declaration of the war. There is a poignant story behind this episode, because the most celebrated poet of Urdu had to defend himself against this charge for the rest of his life. During the war, the composing of the verse chronogram by Ghalib was reported by a spy, Gauri Shankar, to the British, and thus after the fall of the Mughal king, when Ghalib moved for the restoration of his ancestral pension and his place in the *darbār* (Court), he was tersely told by the British that he had maintained relations with the mutineers during the rebellion, and that subsequently his pension and *darbār* were suspended. To one of his friends Ghalib wrote about this: "The charge of composing a verse (chronogram) has hit me like a bullet or a cannon-ball; whom should I speak to, who can testify for me?" Incidentally, the verse being ascribed to Ghalib by the British had actually been composed by someone else, so Ghalib was right in his denial, but his denial never helped him, because this too was a fact that Ghalib had composed a verse commemorating the rebellion, which was presented to the king and that verse has now been traced and found in the manuscript of the spy reports of yet another intelligence agent, Jivan Lal. The manuscript is preserved in the British Museum, and Ghalib's verse reads as follows:

> *Bar zar-e-āftāb-o-nuqrah-e-māh*
> *Sikka zad dar jahān Bahādur Shāh*

On the gold of the Sun, and silver of the Moon,

> Bahadur Shah, the Emperor, struck his coinage, and circulated it in the world.

Therefore, after the rebellion, Ghalib had to suffer. He not only lost his salary from the Red Fort, but also his ancestral pension, and his place of honour in the Court, and, on top of that, his hope of being nominated the official Poet Laureate vanished for ever. Consequently, during this period, Ghalib's financial condition deteriorated. Describing it in *Dastambū*, he wrote:

> I now see no way of getting back the pension I once had from the British. I am carrying on by selling my bedding and clothing; other people eat bread, I eat clothing.

For Ghalib's real feelings about the uprising and the British, one must turn to his private letters to his friends which, freed from the need of expedience, display more forcefully his true feelings. Ghalib felt very deeply the terrible cruelties inflicted on the Indians by the British after the uprising, and his description of the ruin, both of his class and of the city, are very painful. After the reoccupation of Delhi, no one could of course speak out against the British, yet Ghalib, in his letters, points very strongly to the excesses and cruelties. And though he wrote with circumspection, much of what conditions must have prevailed in Delhi during those times comes through. To Shahabuddin, he wrote:

> Think of my situation: I am writing, but what can I write? Can I really write anything, and is it proper to write? This much is true: you and I are still alive. Neither of us should say any more than that.

In another letter Ghalib clearly describes what difficulties the people of Delhi had to endure, and in one part in which he speaks of the cruelties of the British, we see clearly the intensity and boldness with which he describes the reality of the situation:

> The city has sustained five attacks. The first was that of the army of native sepoys, who robbed the confidence of the people of the city. The second was that of the army of the

British who destroyed life, wealth, honour, property, indeed, all the signs of our life...

Again, it was in a letter to one of his friends that Ghalib wrote the celebrated *qat'ah*, in which he describes the ruin of Delhi, and in particular, the plight of the Muslims:

Baske fa'āl-e-māyurīd hai aaj,
Har silh-shoor inglistān kaa.
Ghar se bazaar men nikalte hue,
Zahra hotā hai aab insān kā.
Chowk jis ko kahen wo maqtal hai,
Ghar banā hai namoona zindān kā.
Shahr-e-Dillī kā zarra zarra-e-khaak,
Tashna-e-khoon hai har Musalmān kā.

Surely today every English tommy considers himself God.
Everyone going from his house to the bazaar is struck with panic.
The market-place (Chandni Chowk) looks like a slaughterhouse,
And the houses look like prisons.
As if every particle of dust in Delhi
Thirsts for the blood of the Muslims.

The tragedy of 1857 was so close and deep to the bone of the Delhi poets that many of them composed elegies and *Shahr Āshobs* on the fall of the capital, and about the deportation of Bahadur Shah Zafar to Rangoon. Twenty-seven of such poems were compiled in a book, *Fughān-e-Delhī*, The Lamentations of Delhi, by a disciple of Ghalib, Tafazzul Husain Khan Kaukab. One of the important poems of the period is a chronogramatic poem commemorating the beginning of the uprising composed by Muhammad Husain Azad, which appeared in the *Delhī Urdū Akhbār.* This newspaper was owned by Azad's father, Maulvi Muhammad Baqar, who was later killed by the English, and his press confiscated. The young Azad had to flee for his life. This poem appeared in the 24 May 1857 issue of the *Delhī Urdū Akhbār*, a copy of which is still preserved in the National Archives of India. Bahadur Shah Zafar himself was a poet of merit, and the poetry composed by him during his last years in exile, bears proof of his misery and deprivation.

The poets of 1857 were followed by Hali. Though the harbinger of modern age in Urdu poetry, he was moderate by temperament, and under the impact of the reformist movement of Sir Syed Ahmad Khan, he settled for moral regeneration and social reform. But the distinction of being the first modern nationalist poet of Urdu clearly belongs to Shibli. He was one of the band of devoted *Ulamā*, religious scholars, who not only championed the cause of freedom, but also urged upon their fellow-Muslims to join the mainstream of national struggle. Shibli, by his poems and articles, denounced the separatist politics of some of the Muslim leaders, and pleaded for the independence of the country as soon as possible. Romantic by character, whenever he wrote on political themes, his poetry was full of fire and verve, and deeply anti-colonial in tone and temper. Simultaneously, the close of the nineteenth and the beginning of the twentieth century saw the rise of two major patriotic poets of Urdu, Durga Sahay Suroor Jahanabadi and Muhammad Iqbal. Iqbal's early poetry is permeated with his love for India, and to him goes the credit of composing some of the finest patriotic songs of Urdu, like *Himāla, Āftāb* (translation of Gayatri Mantra of the Vedas), *Nayā Shivāla, Swāmī Rām Tīrath, Rām, Nānak,* and the most famous of all, *Tarāna-e-Hindī* which is sung even today in India, and is one of the most popular national songs among Indian children:

Sāre jahān se acchā Hindostān hamārā
Ham bulbulen hain is kī yeh gulsitān hamārā . . .

India, our country, is the most beautiful in the world
This is our garden, we its nightingales . . .

Though, later on, Iqbal concentrated more on his message of Pan-Islamism, still with his recurrent theme of the infinite potentiality of man as partner with God in shaping the destiny of the universe, and the universal approach for the quest of the Perfect Man, Iqbal's poetry harmonized with the awakening of man throughout the countries of Asia and Africa. He remained firm in his anticolonial stance as is reflected in poems like *Tasveer-e-Dard* (Picture of Pain) which is one of his earliest, and *Shu'aa-e-Umeed* (Ray of Hope) which is one of his last. It is not widely known that Iqbal spontaneously composed a *Qat'ah*, a short four-line poem, on the massacre of the Jalianwala Bagh in Amritsar, where the British opened fire on an unarmed peaceful crowd of thousands of people who had gathered there to listen to the speeches of the national leaders:

Har zāir-e-chaman se yeh kehtī hai khāk-e-bāgh
Ghāfil na rah jahān men gardon kī chāl se
Sīnchā gayā hai khoon-e-shahidān se is kā tukhm
Too ānsuon ka bukhl na kar is nihāl se

To every visitor, the dust-particles of this garden declare:
Beware of the treachery of the times
The seed (*of freedom*) here was sown with martyr's blood
Which you must now nurture with your tears.

Around the First World War, the nationalist verse of Urdu was further enriched by stalwarts like Chakbast and Hasrat Mohani. Chakbast, being a moderate, was inspired by leaders like Bipin Chandra Pal, Gokhale, and Mrs. Annie Besant. His poems, *Khāk-e-Hind, Āwāza-e-Qaum* and *Hamārā Watan Dil se Pyārā Watan* portray the liberal-moderate aspect of our freedom movement, whereas Hasrat was an extremist and he never settled for anything less than full freedom. His political mentor was Bal Gangadhar Tilak and, like him, Hasrat always emphasized on full freedom, *swarāj*, as goal of the Indians. He was a down-to-earth man, lived a simple life, wore *khādī*, suffered imprisonment several times and was always daring and undaunted in expressing his patriotic convictions. Essentially a lyrical poet, Hasrat expressed his political views through the tender medium of the Ghazal whenever he chose to. His poetry thus reflects the extremist element in our freedom movement couched in the sweetest words of the Ghazal mode:

HASRAT MOHANI:

> *Rasm-e-jafā kaamyaab dekhiye kab tak rahe*
> *Hubb-e-watan mast-e-khwāb dekhiye kab tak rahe*
> *Daulat-e-Hindostān qabza-e-aghyār men*
> *Be-'adad-o-be-hisāb dekhiye kab tak rahe*

Let us see for how long the tyranny will rule
Let us see for how long the patriots do not rise from
slumber
India's riches are in the hands of plunderers
Let us see for how long this goes on unchecked.

CHAKBAST:

> *Ye josh-e-pāk zamāna dabā nahin saktā*
> *Ragon men khūn kī harārat miṭā nahin saktā*
> *Ye aag woh hai jo pānī bujhā nahin saktā*
> *Dilon men aa ke ye armān jā nahin saktā*
> *Talab fuzool hai kānṭe kī phool ke badle*
> *Na len bahisht bhī ham 'home rule' ke badle*

This excitement no one can put down,
It's like the life-blood running in our veins,
It's like fire no water can put out,
It's the resolve we will never give up.
Who will barter a flower for a thorn?
We will never accept even paradise in exchange for Home
Rule.

Thus, simultaneous with the Indian freedom movement, assuming mass proportions, and Mahatma Gandhi's emergence as its great leader, and the Khilafat Movement touching the right chord in every heart, Urdu poetry entered a phase where nationalism acquired the distinction of becoming one of its recurring features. During this period there were scores of poets, whose poetry reverberated with sentiments of nationalism, and strong opposition to the foreign rule. Maulana Muhammad Ali Jauhar's following couplet turned out to be a trend-setter:

> *Daur-e-hayaat aaegā qātil qazā ke ba'd*
> *Hai ibtidā hamārī terī intihā ke ba'd*

Qatl-e-Husain asl men marg-e-yazīd hai
Islām zinda hotā hai har Karbalā ke ba'd.

A period of joy certainly will come after the martyrdom
There is a new beginning after every end.
The assassination of Husain is in fact the death of the
tyrant Yazid,
And Islam gets a new life after each Karbala.

This period saw the rise of many poets. To name a few,
Wahidud Din Saleem, Shauq Kidwai, Brijmohan Dattatreya Kaifi,
Zafar Ali Khan, Anand Narain Mulla, Iqbal Suhail, Tilok Chand
Mahroom, Saghar Nizami, Gopi Nath Amn, Ravish Siddiqui, Ali
Jawad Zaidi, Jagan Nath Azad, Makhdoom, Faiz, Majaz, Sardar
Jafri, Kaifi Azmi, Majrooh, and others, whose main poetic
inspiration came from the national struggle and the freedom
movement. However during this period, the voice of Josh
Malihabadi was the loudest. Given to romanticism, Josh's
concept of revolution hardly stands political reasoning, but
endowed with the gift of a highly expressive and powerful
diction, his voice was perhaps best suited for the agitational
poetry echoing the tension and turmoil of the national struggle.
Some of his poems like *East India Company ke Farzandon ke
Nām, Zawāl-e-Jahānbānī* and *Shikast-e-Zindān kā Khwāb*
are memorable in the sense that while being moving pieces of
poetry, they mirror the restlessness and the militant mood of the
Indian freedom struggle, and also preserve its heat at the boiling
point. Josh's poetry has a thundering quality and is known for its
masculinity and boldness. In *Shikast-e-Zindān kā Khwāb*, Josh
compares India to a prison, and the shattering of its gates and
walls to the removal of the vestiges of British domination:

*Kyā hind kā zindān kāmp rahā hai goonj rahī hain
takbīren*
Uktāe hain shāyad kuch qaidī aur tor̤ rahe hain zanjīren

The prison is under attack and the shouts of victory rent the
sky

The prisoners at last have risen in revolt and are shattering the chains .

The nationalist poetry of Urdu, thus, has its peaks and pastures, and its relationship with the yearnings and aspirations of the Indian people is so deep and complex that in a brief sojourn one can touch upon a few landmarks. Still, it is amply borne out that the distinction earned by the Urdu language as being a language of revolt and revolution is not merely because of the freedom movement's slogans like *Inqilāb Zindahbād*, Long Live Revolution, or because of popular songs like:

Sarfaroshi ki tamannā ab hamāre dil men hai
Dekhnā hai zor kitnā bāzoo-e-qātil men hai . . .

Keen is our desire to lay down our lives for the country
Now is the time to challenge the murderer's strength . . .

but because of the deeply realized creative expressions of its innumerable poets who, while echoing the patriotic *zeitgeist*, also participated in creating an emotional climate in which millions rose against colonialism and led their country to the dawn of freedom.

6

The Sound Structure in Iqbal's Urdu Poetry

DR. MUHAMMAD IQBAL (1877-1938) was not only a thinker, but also one of the most important poets of the Indian sub-continent ranking with the highest. With his recurrent theme of the strengthening of individual ego, the infinite potentiality of man in shaping his own destiny and the destiny of the universe, and with his emphasis on the universal approach for the quest of the Perfect Man, harmoniously uniting all of man's creative faculties, Iqbal's poetry cannot be confined to one language or one country. His poetry pulsates with his abounding love for social reform, and is marked by his deeply realised anti-imperialist stance, and his burning desire for the eradication of colonialism from the countries of Asia and Africa. Iqbal was a deeply inspired poet with a mission to accomplish, and his poetic art needs no emphasis. There are many aspects to it. The chief among them is the sound structure of Iqbal's poetic art, through which, coupled with some other features, he casts a spell, and which because of the high degree of his inspiration and his special semantic import, has acquired a mysteriously unique quality, which is a distinguishing mark of his muse.

It could be argued that the use of sound in poetry is neither always deliberate nor conscious. The inspiration, the core of the poem, the idea, the feeling, the choice of words, even the rhyme scheme, all of these have their own compulsions. Hence a poet is not absolutely free to pick or reject all or some sounds. Still the use of language by a poet, or the frequency of certain phonological features in the diction of a poet, reveal certain preferences or choices which lead to the heart of some of the mysteries of the creative art. It is admitted on all hands that Iqbal has a peculiar musicality, and a unique resonant quality which stuns and at the same time fascinates, and which is not met with in other Urdu poets. Iqbal's admirers usually acknowledge this quality of his verse, but they hardly venture to fathom the depths of the secrets of this aspect of Iqbal's creative art.

It is obvious that sounds have no meaning. The operation of meaning by and large starts from the morphological level, and it completes itself at the hierarchy of the syntactic level, or in a unit of discourse. But it cannot be denied that sounds create an impression or mood contributory to the semantic atmosphere of the poem in general. This means that at the highest level of creativity, the use of certain sounds makes an impression on the mind of the reader, or intensifies the denotations or connotations of the words used. Iqbal's beautiful little poem 'An Evening on the Bank of River Neckar, Heidelberg' is a case in point:

> khāmosh hai chāndnī qamar kī
> Shākhen hain khamosh har shajar kī
> Vādī ke navā farosh khāmosh
> Kuhsār ke sabzposh khāmosh
> Fītrat behosh ho gaī hai
> Āghosh men shab ke so gaī hai
> Kuch aisa sukūt kā fusūn hai
> Neckar kā khirām bhī sukūn hai
> Tāron ka khamosh kārvān hai
> Ye qāfila be-darā ravān hai
> Khāmosh hain koh-o-dasht-o-daryā
> Qudrat hai murāqabe men goyā
> Ai dil! tū bhī khamosh ho jā
> Āghosh men gham ko le ke so jā.

The immediate impact of this poem is the feeling of lonesomeness and solitariness. It can be easily seen that this feeling has been created and intensified by the repetitive use of the sounds of s, sh, x (kh) and f, which occur thirty-seven times in this short poem of seven couplets.

The frequency of a particular set of sounds many times is deeply reflective of a poet's creative personality. For instance, Mir Taqi Mir's melancholy and pensive mood cannot be conveyed by sounds used by Ghalib for his iconoclastic and non-conformist defiant attitude. Similarly, Iqbal's dynamism, his emphasis on man's capacity to shape his destiny, and his conceptual framework of the Perfect Man, call for a sound structure packed with power, and which could convey a certain degree of heat and energy to the reader. The majestic vibrance, grandeur and flow of Iqbal's poetic diction generally create an impression as if a mysterious flower is unfolding its petals in the vast openness of the cosmos. Iqbal's voice touches the heart, lifts the soul and carries away the reader in a single sweep. It is sharp, compact, tight, and at the same time so melodious as if a spring were bubbling forth in a lush green valley, or enchanting notes were flowing from the taut strings of a *sarod*. However, while trying to reach the secrets of this unique combination of energy and melody, one has to ignore couplets like:

> *shakti bhi shānti bhi bhagton ke geet men hai*
> *dharti ke bāsiyon ki mukti pareet men hai*

since they form only one aspect of Iqbal's diction, and do not represent the whole or core of his style. To grasp the code of Iqbal's sound structure, one must keep in mind the whole range of Iqbal's poetry, or at least his long representative poems, like *Masjid-e-Qartabah, Zauq-o-Shauq, Khizr-e-Rāh and Sāqi Nāmah.*

A thorough analytical study of *Masjid-e-Qartabah* undertaken by the present writer revealed that Iqbal's semantic and morphological urges lead him to an unprecedented excessive use of 'spirant' sounds like *f, s, sh, z, zh, x(kh)* and *gh*. These coupled with 'continuants', *l* and *r* form the core of Iqbal's phonological code through which he creates his characteristic spell. It must be remarked that the Urdu language is twice as much rich in 'stop' sounds, but their use in no way forms a characteristic of Iqbal's poetic diction. Of the 'stops', eight 'aspirates', i.e., *ph, bh, th, dh, ch, jh, kh* and *gh* plus six 'retroflexes', i.e., *ṭ, ṭh, ḍ, ḍh, ṛ,* and *ṛh* totalling fourteen sounds are indicative of Urdu's Indo-Aryan base, or its Prakritic foundations. But the majority of the 'spirants', i.e., *f, z, zh, x,* and *gh* denote the Persio-Arabic influences. It is through the interplay and blending of these Persio-Arabic and Prakritic elements that the Urdu language acquires its synthetic character. A strikingly interesting feature of Iqbal's poetry is that though it uses the Persio-Arabic 'spirants' excessively, it neither violates nor disturbs the natural fibre of the Urdu language. To explain this paradoxical usage, a further enquiry into other aspects of Iqbal's sound structure is necessary.

Iqbal is very frugal in his use of 'aspirates' and 'retroflexes'. In *Masjid-e-Qartabah's* sixty-four couplets, 'aspriates' and 'retroflexes' have occurred only thirty-nine times, as compared to nine hundred and thirty-one occurrences of 'spirant' sounds, a ratio of one to twenty-four. The hypothesis so derived was further tested by an analysis of *Zauq-o-Shauq* and *Khizr-e-Rāh*, two other long poetic masterpieces of Iqbal. The results fully confirmed the earlier findings. A look at *Sāqi Nāmah, Tulū'-e-Islām, Shuā'-e-Ummīd* and *Iblīs kī Majlis-e-Shūrā* further establishes that Iqbal uses 'retroflexes' and 'aspirates' only when it is absolutely necessary or unavoidable because of the rhyme scheme or verbal usage. It will be recalled that Urdu's verbal system is almost entirely Prakritic, and it is on this level that the 'retroflexes' and 'aspirates' occur freely, or in pronouns, particles and auxiliaries like *mujh, tujh, kuch, phir, bhī, thā, thī*. The average count of 'aspirate' and 'retroflex' sounds in the poetry of Iqbal comes to *less than one* sound per couplet. Keeping in view the poetic conventions, stock similes and metaphors of Urdu, most of which are borowed from the Semitic and Iranian traditions, a question could be raised that the occurrence of 'aspirates' and 'retroflexes' cannot be expected to be on the high side in Urdu poetic usage. But to find the natural usage of these sounds, one has to turn to Mir Taqi Mir, because none else can perhaps represent the 'Urdu-ness' of the Urdu language better than the 'God of Urdu Poesy'. A random analysis for this purpose was undertaken, which revealed that the occurrence of these Prakritic sounds in the poetry of Mir Taqi Mir is *two* sounds per couplet. If this is taken as the mean average of the use of 'aspirate' and 'retroflex' sounds in Urdu poetic usage, then Iqbal scores very low, that is, *less than one* sound per couplet. But this characteristic of Iqbal's Urdu verse is shared by another great poet of Urdu, Mirza Ghalib. Perhaps this is because of the fact that both Ghalib and Iqbal are very fond of Arabic and Persian substantives. Still one cannot hasten to conclude that Iqbal's and Ghalib's sound structures are the same. The reasons for this are not far to seek. The first line of demarcation between the sound patterns of Iqbal and Ghalib can be drawn between the use of the frontal sounds and backward sounds. Iqbal, as we have already noted, is fond of sounds, *f, s, z, sh,* which are mostly produced in the front of the mouth, and are sharp and compact. His stock terminology includes *shāhīn, shuā', sho'la, sham'a, faqr, firishte, aql-o-'ishq, soz-o-sāz, farmān, lāla-e-sahrā, shamshir-o-sinān.* Compared to this, Ghalib's contemplative mood is better conveyed by the sounds produced from the back of the mouth. His stock phrases like *dil-o-jigar, zaxm-e-jigar, da'vat-e-mizhgān, gham-gusārī, marg-e-tamannā, rag-e-jān, rag-e-sang, sang-e-garān, gham-e-āwārgī* abound in sounds of *j, g, gh,* or the voiced ones, which convey heaviness and diffusion.

Nonetheless, the basic difference between Ghalib's and Iqbal's sound structures lies in the use of vowels. Perhaps the touch of heaviness in Ghalib's verse, and Iqbal's bewitching sound impact, can be best explained by taking into consideration the differences in vowel usage in the two poets. It must be remarked that the vowel system of Urdu is the same as that of Hindi, and is one hundred per cent Prakritic. While speaking of the lack of vowel abundance in Ghalib's verse, one must keep in mind that Ghalib's art is oblique, he conceals more than what he reveals. His restrictions are the restrictions of the *genre* of ghazal where everything has to be created on the level of a miniature. Whereas Iqbal's generic possibilities are great, his moulds are large, and his casts are big. His forms are narrative poems, long poems, and stanza poems of different formations and also *Masnawīs*. His art is direct. The tone and temper of his poetry warrant sermonisation, so he can take the liberty to use full verbal structures including pronouns and auxiliaries. In Ghalib's art, his semantic and stylistic compulsions squeeze out all such linguistic redundancies. This obviously has adversely affected the use of vowels, especially the long vowels, in Ghalib. Iqbal's poetry in this regard is as rich as Mir Taqi Mir's common core Urdu usage. The results of a thorough investigation in this regard revealed that as compared to an average of eleven vowel sounds per couplet in Ghalib, Mir and Iqbal use sixteen vowel sounds per couplet. However, not withstanding this *vocalic* similarity, as already discussed, Mir and Iqbal are poles apart in their consonantal usage. They are similar only when it comes to vowel usage. Now, at this stage it is not difficult to answer the question regarding the high degree of musicality in Iqbal, since this quality is closely linked with nasalization, and nasalization occurs freely only where there is an abundance of long vowels. It is, therefore, this feature which renders both Mir and Iqbal phonetically more satisfying than any other poet of Urdu. But Iqbal's own variegated sound structure derives its uniqueness from the masterly blending of the Persio-Arabic 'spirant' sounds with Prakritic simple and nasalized vowels. It is this quality which has given Iqbal's verse a compelling melodious tone, simultaneously with an abundance of dynamic power and energy. It is this sound structure which reverberates and echoes throughout the Urdu poetry of Iqbal, and at its creative zenith becomes, in the words of Iqbal, himself, truly, *yazdāngīr*, a challenger to God, the Creator.

7

Tradition and Innovation in Firaq Gorakhpuri

1

URDU poetry is not written according to conventions, such as one encounters in other Indian languages—either Indo-Aryan or Dravidian, for as a language and as a medium of literature, Urdu developed under different social and historical pressures. Its history, like that of many other Indo-Aryan languages, does not go back to more than seven or eight centuries, when it emerged as a linguistic *modus vivendi* between the two major communities of India. The speech of the majority of the incoming Muslims was Persian, which has a highly developed poetic tradition. Persian dominated the North Indian literary scene as long as the stars of the Mughals were shining brightly, and it is from Persian that Urdu inherited its poetical propensities.

Basically, there are eight feet and nineteen metres in Urdu poetry but, by different permutations and combinations, hundreds of measures can be obtained. The Urdu verse forms can be broadly classified into two categories: *bayāniyah,* (narrative) and *ramziyah,* (suggestive). Many of the verse forms, as the *masnawī* (versified tale) the *qasīdah* (panegyric) and the *marsiyah* (elegy) belong to the first category. The second category is the classical *Ghazal* (love lyric) by far the most popular and most significant genre of Urdu poetry.

To acquaint ourselves with the classical Urdu Ghazal we must take a close look at the following verses:

1.   *tum hamāre kisī tarah na hue*
      warna duniyā men kyā nahīn hotā

      Only you could not become mine
      All else is possible in this world![1]

                                                        Momin

2.   *tum mire pās hote ho goyā*
      jab koī dusrā nahīn hotā

      It seems as if you were with me
      When no one else is present

                                                        Momin

3.   *badnām ho ge jāne bhī do imtihān ko*
      rakkhe gā kaun tum se azīz apnī jān ko

      You'll get ill fame, better just put aside the test:
      Who will hold his own life dearer than yours?

                                                  Mir Taqi Mir

4.   *bijlī ik kaund gaī ānkhon ke āge to kyā*
      bāt karte ke main lab tashna-e-taqrīr bhī thā

      So what if lightning did flash before my eyes?
      If only you had talked, as my lips thirsted to speak.

                                                        Ghalib

5.   *yeh 'uzr-e-imtihān-e-jazb-e-dil kaisā nikal āyā*
      main ilzām us ko detā thā, qusūr apnā nikal āyā

      The test of the heart's response—how did this pretext
      come up?
      I was blaming her; the fault was in fact my own.

                                                        Momin

6. *mat mardumak-e-dīda men samjho ye nigāhen*
   hain jama' suwaida-e-dil-e-čashm men āhen

   Do not think these are glances in the pupils of (my)
   eyes;
   They are sighs collected in the black spot of (my)
   heart's eye.

   Ghalib

7. *nahīn hai zakhm koī bakhya ke darkhur mire tan*
   men
   huā hai tār-e-ashk-e-yās rishta čashm-e-sozan men

   There is no wound in my body that can be stitched up.
   The thread in the needle's eye has become a vexed tear
   string.

   Ghalib

8. *jātā hun dāgh-e-hasrat-e-hastī liye hue*
   hun sham'-e- kushta darkhur-e-mahfil nahīn rahā

   I am leaving, bearing the scar of longing for life,
   I am a snuffed-out candle, not fit to stay in company.

   Ghalib

Verses one and two by Momin belong to the same Ghazal.
Each line is called a *misra'* , and two such *misra's* make a *she'r*.
Usually there are five to twenty-five *she'rs* in a Ghazal. The
ending words of lines two and four demonstrate that the rhyme
does not consist of a single word, but of a full phrase, *kyā nahīn*
hotā and *dusrā nahīn hotā*. The portion *nahīn hotā* is merely
a repetitive element and runs throughout the Ghazal. This is
called *radīf*, literally (one that rides behind). The real rhyming
element is *kyā* and the second syllable of *dusrā;* this is called
qāfiyah (rhyme). So the rhyme scheme can be indicated as a b
z, c b z, d b z. Though the *radīf* adds to the musicality of the

Ghazal, it is not essential; therefore, an easier and more widely used rhyme scheme is a b, c b, d b, and so on.

With these general remarks about the form, let us move on to the meaning of these two *she'rs*. Obviously, it is the lover speaking to his beloved of his love. The first verse is a factual statement of a personal loss, viz., I tried to win you but did not succeed. The second verse is different in that the poet becomes more metaphysical in his concerns. He is speaking of a deeper realization, which has more than one layer of meaning to it. The most obvious level of meaning is the imaginary achievement of oneness with the beloved 'when no one else is present'; that is, not even the lover himself, for the absence of *dusrā* (second, other) semantically guards against any kind of duality. But the word *dusrā* is quite vague; it can also be an allusion to 'other care(s),' meaning that 'when other cares are not on my mind, you are with me'; in other words, I have reconciled myself to the state of loneliness, and think of you only in my free moments.

Both *she'rs* are thus functioning as separate units of meaning. Though there is some kind of progression involved here, that of moving from past to present, this is more a matter of mood or perhaps of rhyme scheme than of meaning.

In Ghazal, each verse is a poem within a poem, complete and satisfying in itself. The only formal connection between different verses is that of the meter and rhyme. On the level of meaning each verse functions by itself. This fragmentary quality causes the Ghazal to appear to a foreign reader, in the first place, as a jumble of disconnected or contradictory ideas.

But the fragmentary quality of the Ghazal forces the poet to make his point, or say whatever he wants to say in only two lines. Therefore, the Ghazal is a very restricted verse form. Still, this 'narrowness of space' *(tangī-e-jā)* has also proved to be an asset, as it requires utmost poetic restraint and concentration, and results in the compactness and selectiveness of this genre. The Ghazal thus assumes an epigrammatic quality and a capacity to express difficult thought in a very condensed form. To illustrate how a *she'r* of Urdu Ghazal can become a marvel of the art of condensation, let us move on to verse five. At the first look the whole thing appears baffling. The second line, "I was blaming her, the fault was, in fact, my own", is somewhat clear. We can see that the situation started with the lover blaming the beloved. Blaming for what? The answer can be supplied by the conventions of the Ghazal, where the beloved is invariably cold and indifferent. Now the last phrase in the second line says, "The fault was in fact my own". In other words the tussle ended with the lover discovering that he himself was to be blamed for the indifference of the beloved. The question naturally arises how this discovery was made, and we revert to the first line. "The test of the heart's response—how did this pretext come up?" Obviously, the emphasis is on the 'pretext', involving *jazb-e-dil* (heart's response), and there is some talk of a 'test' for it. Was not the lover complaining of 'heart's response' on the part of the beloved, and is she not challenging his accusation on the same grounds, making her 'heart's response' a test of something? Now let us ponder over the nature of that thing to which a heart responds. In this context it could only be true love. Hence the beloved's pretext is: had your love been true, it certainly would have evoked a response in my heart; now I am indifferent because you yourself lack real love. Hearing this, the lover had to stop blaming the beloved.

All these steps mentioned above, which can be the subject of a full-length poem, are recounted in one *she'r* of a few words. The poet had no other choice than to confine himself to the narrow limit of the two lines. Much of the success of a Ghazal depends on brevity and the use of a highly suggestive language, and their aesthetic value in this type of art cannot be overemphasized. Conciseness operates on two axes—syntactical and semantic. We therefore note that the beginning of the dialogue is given in the second line. Then all the detail that can be provided by the reader's imagination or his familiarity with the conventions has been omitted. The key words of the argument *'uzr-e-imtibān-e-jazb-e-dil'* are mentioned in the first line, and the ending of the dialogue is given immediately after the beginning in the second line. This completes the whole thought. On the syntactic level, the phrase, *'uzr-e-imtibān-e-*

jazb-e-dil', is no less a marvel of terseness. Translated literally into English it reads: 'The pretext of the test of the responsiveness of the heart.' Note the -e- sounds connecting the four substantives *'uzr-e-imtihān-e-jazb-e-dil'*. This is the Persian *izāfat*, an indication of the genetive frequently used in Urdu which squeezes out from the Urdu syntax the postpositional set, *kā, ke,* and *ki*. Another device of syntactic condensation is the dropping of the pronoun, which, however, is retained in this verse. But if we take a quick look at verses three, four and six, we will see that 'you', 'me', 'your', and 'my' are mere 'fillers' in English translation. In Urdu, however the terminal verb or auxiliary verb like *ho ge* (3), *do* (3), *karte* (4) or *samjho* (6) determines not only the person but also the number and gender.

It is appropriate to point out here that contrary to Persian which has no verbal gender, the Urdu Ghazal uses the masculine gender for the beloved. This is illustrated by *hamāre* (1), *hote* (2), *ge* (3) and *karte* (4). Strangely enough, the lover is also of masculine gender. Does this involve talk of homo-sexuality? The answer at this point is both yes and no. Note that the beloved, whose glimpse we caught in verses 1, 2 and 5, and who is further talked about in verses 3 and 4 is implicitly referred to as being indifferent, cold and careless. She may be cruel, callous and treacherous as well. Consider also verses 6 and 7, where the lover talks of his infinite yearning, of his overflowing 'sighs' and incurable 'wounds'. What type of love is this? Is this a one-sided affair? Or, is the beloved a creation of the poet's own fancy?

To find answers to these questions we must go back to the early Islamic society in which the Ghazal originated. Incidentally, the word *ghazal* literally means 'talking to women'. Rigid and austere, as is the nature of Islam, the early Islamic society was quite puritan. The only physical love permissible was within the four walls of the house, i.e., the *harem*. Of course there developed the institution of the courtesan's quarters, but in fact physical love was proscribed and was frowned upon by society. This was the environment in which the Ghazal originated. The only safe way of referring to one's love in poetry, without, however, giving away her identity, was to talk in universal terms.

(It has already been pointed out that in Persian there is no verbal gender, i.e., male and female are referred to by the same verbal endings.) Hence, with the open and free expression of love impeded, the concept of the beloved, which had a physical entity as its basis, changed, in course of time, to a mere *abstraction*, a thing of dreams. In the Ghazal there are many instances when a lover seems more interested in *'ishq* (love) *per se*, or in the imaginary creation of his desire than in *ma'shūq*, or the object of his desire. This accounts for the despair, resentment and even anger of the lover, and also for the introspection (*dākhiliyat*), which so dominates the Ghazal. Given the social and moral pressures and the restrictions imposed by the form, the Ghazal, using suggestive language for love themes, evolved an elaborate system of symbolic imagery and conventions.

The basis of love in the Ghazal is the inevitable eternal triangle, but it has its own variants. The base might very well represent the lover, the source of the manifestation of love yet dormant, reticent and suppressed. One angle represents the beloved, which in this case can be either a physical entity, a creation of fancy or the idea of the love (*'ishq*) itself. The other side stands for the proverbial *raqīb* (rival) which in the Ghazal can also be the puritan society or orthodoxy represented by *shaikh*, *zāhid*, or *maulavi*. The poetical symbolism and conventions of this triangle work as follows:

1.	*'āshiq*	lover	*ma'shūq,*	beloved	*raqīb*	rival
			'ishq	love	*zāhid,*	ascetic
					muhtasib	censor
					shaikh	
2.	*dil*	heart	*husn*	beauty	*vahm*	doubt
3.	*jazbah*	emotion	*vijdān*	intuition	*'aql*	reason

4.	*āshiyānah*	nest (lover's heart)	*bāgh, chaman*	garden	*barq, bijlī*	lightning (cruelty of fate and of the skies which strike the heart, i.e., nest)
5.	*parand*	bird	*fazā*	open space	*saiyyād, qafas*	hunter (who clips the birds' 'wings' and puts him in a cage)
6.	*bulbul*	nightingale	*gul, bahār*	rose spring	*gul-chīn, bāghbān, khizān*	flower-picker, gardener, autumn
7.	*parvānah*	moth	*sham'*	candle	*sahar*	morning
8.	*brahman*	infidel	*but*	idol	*shaikh*	orthodoxy
9.	*Farhād*	Farhad: a sculptor	*Shīrīn*	Shirin: wife of Khusrau	*Khusrau Parvez*	Khusrau Parvez: a king of Persia
10.	*Majnūn*	Majnun	*Laila*	Laila	*duniyā*	world
11.	*nigāh, nazar*	eye	*rukh, didār, jalwah*	face	*niqāb, pardah, hijāb*	veil

These conventions have another dimension to them also. They are as much applicable to mystic themes as they are to erotic. To pursue this point further we will have to consider the following verses:

9. *hijāb-e-rukh-e-yār the āp hī ham*
    khulī ānkh jab koī parda na dekhā

    I myself was the veil upon my Beloved's face;
    When I opened my eyes, there was no veil.

    Mir Dard

10. *galī men uskī gayā, so gayā, na bolā phir*
    main Mīr, Mīr kar usko bahut pukār rahā

    Mir went into her lane, was lost, did not speak:
    I kept calling him again and again, Mir! Mir!

    Mir Taqi Mir

11. *jab dil ke āstān par 'ishq ān kar pukārā*
    parde se yār bolā Bedil kahān hai ham men

    To my heart's threshold Love came, stood and called.
    Through the veil the Loved One said, "Bedil's not in
    here."

    Bedil

12. *ham muwahhid hain hamārā kesh hai tark-e-rusūm*
    millaten jab miṭ gaīn ajzā-e-īmān ho gaīn

    I am a monotheist, my religion is to reject all Externals.
    When the creeds were ground down, they became
    elements of the Faith.

    Ghalib

13. *ghāfil tū kidhar bahke hai ṭuk dil kī khabar le*
    shisha jo baghal men hai usī men to parī hai

    Silly man, where are you wandering? Just note your
    heart.
    The glass under your arm—it's what contains the Spirit.

    Mir Dard

14.   *mat jā tar-o-tāzgī pe is kī*
       'ālam to khayāl kā čaman hai

       Don't be swayed by its flourishing freshness:
       The world is a garden of fancy.

                                                    Mir Dard

15.   *parastish kī yān tak ke ai but tujhe*
       nazar men sabhon kī khudā kar čale

       I worshipped you so much, O Idol, that
       In the eyes of all I made you a god.

                                                    Mir Taqi Mir

Let us take a look at verse 9 (compare this with the last convention). Obviously, *hijāb*, *rukh-e-yār*, and *pardah*, are part of erotic imagery, but the phrases *āp hī ham* (I, myself), and *ānkh khulnā* (the eye to open), have overt mystical connotation, and anyone with some familiarity with the Islamic mystical concept of *ma'rifat* (spiritual knowledge; or the Indian concept of *jnāna*) can see that clearly. This double play of the imagery developed during the eighth and ninth centuries, especially in Iran and its bordering countries, following the rise of *tasawwuf* (mysticism). We will not belabour the point as to whether Islamic mysticism was a rationalization on the part of the non-puritan elements, or whether it was a reaction on the part of the Aryan race accepting Islam. Whatever its nature, it rebelled vehemently against the established orthodoxy and restraints on physical love. With this, the Ghazal entered into a new phase in its development whereby physical love was made the basis of spiritual love; *almajāz qantratal-haqīqa*, (physical phenomenon is the bridge to the reality). The poets freely talked of their revelries and drinking bouts, a trend which coincided with the vogue in Iran of homosexuality. This practice had already marked its beginning in Arab countries during the Islamic wars and flourished with the influx of handsome turkish boys brought back as war captives to serve as slaves and cupbearers. In mystic poetry the boys are referred to as *mazhar* (exhibitors of the beauty of God). The poets had a prolonged spell of physical as well as 'gnostic' honeymooning with them, and traces of this love are still found in the dual reference, masculine-gender-oriented imagery of the Urdu Ghazal, but as a poetical subject this type of love soon died out. However, the mystic themes were pursued further. The number of practising mystics was always very small, but as mysticism was considered a mark of cultural attainment, almost every poet talked in terms of mystic imagery.

The conventions of mystical poetry can be outlined as follows:

1.	*'ishq*	divine love	*vasl* *didār*	union: revelation of divine mysteries	*hijr* *firāq*	separation: non-attainment of oneness with God
2.	*nūh*	soul	*khudā*	God	*dair-o haram*	temple and 'sanctuary'
3.	*musāfir,*	traveller	*manzil*	destination (attainment of communion)	*khār*	thorn
	rāh-rau		*rāh*	way, path	*sar sar*	strong wind
					rahnumā	guide
					rāhzan	robber
4.	*rind*	drunkard, libertine (one who is heedless of and defies social conventions)	*mai,* *sharāb,* *sāqi,*	divine wine, cupbearer, spiritual instructor	*muhtasib*	censor

			maikhānah	tavern (where one relinquishes his fame and pride)		
5.	*junūn*	divinely inspired madness	*haqīqat*	truth	*'aql, khirad*	empirical knowledge (has a traditional rivalry with *junūn*)
6.	*Mansūr, mujāhid, bebāk*	name of a celebrated sufi, fighter for the faith, fearless	*dāro-o-rasan*	scaffold	*hākim*	ruler
7.	*diwānah*	mad (frenzied, inspired)	*sahrā, virāna, bahār*	desert, wasteland, spring	*zanjīr* *zindān*	chain prison
8.	*sūfī*	mystic	*ma'rifat*	spiritual knowledge	*maulavī, shaikh*	theologian orthodoxy
9.	*sālik*	devotee	*fanā*	extinction, submission	*anā*	ego, (that only through complete annihilation of ego, the lover can seek oneness with the perfect beauty)

10. *khud*   self   *bekhudī*   self   *khudī*   self
                                    forget-   conscious-
                                    fulness   ness

The mystical tradition of the classical Urdu Ghazal can be represented by three circles going round the triangle.

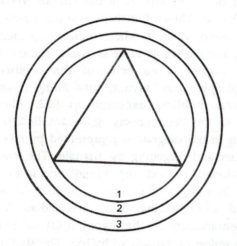

The elements of the eternal triangle will now have to be re-defined slightly for the mystical tradition: the base represents the *sūfī* (mystic); one side the *mazhar*(exhibitor, or wine or tavern); and the other side *shaikh-o-muhtasib* (the religious orthodoxy or material delights). The goal of the mystic is union with God, the state which is referred to in verse 10, of Mir Taqi Mir. *Galī* (her lane) and *so gayā* (was lost) stir our imagination on the physical plane. But in the next line when we see the image of the lover splitting into two, the self-conscious or assertive *main* (I) speaking to the unconscious or submissive Mir, the poet, we realize that we must look beyond the erotic imagery. Note that though the elements of double-play function aesthetically on the same plane of time, the valid meaning is the realization of becoming one with God. This negation of self or union with God, referred to as *fanā* (annihilation) of the 'limited ego' in mysticism, is represented by the first circle circumscribing the triangle. At this point, we have to assume that this is the only circle around the triangle. God is all-embracing; the mystic, his desire and the material phenomena are all His creations and within Him. In this type of union, the mystic loses his identity and what remains is God.

Consider, at this point, the excellent verse by Bedil (verse 11). This verse at once reminds us of the famous Vedantic saying, *tatvamasi* (That art Thou). But there is another side to the coin. Take, for example, verse 9, where there is no mention of any other person, and the whole verse is based on the first person *āp* (I). Dard's couplet is an echo of the celebrated mystic Mansoor's 'blasphemous' saying, *anal-haqq!* (I am God), for which he was publicly executed in 922. Also note the resemblance to the Vedantic saying, *aham Brahma'smi* (I am Brahma). This in our diagram is represented by taking the three circles together and forgetting the triangle. The 'core' circle, as already mentioned, is God, the 'fringe' one is the self of the mystic, who in a flight of intuition visualizes himself as God, supreme and all-embracing. The 'intermediate' circle is the material phenomenon or the hypocritical orthodoxy which obstructs the union of the self with God. The starting point, the centre of the circles, is common to them. This is the 'Love', which according to mystic poets, is the source of both self and non-self. In the words of Mir, *ārzū 'ishq mudda'a hai 'ishq* (the desire is Love, and the goal of desire is also Love). Thus, in this type of poetry, differences of creed, colour and religion pale into insignificance, as exemplified by verse 12, one of the finest from Ghalib.

Lastly, it should also be mentioned that in the classical Ghazal inanimate or abstract images are usually personified and given animate attributes. Three of the most common sets of images as discussed by Muhammad Husain Azad in *Āb-e-Hayāt*, (Lahore 1881, pp. 55-56) are given below:

GARDEN : with its flowers and birds is the human society. Spring enters with her henna-coloured feet after the grey old lady—autumn—has left. The nightingale and the rose play the game of hide and seek. The Zephyr (messenger) whispers something into the ears of the buds, and they start smiling (opening) and laughing (blooming). The dew puts together a necklace, but also weeps because the life (of the rose) is so short.

FLASK : has a long, elegant neck like a damsel. She bends herself gracefully and laughs and sobs as the wine is poured out of it.

CANDLE : is a tall and slim beauty, standing proudly with a golden crown of flame over her head. The dark central area of the flame is the *dāgh-e-dil* (the black scar in the heart), the mark of her grief at the sad end of her lover, the moth, or it may denote her own longing for life; as long as she lives, she keeps consuming herself and sheds tears of sorrow.

2

FIRAQ GORAKHPURI: Having acquainted ourselves with the tradition, let us now move on to the poetry of Raghupati Sahay Firaq Gorakhpuri. Born on August 28, 1896, at Gorakhpur, Uttar Pradesh, Firaq graduated from Allahabad in 1917. After graduation, he was nominated for the Civil Service, but he preferred to join the freedom struggle, and after serving a term in the prison, he was appointed Under Secretary of the Indian National Congress Party. In 1930 he became a Lecturer of English at Allahabad University, from where he retired in 1959. He published more than half a dozen volumes of poetry, and was recipient of the highest literary awards of India given by the Sahitya Akademi (1960) and the Bharatiya Jnanpith (1969). Firaq was both a poet and a critic, and is remembered for his penetrating essays on Mus-hafi, Zauq, and Urdu love poetry. He passed away in 1982.

Firaq's poetry, like Wordsworth's and Mir Taqi Mir's, is uneven. At its best, it ranks with the highest, and at its worst it is flat and trivial. Here we shall, however, take into consideration only the former aspect and discuss the innovative element of his poetry. Here are some verses from Firaq:

1. *māil-e-bedād woh kab thā Firāq*
   tū ne us ko ghaur se dekhā nahīn

   When was she inclined to harshness?
   You have not observed her carefully.

2. *sitāre jāgte hain rāt lat chatkāe sotī hai*
   dabe pāon ye kis ne ā ke khwāb-e-zindagī badlā

   The stars keep vigil, night with loosened tresses sleeps.
   Who, coming on soft foot-falls, has changed the dream of
   life?

3. *zarā visāl ke bā'd āina to dekh ai dost*
   tire jamāl kī doshīzgī nikhar āī

   Just look into the mirror, O dear one, after love's
   consummation
   Your virgin youth has blossomed still.

In the first verse, Firaq is challenging the traditional view that
the beloved is harsh and indifferent. Addressing the conformist,
he says that you yourself have not given enough thought to the
beloved's nature, suggesting that she is normally responsive, and
if you find her otherwise, perhaps it is because of some external
forces over which she has no control. Note the phrase 'inclined
to harshness' in the first line, implying that 'harshness' is not the
nature of the beloved. The positive tone suggests that in this case
love is not a mere abstraction, but a deeply realized experience.
Consider how Firaq, starting from a traditional concept, weaves
his delicate idea into the fabric of the verse, deviating markedly
from the beaten track. On the formalistic level, he has not
introduced a single change in the Ghazal, and has even retained
the traditional use of the masculine gender, as shown in this
verse by the use of the auxiliary verb *thā* (he was). This helps
retain the universality of the Ghazal and maintain a sense of

decorum, a highly cherished value of the composite Indian culture.

Verse 2 also refers to a feeling based on an actual experience. The first line is in the present tense, somewhat unusual in the classical Ghazal. Now the poet no more speaks in terms of 'this happened' or 'this was so', but rather, 'this is so' or 'this seems to be so'. *Sitāre* (stars) and *rāt* (night) metaphorically stand for the male and the female, a fact which is further established by their grammatical nature, for *sitāra* is a masculine, and *rāt* a feminine noun. The word *soti* (sleeps), together with *rāt* (night) is suggestive of the physical presence, the intensity of which is revealed in the second line, "Who, coming on soft foot-falls, has changed the dream of life"? That is, the impact is such that it has changed the life of lover; and the earlier life, compared to the present, looks unreal, like a dream; or the present life is as pleasant as a dream. Also note the beautiful use of *ri'āyat-e-lafzi* (use of the morphologically linked images), as 'stars', 'night', 'dream', 'sleep' and 'vigil'.

Moralists have often criticized the third verse as obscene. The mention of *visāl* (union) is nothing new in the Ghazal, but the difference is that this time one can feel the beat of the pulse. The poet is speaking of the sheer delight of an experience shared by both the lover and the beloved. In this verse the poet, paradoxically, is demolishing the conventional idea of chastity by implying that it is more a state of mind than a state of body, and emphasizing that the consummation of love does not lessen but, rather, enhances the charm of the beauty.

Firaq's forte is that he can clothe the traditional imagery of classical Ghazal with a new awareness and sensibility all his own. He possesses a 'historical sense', similar to that of T.S. Eliot. Such a poet "lives in what is not merely the present, but the present moment of the past..., not merely with his own generation in his bones, but with a feeling that the whole of the literature has a simultaneous existence." ('Tradition and the Individual Talent', *Selected Essays, 1917-1932*.) Firaq's Ghazal shows that he first digested the tradition he inherited, and only then introduced to it new lyrical dimensions.

From classical Ghazal to Firaq is not a big jump.
Modernization of the Ghazal started with Hali and was carried
on by Iqbal, Hasrat, Asghar, Fani and Jigar. Some of them,
especially Hasrat and Jigar, spoke of humanistic love, but it was
left to Firaq to speak of love in terms of its totality, in terms of its
tenderness and coarseness, its significance and meaninglessness.
His is a full-blooded response to love in its bewildering
complexity.

Perhaps this totality needs some elaboration. Firaq essentially
speaks of the timeless human relationship, with its joys and
sorrows, union and separation, but he has a capacity to capture
the intense excitement of love, and he speaks of it in a state of
heightened sensibility. His poetry, therefore, is not bound by the
temporal, but marked by the universal. He added no new
emotions in Urdu Ghazal, but he writes of some old ones with
new feeling. Furthermore, the lover and the beloved of Firaq's
Ghazal are deeply conscious of the complexity and anxiety of
their age. Things for them are not as clear as they were for the
classical poets. Here are some illustrative verses:

4. *kis liye kam nahīn hai dard Firāq*
   ab to woh dhyān se utar bhī gae

   Why does the pain not lessen, O Firaq,
   Now that she from my thoughts has gone away?

5. *tujhe to hāth lagāyā hai bārhā lekin*
   tire khayāl ko chūte hue main ḍarta hūn

   I have fondled you so many times,
   But I fear even to caress the thought of you.

6. *faza tabassum-e-subh-e-bahār thī lekin*
   pahunć ke manzil-e-jānān pe ānkh bhar āī

   The scene was like the smile of a spring morning.
   But when I reached my love's abode tears filled my eyes.

7. *batāen kyā dil-e-muztar udās kitnā thā*
   ke āj to nigah-e-nāz ne bhī samjhāyā

   How can I explain why the restless heart was so sad
   Even though today the dear one's looks consoled?

8. *tum mukhātab bhī ho qarīb bhī ho*
   tum ko dekhūn ke tum se bāt karūn

   You are attentive, and you are close.
   Shall I look at you? Or speak to you?

In verse 4, the line, "she from my thoughts has gone away", alludes to the customary view that it is the memory of an unattainable ideal that brings one pain. The first line, where the poet claims that in spite of his forgetting the beloved, the pain is no less suggests that there is much more to life than mere haunting, painful memories.

Observe, too, the subtle ambiguity of the verse. Firaq, here and elsewhere, after mentioning a common belief, takes an unconventional or startling positon, and sets the reader to thinking. He does not narrate but only suggests, for there is much in the emotional conflicts or problems of the modern man that has no clearly definable nature. In such verses, his images are often times fused. Though he points his finger, he never says, "this is a vague feeling"; rather, he suggests the situation where the impact of that vague feeling is deeply felt. It is this imprecise, amorphous feeling, an undefinable element, that forms the third element of the traditional love triangle in Firaq's poetry. It does not make any allowance for the conventional *raqīb* (rival) or *muhtasib* (censor, ascetic or *shaikh*). He suggests that the free flow of love from its fullest expression is perhaps obstructed by the anxiety of the age, the very consciousness of the burden of life. The verse that follows will further verify this point.

Verse 5 suggests that they both were friendly some time back, but now the mere idea of thinking about the beloved is sheer torment. Why that is so is not mentioned. Perhaps it reminds the lover of the problems that could not be solved, or perhaps of problems which are not easy to understand.

In verses 6 and 7 the poet is again juxtaposing two opposites. Note the words 'smile' in the first line and 'tears' in the other. Conventionally, the lover is expected to feel happy when he gets to the abode of his beloved. But "love" as we know, "is a many-splendoured thing", and who can tell what these tears are about? Perhaps they are of relief, anguish, excitement or some such feeling that cannot be defined precisely. The same is the nature of the expression in verse 7, where, in spite of all the assurance, the lover's heart remained as restless as ever. This again is both a negation of a traditionally held view and an allusion to the complexity of the nature of love and life.

Verse 8 is a marvel of simplicity and the suggestive clarity of expression, as both the figure and the speech of the beloved are made equally fascinating and absorbing. The poet is avoiding direct compliments and is speaking in terms of his own realization of the beauty of the beloved, implying that each single aspect of beauty is as innately fascinating as the wholeness of beauty.

As mentioned earlier, Firaq is the poet of the totality of love, which also implies that the beloved we find as the subject of his poetry is more truly human, vivacious even voluptuous. Conversely, while the traditional poets also talked of the beloved, it was more of an idea, an image, an illusion than a physical reality. We read much of the ruby lips, almond eyes, night-black tresses, rosy face and darting gestures, but all this expression was, at its best, merely two-dimensional, lacking a third, more human dimension. Thus, it was inevitably flat, though colourful. This is somewhat different with Firaq; his poetry has a deep, sensuous tone, perhaps the most sensuous in all Urdu poetry, and like Keats', is a riot of sounds and colours. He achieves this effect not so much by merely listing such words as touch, feel, form, warmth, glow, fragrance, melody, etc., as by putting them to a more ingenious use whereby they become full of life, giving the reader a living sensation of being close to someone's vital, intimate presence—a presence charged and tense with emotions, filled with the gently swaying figure of a youthful form that one can almost touch, and fragrance that one can drink deep—such is the effect of Firaq's language.

The following three of Firaq's quatrains present the woman in her simultaneous totality—as a virgin, wife and mother:

1. *doshīza fazā men lahlahāyā huā rūp*
   ā'ina-e-sub-h men jhalaktā huā rūp
   yeh narm nikhār, ye sijil dhaj, ye sugandh
   ras men hai kunwāre-pan ke dubā huā rūp

   Against the immaculate air, this undulating Beauty
   In the mirror of the dawn, this shimmering Beauty
   The soft glow, the elegant figure, the fragrance
   Steeped in the elixir of virginity, this Beauty.

2. *dhalkā ānčal damakte sīne pe alak*
   palkon kī ot muskurāhat kī jhalak
   woh māthe kī kahkashān, wo motī bharī māng
   woh god men nanhā sā humaktā bālak

   The slipping anchal, the gleaming bosom's glow
   The eyelids cover the sparkle of a smile
   The forehead a Milky Way, hair-part studded with pearls
   And in her lap, a tiny bouncing baby.

3. *hai byāhatā par rūp abhī kunwārā hai*
   mān hai par adā jo bhī hai doshīza hai
   woh mod bharī, māng bharī, god bharī
   kanyā hai, suhāgan hai, jagat mātā hai

   She is married, but her Beauty still is virgin
   She is a mother, but all her charm is still untouched
   She is joy-filled, her hair-part filled, her lap is filled
   She is a daughter, a happy wife, the mankind's mother.

Firaq's use of language also deserves mention. He was a great advocate of *Khārī Bolī Hindustānī*, which forms the common base for both Hindi and Urdu. The more one deviates from it by using *tatsama* forms in Hindi and pure Persio-Arabic forms in Urdu, the more removed he is from the common usage. Firaq's language attempts a happy blending of the forms drawn from both sources, while trying to keep as close to the base as possible. Any one of his above-quoted verses, for instance, his second quatrain, demonstrates this fact. On the phonological level it employs three retroflex sounds, *ḍh* in *ḍhalkā*, *ṭ* in *oṭ* and *ṭ* again in *muskurahaṭ;* and three aspirate sounds, *ḍh* in *ḍhalkā*, *th* in *māthe*, and *bh* in *bhārī* but not a single glottal or spirant velar sound of the Persio-Arabic origin. This is not to say that he completely opposes their use; rather he uses them where they are naturalized in Urdu. On the lexical level, the first, second, and third lines have one Persian word each, and the fourth has none. In each line the loan word is semantically tied to an indigenous word:

sīna	to	*āncal*
palak	to	*oṭ, and*
kahkashān	to	*māthā*

The quatrain opens with *ḍhalkā*, and closes with *bālak*, both native words. In this particular quatrain it is significant that there is no Persian *izāfat*, though the meter and rhyme-scheme are of Arabic origin. *Izāfat*, however, is not entirely avoided, but where used, Firaq ensures its blending with the rest of the language.

Through this type of verse, both on the semantic and expression levels, Firaq introduced a new tenderness and a new intimacy to Urdu lyric poetry. His sensuousness reminds one of Sanskrit literature. Obviously, he has been influenced by the Indian classical literature and the traditional theory of *Rasa*, and one can make a study of the parallels between the two. He seems to have the mind of a modern man but the heart of an ancient Aryan, and he repeatedly said that he wanted to make his poetry the voice issuing forth from the very soul of India. Under the impact of his verse Urdu poetry has gradually become conscious of its Indian heritage, and as well acquired modern sensibility.

Note

1. All translations, quoted here, unless otherwise stated, are by the author and Richard H. Robinson.

8

Tradition and Innovation in Faiz Ahmad Faiz

FAIZ AHMAD FAIZ (1911-1984) is widely acclaimed as a significant 20th-century poet of Urdu, and an understanding of contemporary Urdu poetry is not complete without a recognition of the importance of his work. The other major voices of the post-Iqbal period include Josh Malihabadi, Firaq Gorakhpuri, Meeraji and N.M. Rashid, who had also influenced the contemporary literary scene in their own right in the last few decades. Nonetheless, Faiz gained in popularity over the years, and an understanding of what he had inherited from the tradition, and what he added to it by way of the socio-political content is in fact essential for an overall appreciation of the significance of his contribution to the last fifty years of Urdu poetry.

Faiz Ahmad Faiz was born in Sialkot, West Punjab, received his education at Lahore, and started his career as a lecturer in English. Later, he served in the army for five years, and in 1946 was made the Editor of *The Pakistan Times*. In 1951, he was arrested along with some other political and military figures on charges of conspiracy aimed at overthrowing the government, and remained for some time in danger of a death-sentence, but was later released in 1955. He had socialistic leanings from the beginning, and remained an active member of the Progressive Writers' Association during the nineteen-thirties and forties. Faiz published seven collections of poems. His collected works, *Sāre Sakhun Hamāre,* appeared from London in 1982, and *Nuskha-hāe-Wafā* from Lahore and Delhi in 1984. In 1962, he was awarded the Lenin Peace Prize, the first South-Asian poet to receive this honour.

Faiz, in spite of his leftist leanings, was not a rebel poet in the real sense of the word. He was an admirer of the classical imagery of Urdu Ghazal, and his style bears traces of the language of both Ghalib and Iqbal. He had accepted and assimilated much that was in the tradition and used the classical conventions and imagery with such depth and ingenuity that his poetry reflects at once the heritage of the past and the quest and restlessness of the present.

Faiz was essentially a lyrical poet. He has written both Ghazals and *Nazms,* a comparatively new verse form in Urdu poetry based on the western models. Here we will quote from both his Ghazals and *Nazms* simply to demonstrate his introduction of the Ghazal imagery to the comparatively new genre of *Nazm.* These lines are from his *qat'ah,* 'Because We Live':[1]

> *hamāre dam se hai kū-e-junūn men ab bhī khajil*
> *'abā-e-sheikh-o-qabā-e-amīr-o-tāj-e-shahī*
> *hamīn se sunnat-e-Mansūr-o-Qais zindah hai*
> *hamīn se bāqī hai gul-dāmanī-o-kaj kulahī*

Still, because we live, folk in Madman's Alley can laugh at Sheikh and Shah and Emir, mantle and ermine and crown.
We are the heirs of Mansur the God-crazed, Majnun the smile-crazed; we
Keep from extinction the gay cap and the flower-chequered skirt.

Note the words 'madman's alley', 'sheikh', 'Mansur', 'Majnun', 'gay cap', 'flower-chequered skirt', and 'extinction'. These are all drawn from classical imagery. Majnun is the legendary lover of

Laila, and Mansur the celebrated heretic who was executed in Baghdad for his boldness and courage to speak the truth in matters of divine love. Here the meanings have been enlarged and they stand for the spirited patriots. The 'gay cap' is the mark of Mansur, the mystic, and 'flower-chequered skirt' of Majnun, the ideal lover. Hence, 'madman's alley' is here the street inhabited by the socially-inspired patriots. The 'Sheikh and Shah and Amir' are conventionally the symbols of the oppressive orthodoxy. Here, therefore, they stand for the soulless bureaucracy or the imperialists. The anti-colonial message of this short poem is now clear. Faiz has taken all the key words from the repertoire of the classical poetry, and added none of his own; still, he is completely successful in conveying a contemporary social and political idea. At one place Faiz has remarked :

> Let us talk of Farhad and Parvez, O Faiz
> For those who understand will see the truth.

The imagery of the classical Ghazal was developed and perfected in Persian for love poetry. Later, in the course of centuries, the same imagery was further developed and expanded for the expression of mystical and metaphysical themes as discussed earlier in the introduction to the section on Firaq. This practice continued for long, and though once in a while the same imagery was used with socio-political nuances, it was in the twentieth century that a new dimension was added to it by Iqbal, Chakbast, Hasrat and others who sought to make use of classical imagery for political themes. They were followed by Faiz and his contemporaries, who, responding more and more to the demands and stresses of the modern age, used it for socialistic and nationlistic themes, thus broadening its scope and introducing still newer shades of meaning into it. The underlying pattern of such poems is the same age-old love triangle. The first person of the poem is again the 'āshiq (lover), that is, the revolutionary, the nationalist or the socialist. The ma'shūq (beloved) is the country, the society or the people. The third element of the triangle, the *raqīb* (rival), is now the imperialism, foreign tyranny, or the capitalist and the bourgeoisie. Similarly, the set of symbols containing *junūn* (madness), *dār-o-rasan* (scaffold), *maikhānah, sharāb, pyālah* (tavern, wine and cup) and *bulbul* (nightingale) are very common in Faiz's poetry. The following table sums up some of these three-dimensional elements of Faiz's poetic structure:

1.	*āshiq*	(lover) patriot, revoluti- onary	*ma'shūq*	(beloved) country, people	*raqīb*	(rival imperialism, capitalism, tyranny, exploita- tion
2.	*'ishq*	(love) revoluti- onary zeal	*visāl*, *didār*	(union) revolution social change	*hijr*, *firāq*	(separation) the state of the reactio- nary controls or oppresssion
3.	*rind*	(libertine) rebel	*sharāb*, *maikhānah*, *piyālah*, *sāqi*	(wine, tavern, cup, cup- bearer) sources of social and political awareness	*muhtasib*	(censor) the colonial system, the capitalist state establ- ishment
4.	*junūn*	(sublime madness) zeal for social justice	*haq*	(truth) socialism	*khirad*	(empirical knowledge) capitalism, establish- ment

5. *mujā-* (fighter)   *zanjīr* (chain)   *hākim* (ruler)
    hid   freedom-   unjust ruler,
            fighter   colonialist
                                                or dictator

                          zindān, (prison)
                          dār-o- (scaffold)
                          rasan   political
                                    imprison-
                                    ment, or
                                    execution

6. *bulbul* (nightingale) *gul*   (rose)   *bāghbān* (gardener)
            nationalist   political ideal   usurper,
            poet   or corrupt
                                                        system

To appreciate further the socialistic and nationalistic implications of the above structure, let us consider the following verses of a Ghazal:

> *mai-khāna salāmat hai to ham surkhī-e-mai se*
> *taz'īn-e-dar-o-bām-e-haram karte rahen ge*
> *baqī hai lahū dil men to har ashk se paidā*
> *rang-e-lab-o-rukhsāre-e-sanam karte rahen ge*

While yet the Tavern stands, with its red wine
Crimson the Temple's high cold walls; and while
My heartblood feeds my tears and lets them shine,
Paint with each drop the loved one's rosy smile.

In these lines, the 'Tavern' and the 'red wine', which conventionally stand for divine inspiration, represent the sources of political and social awareness here. The 'loved one' obviously represents the masses, or the society. Similar structure is found in the following verses of another beautiful Ghazal:

> *yahī junūn kā yahī tauq-o-dār kā mausam*
> *yahī hai jabr, yahī ikhtiyār kā mausam*

qafas haì bas men tumhāre, tumhāre bas men nahìn
chaman men ātash-e-gul ke nikhār kā mausam
sabā kì mast khirāmì tah-e-kamand nahìn
asìr-e-dām nahìn hai bahār kā mausam
balā se ham ne na dekhā to aur dekhen ge
farogh-e-gulshan-o-saut-e-hazār kā mausam

This hour of chain and gibbet and of rejoicing,
Hour of necessity and hour of choice.
At your command the cage, but not the garden's
Red rose-fire, when its freshest hour begins:
No noose can catch the dawn-wind's whirling feet,
The spring's bright hour falls prisoner to no net.
Others will see, if I do not, that hour
Of singing nightingale and splendid flower.

This Ghazal was written in a prison cell in the spring of 1951 when Faiz was facing a death-sentence. The imagery, 'chain and gibbet', 'rejoicing', 'noose', 'net', 'garden', 'wind', 'rose', 'spring', 'nightingle', etc., throughout these lines, is basically classical, but is pregnant with contemporary meanings. So is also the case of the poem, 'Sar-e--Maqtal' (At the Place of Execution), where the 'fiery grape' is the desire for freedom, 'street of reproach' is the political prison, 'flask and cup' the national ideal, and so on. Faiz demonstrates how a fine poet can transcend the circumscribing restrictions placed upon him by the conventions, for he has not only infused the conventions with socio-political meanings, but at the same time retained their universal structures—erotic, mystic and spiritual. The different connotations exist side by side, reinforcing each other whereas the 'meaning' is derived either through a familiarity with relations obtaining between elements of these structures, or through the help of some other 'pointer' such as direct expression or the title of the poem itself.

But to say that Faiz is a poet of socialist realism is just a part of the tale. A close look at the poem, 'Sarūde-e-Shabānah' (Nocturne), will emphasize this fact:

nīm-shab, c̄and, khud-farāmoshī
mahfil-e-hast-o-būd vīrān hai
paikar-e-iltijā hai khāmoshī
bazm-e-anjum fasurda-sāmān hai
ābshār-e-sukūt jārī hai
c̄ar sū be-khudī si tārī hai
zindagī juzv-e-khwab hai goyā
sārī dunyā sarāb hai goyā

so rahī hai ghane darakhton par
c̄āndnī kī thakī huī āwāz
kahkashān nīm-vā nigāhon se
kah rahī hai hadīs-e-shauq-e-niyāz
sāz-e-dil ke khamosh tāron se
chan rahā hai khumāre-e-kaif-āgīn
ārzū, khwāb, terā rū-e-hasīn

Midnight, moon, oblivion—
The sum of things all chill and wan,
Desire inaudible;
Listless the fellowship of the stars,
Streaming the cataract of silence;
All round a self-forgetting spread;
Life, fragment of a dream—
Earth, all a shadow-play.

Slumbering in the dense woods,
Moonlight's exhausted murmur;
Eyes half-opened, the Milky Way breathes
Legends of thirst of self-surrender
From the heart's unplucked strings
Drifting echoes of exultations;
Longings, dreams, and your charmed face.

The poem functions in two sets of tangible and intangible images. The first stanza opens with the word, 'midnight', then we have a tangible image, the 'moon', and then 'oblivion', originally *khud-farāmoshī* (self-forgetfulness), vague as a state of mind, but quite tangible as an image which involves the 'self'. Considering *khud* (self) as the starting point, let us move on to 'desire', 'fellowship' and 'silence', which again are followed by *bekhudī* (All round a self-forgetting spread). Then, the poet goes to the source of all activity, 'life', and calls it a 'dream'; hence 'Earth all a shadow-play'. If we try to stretch the imagery a little further, we will see that personal feelings can be identified with something wider. The 'sum of things' originally, *mahfil-e-hast-o-būd* (the assembly of old and new) can refer subtly to political ideologies, old or new. Similarly, 'Desire' can stand for the personal choice, and 'fellowship of stars' for the national or political leaders.

Structurally, the first stanza opens with a vague image, 'midnight', dwells on 'self' as its core, fading eventually, into vagueness, 'dream, a shadow-play'. The second stanza follows the opposite pattern. Beginning as it does with the tangible image of 'dense woods', it soars up to the airy 'Milky-Way', and then ends with the tangible 'charmed face'. The imagery in this stanza again is romantic, and the word 'dense' at once revives the memories of black tresses. This is further supported by 'eyes half-opened, the Milky-Way breathes'; and the poem closes with a deep yearning for the beloved. The poem is one of the finest examples of Faiz's subjective moods and his impressionistic style.

As noted by Al-e-Ahmed Suroor in the preface to the Aligarh edition of *Zindān Nāmah*, "Faiz's poetry is oblique rather than direct", a fact which should be kept in mind as we now turn to another excellent poem, '*Tanhāī*' (Solitude):

> *phir koī āyā dil-e-zār! nahīn koī nahīn!*
> *rāh-rau ho gā, kahīn aur čalā jāe gā*
> *dhal čukī rāt, bikharne laga taron ka ghubār*
> *larkharāne lage aivānon men khwabīdah čarāgh*
> *so gaī rāsta tak tak ke har ik rāh-guzār*
> *ajnabī khāk ne dhundlā diye qadmon ke surāgh*

gul karo sham'en, barhā do mai-o-mīnā-o-ayāgh
apne be-khwāb kivāron ko muqaffal kar lo
ab yahān koī nahīn, koī nahīn āe gā!

Someone has come at last, sad heart! no, no-one is here.
A traveller must be going by, bound some other way.
The starry maze is wavering, night grows to its decline;
About the halls the nodding lamps gutter and go out.
Each highroad drops asleep, worn out listening for steps;
An alien dust has buried deep every trace of feet.
Put out those candles, take away wine and flask and cup;
Close your high doors that know no sleep, fasten bolt and bar;
No-one, no-one will come here now, no-one any more.

In this poem personal feeling can again be seen identifying itself with something wider. Kiernan pointed out that the deserted halls are not only the poet's fancied residence, but an old culture or society mouldering away. The next line, "Each highroad drops asleep worn out listening for steps", alludes to the failing effects of the different strands of the freedom movement. The imagery is further reinforced in the following line: "An alien dust has buried deep every trace of feet"; The 'alien dust' here refers very deftly to the withering touch of imperialism. (Note that the symbol *ajnabī* is also used for 'foreign yoke' in other poems of Faiz, as in 'A Few Days More': "Under this load beyond words of a foreign yoke we must submit for a while, not forever submit.") The poem opens with a note of hope "Some one has come at last, sad heart", and ends on a note of dejection "No-one, no-one will come here now, no-one any more." It thus reflects the contemplative and despondent mood of India in the late thirties and early forties.

Still, Faiz is as deeply concerned with purely personal themes as he is with the nationalistic and socialistic. Frequently, the two emerge as poles, pulling him in two different directions. In his poem, *'Mujh se pahlī sī muhabbat mere mahbūb na māng'* (Love, Do Not Ask), he speaks of his beloved whose "beauty kept earth's springtimes from decay" as one pole, and of "men's bodies sold in street and marketplace, . . .with festered sores dripping corruption" as another pole. One is calling for love, the other for action. To Faiz, both are dear. He wants to respond to the individualistic urges as well as to the call of the exploited society. Hence, the request, "Love, do not ask me for that love again." The emphasis is on the words *pahlī sī* (that), as individualism completely divorced form the plight of society is meaningless to Faiz. This cleavage between human passions and socialistic obligation, or the division of loyalty between reality and ideal, classical and modern, or love and faith, runs its contradictory course throughout the poetry of Faiz.

In poems like *'Mauzū'-e-Sukhan'* (Poetry's Theme), *Do'Ishq* (Two Loves) and *'Do Āwāzen'* (Two Voices), he speaks very clearly of this cleavage. In 'Poetry's Theme', speaking of the beloved's 'loveliness... languorous eyes', and the 'henna's delicate stain', he resolves that 'here is the chosen world of rhyme and dream'. Then, comparing it to 'swarming progeny' and 'hunger wave', he affirms:

> *yeh bhī hain, aise kaī aur bhī mazmūn hon ge*
> *lekin us shokh ke āhista se khulte hue hont*
> *hāe us jism ke kam-bakht dil-āvez khutūt*
> *āp hī kahiye kahīn aise bhī afsūn hon ge*
> *apnā mauzū'-e-sukhan in ke sivā aur nahīn*
> *tab'-e-shā'ir kā vatan in ke sivā aur nahīn*

> Here too are subjects; many more there may be.
> But—oh, the slow-parted lips of that sweet wretch!
> Oh, those cursed limbs that curve so ravishingly
> Tell me where else on earth is such a witch!

> No other theme will ever fit my rhyme—
> Nowhere but here is poetry's native clime!

But deeply touched by the suffering of mankind as Faiz is, he cannot be trusted too long for his above resolve. In *'Do 'Ishq'*

(Two Loves), he holds the scale once again, this time trying not
to tilt it to any one side:

is 'ishq na us 'ishq pe nādim hai magar dil
har dāgh hai is dil men bajuz dāgh-e-nadāmat

—My heart neither this love
Nor that love repents;
My heart that bears every
Scar, but regret.

The *dāgh*(scar) refers to the just or unjust criticism of friends
and foes, writers and critics, both literary and political.

This so-called tension between the humanistic and idealistic
impulses, or between the devotion to art and country, or to the
self and society is nothing new. As suggested by Faiz's translator
Kiernan, "It is the common fate of the progressive movements
all over the world". Wherever the writer is beset with social
problems and is given the freedom to speak through his
conscience, he will feel the cleavage between duty and choice,
the ideal and the practical. But what lends a unique quality to the
duality of Faiz's poetry is the fact that besides being true to his
personal feelings, and writing lyrical verse of great ecstasy, he
has transformed some elements of the classical poetic tradition
by infusing them with socio-political meanings.

Speaking of his nationalistic poetry, we have already
mentioned that its underlying structure is the same conventional
three-dimensional triangle; that is, Faiz speaks of suffering
humanity in terms of the beloved of classical poetry. But the
reverse is not true. If the conventional triangle in Faiz's poetry is
taken to represent both his subjective and socialistic themes,
then we will have to assume that there are two triangles
functioning on different levels, and the two can never coalesce,
that is, Faiz can identify the socialist ideal with the beloved of
classical poetry, but not his beloved with the socialist ideal. This
unique feature of his duality can be satisfactorily explained only
in terms of his deviation from the tradition. Faiz, it should be

recalled, appeared on the literary scene when Iqbal was about to depart. Faiz inherited from Iqbal what Iqbal, in his turn, had inherited from Ghalib. Faiz's diction thus bears a clear stamp of the style of both Ghalib and Iqbal. His language is not the common-core Hindustani, but that delicately-decorated medium which re-establishes Urdu's relationship with Semitic and Iranian languages, a relationship which opens to Urdu their "nostalgic world of rose-garden and nightingale, and goblet and grapes". Iqbal's majestic voice, though it added new grandeur and charm to Urdu poetry, made it a tool of revivalism. But Faiz, imbued with the spirit of the age, rejected the message of revivalism. As a freethinking man, earnestly desiring to find a solution for the suffering and exploitation of humanity, he turned to socialism, an ideology that offered some hope. However, Faiz is tenaciously rooted in the tradition and, therefore, was not swept off his feet by the winds of political exigencies. Many of his poems remind us of the dreamy monologues of the Ghazal, and recall the same mood of melancholy. And the captivating musicality of his verse is yet unsurpassed in contemporary Urdu poetry. He is a lyric poet *par excellence*. The humanistic values of Urdu Ghazal have also saved Faiz from being indignant or violent. Nowhere is he eager to seek the help of the 'midwife' called 'force'. He strongly feels that poetry should come out of its ivory tower and take notice of human misery, but also believes that poetry should serve Beauty and must not be subservient to anything other than the aesthetic or artistic values. Some of these views are not consistent with an ideal left philosophy, and thus, in the strict sense of the term, Faiz is not a 'true believer'. Nor is he a mystic; otherwise he might have reconciled the 'Two Voices' in some obscure way. But is it necessary that the poet must reconcile these two so-called contrary visions of life, or he should be true to the poet within him, and speak of his internal feelings, riddles and doubts also, as sincerely as he can. Obviously, Faiz has chosen the latter, and in him the two, i.e., the ideal and the personal, coexist, one to the fulfilment of the other.

Urdu poetry has thus come a long way from the classical tradition. It has undergone quite a transformation at the hands of Faiz, and he has, in fact, revolutionised its spirit and content, both in the lyrical, as well as in the socio-political sense.

Note

1. All translations of Faiz quoted above are by V.G. Kiernan, *Poems by Faiz Ahmad Faiz*, New Delhi 1958. Urdu text is from *Harf-Harf*, Rampur 1965.

9

Modern Urdu Poetry: The Indian Panorama

MODERN Urdu poetry in the post-Independence period in India has undergone a tremendous change both in content and expression. With the partition of the Indian subcontinent in 1947, Urdu literature entered an era of frustration, depression and outrage. The partition of India was perhaps the most important historical event to influence Urdu literature, for the dreams inspired by the idealist romantics were shattered, and the concept of the compositeness of Indian culture received a severe setback. Writers suffered materially, for, with the country's partition, their families, audience and readership were likewise divided. Apart from the mutual mistrust, loss of life and property, the loss of values was most devastating. Freedom having been achieved, nationalistic and patriotic themes sounded old and stale, and lacked purpose and appeal. The Progressive Writers Movement, which had proved the source of inspiration during the previous decade, declined in influence, and there was widespread disillusionment and disenchantment with the role of politics in literature. Writers questioned preconceived ideas, manifestoes and regimentation in any form. The concept of socialist realism as practised by the Progressives was rejected by the younger writers as defective and insufficient.

The generations that followed generally felt that freedom of mind was the most important basic value, and that the writer should not be subjected to any sort of external control. The moderns, the rebels, and the deviationists advocating the autonomy of arts, entered into long debates with the Progressives on the nature of the creative process, and the role of literature in society. It was argued that the mere subject-matter or specific themes did not determine the quality of literature, and the poet was free to choose his own subject. The discussions about the purposiveness and aesthetics of literature ushered in a new era in Urdu literature dominated by the Modernists. Though the Modernists did not form associations or groups, nor issued manifestoes or guidelines, opposed as they were to these things, still, because they influenced the literary scene tremendously and popularized new trends, they formed part of a literary movement which had an all-round impact. In the present study, though mainly the poetic scene in India will be discussed, yet since the events and trends on either side of the border influence each other, the Pakistani poets will also be mentioned to give an idea of the total perspective of the modern Urdu poetry.

The Modernist Movement was blessed by senior critics like Al-e-Ahmad Suroor in India, and Mohammad Hasan Askari in Pakistan. The process of change was accelerated by journals like *Saughāt* (The Gift) of Mahmood Ayaz from Bangalore, and *Sabā* (The Breeze) of Sulaiman Arib from Hyderabad. They played a leading role in popularising the new literary concepts. Khalilur Rahman Azmi wrote freely on the new movement and new writers in *Hamārī Zabān* (Our Language). Besides, *Talāsh* (The Search) and *Mahvar* (The Axis) from Delhi, and *Kitāb* (The Book) from Lucknow also projected and introduced the new writers. But many of the younger Indian poets were first introduced by the Pakistani journals *Saverā* (The Morning), *Nusrat* (The Victory), *Sātrang* (The Rainbow), *Adabī Duniyā* (The Literary World) and *Adab-e-Latīf* (The Belles Lettres), and a little later by Dr. Wazir Agha's *Auraaq* (The Pages), because Modernism as a literary phenomenon first gained currency in

Pakistan, since the Progressive Movement was never so deeply rooted in Pakistan as it was in India, and secondly because of the liberating influence of the poets of *Halqa-e-Arbāb-e-Zauq* (The Lahore Group): the Pakistani journals and readership at that time were more receptive to new ideas and experimentation. Thus, during the late 1950's and early 1960's *Jadīdiyat*, the Modernist Movement steadily gained in popularity and swept the whole of the subcontinent becoming a forceful literary movement deeply influencing both poetry and fiction.

The Modernists presented the writers of *Halqa-e-Arbāb-e-Zauq* (The Lahore Group) of the 1940's as their precursors, and sought inspiration especially from the poetry of Meeraji (1912-1949) and N.M. Rashid (1910-1975). At that time there was a dearth of Urdu literary journals in India. After some years this need was met by *Shab-Khoon* (Night-Attack) of Shamsur Rahman Faruqi which appeared from Allahabad in the mid-1960's. The *Shab-Khoon* gave an impetus to the new trends, literary freedom and experimentation, and played a historic role in introducing and establishing many an emerging Urdu poet and writer. By then Nasir Kazmi (1925-1972), Majeed Amjad (1914-1974), Ibn-e-Insha (1926-1978), Saleem Ahmad, Jamilud Din Aali, Aziz Hamid Madani, Ada Jafri, Wazir Agha, and Shahzad Ahmad from Pakistan; and Khalilur Rahman Azmi (1927-1978), Bani (1932-1981), Baqar Mehdi, Balraj Komal, Muhammad Alvi, Qazi Saleem, Amiq Hanfi, Krishan Mohan, Hasan Naim, Khurshidul Islam, Mazhar Imam, Shaz Tamkanat from India, who had gained prominence earlier were joined by the next generation of younger poets like Shakeb Jalali, Saqi Faruqi, Ahmad Mushtaq, Kishwar Naheed, Iftikhar Arif, Shabnam Romani, Joan Alia, Mahboob Khizan, Asghar Nadeem Sayyid, and Javed Shaheen in Pakistan; and Shahryar, Kumar Pashi, Bimal Krishan Ashk, Basheer Badr, Bashar Nawaz, Nida Fazli, Zubair Rizvi, and Salahud Din Parvez in India. Along with these younger poets some senior poets like Akhtar-ul-Iman, Munir Niazi, and Munibur Rahman who had been writing for the last many years and had been ignored because of their highly individualistic and subjective tone, now received full attention, and were rediscovered by the younger generation. Of these Akhtar-ul-Iman wielded a strong influence over his contemporaries for quite some time.

Though similar in essence to the Modernist Movement in the West, the Urdu *Jadīdiyat*, Modernism has some characteristics which cannot be explained only in terms of Western influences. The Urdu writers, since the times of Hali and Azad have been trying to create a new value system which incorporated Western as well as Islamic and Indian ideas. However much the *Jadīd*, i.e., Modern poets, may refer to imagism, symbolism and existentialism, they draw heavily on Islamic, Hindu and Buddhist traditions. Amiq Hanfi and Adil Mansoori, for example, synthesize Islamic and existentialist thought, whereas Krishan Mohan, Kumar Pashi and Nasir Shahzad seek inspiration from Indian mythology and indigenous tradition. The *Jadīd*, Modern Urdu poets, urgued for art as an expression of the individual rather than as an instrument for social reform. The Modernist poets increasingly felt that the romantic idealism and relatively simplistic literary techniques of the Progressive writers had not been able to answer the challenges posed by social change in the post-Independence period and the growth of an urban industrial society. The emphasis, therefore, shifted from an attempt to effect reform to the author's inner feelings and search for meaning. Thus, there has been a growing trend away from viewing man through society, and towards focusing on the inner individual. That is, there has been a shift from socio-political concern to human existential concern. The emphasis of the earlier writers on society, family, or group was corrected by attention to the individual, the self, through interiorization and introspection. However, this does not mean that the Modernist poets have been divorced from social reality or processes of social change. On the contrary, the modernists maintained that their relationship with society was more dynamic and meaningful than that of their predecessors. They believed that the individual is individual first and last, and should be portrayed as such, and only that view of society was genuine and authentic whereby society was viewed through the individual.

Any other relationship with society which is not based on freedom of the individual is non-creative, and therefore, is harmful to the arts.

Many poets of this age are individualists. Most important of these is Akhtar-ul-Iman. Thematically, Akhtar-ul-Iman's poetry strives to express both an understanding of external life and a sense of the complexity of the individual's inner life. Many of his poems deal with themes such as oblivion and eternal life, the decline of moral values, the tension between outer and inner life, and the struggle between dream and reality. A profound humanism characterizes most of Akhtar-ul-Iman's poems. The main character of his poem, '*Ek Larkā*' (A Boy) is a metaphor for human consciousness, while the poem '*Yāden*' (Momories) could be the universal story of the contemporary age. Similarly, the poem '*Mufāhamat*' (Compromise), which is one of his best, deals with the fundamental relationship between human sorrow and joy, pleasure and pain. Akhtar-ul-Iman has bequeathed a substantial legacy to the next generation of *Nazm* writers. Apart from the acceptance of his poetry in the late 1950's by critics and readers, his influence has percolated to modern poetic trends and modern Urdu literature as a whole. Moreover, Akhtar-ul-Iman has set the thematic direction of the contemporary *Nazm* with his emphasis on philosophical humanism. In addition, he has ifluenced others with his use of the monologue as a mode which continues to characterize his work.

Another major poet, Balraj Komal, disdaining the *Ghazal*, like Akhtar-ul-Iman, has expressed himself only in the *Āzād Nazm*. Although his tone is generally inward and the character of his poetic experiments private and personal, Balraj Komal generally builds his poem on a common experience of life, either some current event or a scene from domestic life. His fertile imagination reveals in these experiences glimpses of fundamental human truth and eternal verities to which he attempts to give symbolic expression. Consequently, as his well-known poems '*Ambulance*', '*Radio*', '*Kāghaz kī Nāo*' (Paper Boat) and especially '*Sarkas kā Ghorā*' (Circus Horse) testify, he is not a topical poet but rather one who records the timeless moment in time.

Qazi Saleem also is a poet of *Nazm*. Unique in his thought and innovative in his choice of subject, Qazi Saleem cogently expresses the disillusionment produced by the decline of old ideas and values. As is evident from his collection of poems, *Najāt se Pahle* (Before Salvation), free verse is his forte. He has given particular attention to the composition of his poems, using to good advantage, new permutations in the present system of prosody. He has also experimented with metres based on *pingal*, the traditional Hindi method of prosody. His poetry is known for boldness and courage of conviction. He raises his voice like a crusader, and attacks false values, hypocrisy, sectarianism and double standards in public and private life. His poetry is a happy blending of the human-existential and socio-political concerns, and is marked by vigour and exuberance of expression.

In contrast to the individualistic modernism of poets like Akhtar-ul-Iman, Balraj Komal and Qazi Saleem, there is a strain of a return to romanticism in the poetry of Munibur Rahman. Initially reckoned among the Progressives, Munibur Rahman expressed progressive social ideas in a general way in his early topical poems. However, in his later poems, especially those of the collection *Bāzdīd* (Return Visit), he almost completely gave up the Progressive position. Instead, he now inclines towards indirect expression, monologue, interiorization and symbolic references. What is more important, he has given new life to romanticism in his treatment of personal and delicate subjects.

Balancing the subjective and romantic strains, Baqar Mehdi, a noted radical poet, registers a lyrical social protest in his poems. He exemplifies the angry and rebellious mood of modern Urdu poetry. A committed modernist, through the *Nazms* of his colletions: *Kālē Kāghaz kī Nazmen* (Poems on Black Paper) and *Tūṭe Shīshe kī Ākhīrī Nazmen* (Last Poems of Broken Mirror) and his many thoughtful critical essays, he has attempted to propagate radical, revolutionary modernism as a substitute for outdated and false literary standards. More importantly, Baqar Mehdi's anger has not only been salutary in a climate of political expediency and literary compromise, but it has also kept his poetic voice distinct.

In addition to the evolution of the *Nazm* in thematic terms, modern Urdu poetry has also been characterized by experimentation with the form of the *Nazm*. Besides experimentation with the metres and freedom from rhyme schemes in the free verse, there have been experimentations in the length of the poems, both narrative like poems and very brief ones, *Mukhtasar Nazm*. Though brief poems have been written even before Independence, yet the credit for developing and popularizing the true brief *Nazm* of only a few compressed and unified lines undoubtedly goes to Akhtar-ul-Iman. The Indian poets who are especially accomplished in using the brief *Nazm* are Mohammad Alvi and Shahryar. Although Mohammad Alvi has clearly been influenced by Munir Niazi in his use of the brief *Nazm*, his most striking poetic trait is his use of visual imagery. He has aptly been characterized by Mahmood Ayaz as "a poet of the eyes." However, some of Alvi's poems have provided insight into larger problems. This is particularly apparent in his brief lyric *'Akhiri Din ki Talash'* (In Search of the Last Day), which ridicules hypocritical religious values and alludes to the restlessness of modern life.

Unlike many other modern poets, Shahryar neither equates modernism with the denial of social responsibility, nor is he willing to submit to externally imposed formulations. Moreover, he often returns to a classical usage in his language and style. However, because of the intensity and freshness of his thought and tone, his poems remain totally compatible with the modernist current. Shahryar is fundamentally an intellectual poet, whose poetry strongly expresses an ideological non-commitment, whose roots lie in the poet's desire for self-realization and his attempt to understand modern problems. Combining economy of picturization with suggestivity, characteristic of *Ghazal*, he has dealt even in his brief poems with the problems of contemporary life in an extraordinarily vivid way. Shahryar is not concerned in his poetry with messages or conclusions. Rather, he expresses the spiritual suffering and psychological conflicts of what he regards as the wounded modern person. Suspended between the two harsh realities of time and death, yet wanting to live fully in the present moment, he tries to see the true face of life in brief moments of joy and sorrow.

In contrast to those who have excelled in short poems, there are poets who have constantly attempted *longer Nazms*. They include Abdul Aziz Khalid, Jafar Tahir and Wazir Agha of Pakistan, and Amiq Hanfi of India. Like Ibn-e-Insha, Amiq Hanfi too put the legendary figure of Sindbad to a new use in his famous long *Nazm 'Sindbād'*. In this poem he focusses on the figure of Sindbad, whose wanderings in search of a new faith lead him towards Greek and Hindu mythology. Through the figure of Sindbad, Hanfi thus presents his view of the modern predicament: despite our desire to be liberated from the past, the past is rooted not only in our minds but in our every cell. Although Hanfi's other long *Nazms,* including *'Shahrzād'* (City-born) and *'Shabgasht'* (Night-stroll) are technically more unified than *'Sindbād',* they are not as effective.

Another feature of the age is the revival and popularity of the traditional folk forms of *Dohā* and *Geet* in Urdu. With the publication of Jamilud Din Aali's collection, *Ghazaleen Dohe Geet* in the mid-fifties in Pakistan, Urdu poets have turned enthusiastically to exploit the potential of indigenous *Dohā* form. Aali, the former Secretary of the Pakistan Writers' Guild, and the present Secretary of the Anjuman Taraqqi-e-Urdu (Pakistan) has been a trend-setter in this regard, and it is mainly due to his efforts and experimentation of *Dohā* with the Bengali *Bhaṭiyāli* style, that the *Dohā* has gained acceptance in Urdu. His renewal of an indigenous model and his use of the *Rasa* vocabulary producing thereby a *Geet*-like feeling have influenced the contemporary trend. Of the poets associated with this trend, Nasir Shahzad, Partau Rohila and Taj Saeed have been prominent in Pakistan, and Krishan Mohan, Kumar Pashi, Nida Fazli, Salahud Din Parvez and Sheen Kaaf Nizam have distinguished themselves in India.

The search for Indian roots therefore is a distinguishing feature of modern Urdu poetry. It is not only the premodern past or the medieval India, but the ancient past, the prehistoric or the Buddhistic India that has been evoked by the contemporary poets. Some of them aim at the metaphysical revelation to discover an illuminated, unified vision, to return to the archetype of consciousness, which is man's true nature and essential being. This approach to art also seeks to combine the invisible world of spirit with the world of physical sense, to see both sides at once, or one might say that the awareness of the cumulative unconscious supercharges the physical with energy and creative delight so that contemporary reality is entered and revealed. Although traces of this trend are visible in the works of almost all modern poets, the search for Indian roots is most visible in the poetry of Krishan Mohan, Kumar Pashi, and Salahud Din Parvez. A prolific poet, Krishan Mohan has written with felicity and grace in almost all forms and on almost all subjects, building in his poems his own unique aestheticism and thematic world. In contrast to Krishan Mohan, Kumar Pashi's poems, whatever their form, suggest the sweetness, softness and fluidity of the song. Entering those regions of the intuitive mind to which the poetry of others rarely gains access, his poems suggest a sense of the boundlessness of time. The subject matter of Kumar Pashi's poetry has also clearly been influenced by classical Indian mythology.

Salahud Din Parvez is different in that he seeks inspiration from both the Islamic and Hindu traditions, and uses legends and motifs from both the Indian and the Arab past. He has used the traditional form of *Na'at, Hamd,* and *Salaam* to express his devotion to the Prophet, but at the same time his poems are refreshingly modern. He displays a unique creativity and spontaneity, and is not at all conscious either of the tradition, or deviation from it. His is a carefree, playful voice experiencing the ecstasy of communicating at different levels of consciousness. One finds the echoes of the centuries of India's past and that of the early glory of Islam in his poetry. His diction is tender and soft, and he freely uses the Prakritic Hindi element for enhancing the expressive qualities of his language.

In a period which has seen both the rise and fall of various literary movements and the acceptance and growth of the relatively new form of free verse, *Azād Nazm*, one of the most surprising developments of the post-Independence period has been the survival and durability of the classical *Ghazal*. Although few contemporary poets limit themselves solely to the *Ghazal*, many write both *Ghazals* and *Nazms* with equal ease, and some have even attempted other classical forms as well. However, all those who have preserved the *Ghazal* tradition, have demonstrated that, despite its classical origins, the *Ghazal* is still admirably suited to the expression of a modern sensibility and the depiction of contemporary concerns. The most distingushed modern *Ghazal* poets being the following. In India: Khalilur Rahman Azmi (1927-1978), Bani (1932-1981), Zeb Ghori, Bimal Krishan Ashk, Hasan Naim (since deceased), Mohammad Alvi, Mazhar Imam, Shahryar, Bashir Badr, Shuja Khavar; and in Pakistan: Nasir Kazmi, Shakeb Jalali, Ibn-e-Insha, Saleem Ahmad (since deceased), Aziz Hamid Madani, Shahzad Ahmad, Saqi Faruqi, Zafar Iqbal, Ahmad Mushtaq, and Iftikhar Arif. Bearing marks of the influence of Mir Taqi Mir, as well as of Firaq and other contemporary poets, Nasir Kazmi, who died young in 1972, developed the *Ghazal* into a modern art-form which transmuted the classical tradition into something at once modern and unique. His *Ghazals*, reflecting the pervasive influence of the *Ghazals* of Mir, have transformed the traditional pessimism of the *Ghazal* into an expression of the sorrow, despair and anguish of the twentieth century.

Nasir Kazmi's contemporary Khalilur Rahman Azmi declared his rebellion against Progressive ideology. Consequently, his early *Nazms* and *Ghazals* reflect not only his own personal openness and liberality of spirit but also his respect for tradition gained from a study of classical poetry. What is more important, Khalil made renewed use of a romantic tone based on monologue, introspection and the depiction of individual, personal experience. In addition to using this romantic tone to describe everyday events, he also expresses, in his early lyrics nostalgia for his village, home and childhood and feelings of the lack of identity and uprootedness characteristic of city life. What is perhaps most important about Khalil's later poetry is that *Ghazals* predominate in it. Written entirely in a classical style, these *Ghazals* reflect not only Khalil's temperamental affinity for the *Ghazal* but also his ability to express contemporary concerns through it.

In contrast to other contemporaries, the *Ghazals* of Bani are not only highly individual in their use of language but also intensely modern in their thought. Bani's linguistic individualism is in his use of new and unusual metaphors and in his ability to invest even the traditional symbolism of the *Ghazal* with new semantic dimensions. Bani has also stretched its capacity to deal with contemporary concerns. In many respects a neo-classical poet, Bani avoids both the physical and emotional aspects of love in his *Ghazals*. Instead, in a manner reminiscent of Ghalib, he combines an expression of the scepticism, restlessness and disillusionment common to much modern literature with a special quality of abstraction and refinement.

Like Khalil and Bani, Hasan Naim has also put his personal stamp on the contemporary *Ghazal*. His deep attachment to the classical tradition has not prevented him from dealing with contemporary realities in his *Ghazals*. Viewing the totality of life, he attempts to plumb both the deep mysteries of human relationships and the complex secrets of everyday phenomena. Rejecting a sentimental notion of love, he explores its complexities in the context of both psychological insight and contemporary conflicts. Moreover, he has taken a stance of self-affirmation, seeing hope in disappointment and constantly, even restlessly, striving for happiness.

The other poets of the *Ghazal* include Mazhar Imam, who has equal command over both the *Ghazal* and the *Nazm*, and who has treated both individual and topical events in a style that strikes a balance between metaphorical and direct expression. He has also been experimenting with a different verse-form,

Āzād Ghazal, on the lines of *Āzād Nazm,* where the two hemistitchs can be of uneven length.

Yet another feature has been the emergence of a feminist trend in the modern Urdu poetry. The harbinger has been Ada Jafri with her elegant and refined expression, but Kishwar Naheed is more versatile and influential, closely followed by the strident Fahmida Riaz and the tasteful Parveen Shakir. This trend is somewhat weaker in India as old timers Sajida Zaidi and Zahida Zaidi are mellower, and Shafiq Fatima She'ra is comparatively frugal.

The Modernist Movement has its devout advocates on both sides of the border. As Askari and Saleem Ahmad passed away early, Wazir Agha and Intizar Husain have been the literary trend setters in Pakistan. The credit for spearheading the Modernist Movement in India belongs to A.A. Suroor, Khalilur Rahman Azmi, Baqar Mehdi, Waris Alvi, and more so to Shamsur Rahman Faruqi. Recognized as an important critical voice in the evolution of contemporary poetry, Faruqi in the sixties and seventies fostered the growth of the Modernist Movement through his journal *Shab-Khoon* (Night-Attack), as Wazir Agha has been doing through his journal *Auraaq* (Pages). Paralleling their efforts in their critical articles to establish the validity of the modernist approach, Wazir Agha and Faruqi are different in their poetic expression. Wazir Agha, influenced by Meeraji, has taken a consciously symbolist approach moving away from classical tradition, while Shamsur Rahman Faruqi has been strongly influenced by the classical tradition. With its effective expression of a modern sensibility within the bounds of classical diction, Faruqi's poetry, despite his own critical theory, clearly suggests that, in one sense at least, modernism in Urdu poetry is a renaissance of classicism.

Despite their rebellion against Progressive domination of literary canons of the preceding two decades, the Modernists discussed so far advocated a relatively moderate modernism. As their poetry reveals, they continued to respect certain established literary values despite their modernist persuasion. Alongside them, however, a group of angry young men existed, who, rejecting the entire poetic tradition of Urdu, espoused a radical modernism that sought to lead Urdu poetry in an entirely new direction. Led by Iftikhar Jalib, this group takes its theoretical orientation from Iftikhar Jalib's *Nai Shāirī* (New Poetry) and *Lisānī Tashkīlāt* (Linguistic Reconstructions) and from Anis Nagi's *Sherī Lisāniyāt* (Poetic Linguistics). In addition to Iftikhar Jalib, this group of radical modernists included Anis Nagi, Jilani Kamran, Zafar Iqbal and Zahid Dar in Pakistan, and Adil Mansoori and Ahmad Hamesh in India. (Ahmad Hamesh later went back to Pakistan.) These poets have attempted to lead Urdu poetry in a radically new direction through their highly unusual approach to structure and language in their *Nazms*. Lately, some of them have relented in their efforts and have retracted their position somewhat.

Although Modernism is the most predominant feature of the post-Independence period, yet it must not be overlooked that stalwarts like Firaq Gorakhpuri and Anand Narain Mulla; poets of the Lahore Group like Meeraji, N.M. Rashid and a loner like Majeed Amjad; and Progressives like Josh Malihabadi, Faiz Ahmad Faiz, Ahmad Nadim Qasmi, and Ahmad Faraz of Pakistan; Makhdoom Mohiuddin, Jan Nisar Akhtar, Ali Sardar Jafri, Kaifi Azami, Majrooh Sultanpuri, Khurshidul Islam, and Waheed Akhtar of India have also been living and contributing during this period, but their poetry is not discussed here as this is not part of the movement under study. Meeraji passed away in the forties, Makhdoom in the sixties, Majeed Amjad, Jan Nisar Akhtar and N.M. Rashid in the seventies, and Josh, Firaq, and Faiz in the eighties, while the remaining are making worthwhile contribution to the Urdu poetry till today. Of these Faiz Ahmad Faiz's subjective stance and obliqueness of style were acceptable even to the Moderns, whereas the poetry of Makhdoom and Jan Nisar Akhtar underwent a subtle change. They even showed the acceptance of the modern poetry's emphasis on self, interiorization and indirect expression. Jan Nisar Akhtar's *Ghazals* published in his last collection *Pichle Pahar* (Late Hours) which were proclaimed as his best by both the Progressives and the Moderns are reflective of his subjective mood, and clearly established his having been influenced by modern sensibility. Makhdoom also received the modern influences open-heartedly, and some of the poems of his last years like *'Chānd Tāron kā Ban'* (Forest of Moon and Stars), *'Lakht-e-Jigar'* (The Son) and *'Sannāṭā* (Uttier Silence) are considered his best. Even Ali Sardar Jafri's poetry has undergone a slight change. It is mellower, softer and adopts an oblique tone with an eye on imagery and semantic layeredness.

The main contribution of modern poetry in this period has been the rejection of preconceived ideas and trite subjects, disuse of the direct idiom, oratory or rhetorical devices and the emphasis on literariness or poeticality of the poem itself as the basic aesthetic prerequisites. It has opened new vistas for creative and emotive use of language encoding deeper meanings, or meanings of meanings. There is a clear shift from the cliche-ridden predetermined social concern to the truly felt human existential concern, providing freer play for the intellect and the imagination. The ambiguity and obliqueness of style, search for fresh imagery and the use of metaphorical, symbolic, and mythological idioms are the distinguishing stylistical features of present-day poetry. The notion of dichotomy between content and form is considered non-literary and the awareness of an organic relationship between the elements of creation has steadily increased. The modern Urdu poetry is the poetry of free mind, unfettered and unimpeded, and with its present boldness of experimentation and growth, it is expected to open new horizons of human consciousness.

10

Major Trends
in the Urdu Short Story

THE Urdu short story as it exists today is a literary phenomenon of recent origin. Its present development owes much to the inspiration of the West. Of course, storytelling as such was a favourite pastime in India, but the modern short story is different from the age-old tales which were still being written in Urdu at the turn of the century.

The short story in Urdu really originated with Premchand (1880-1936), universally considered as one of the greatest fiction writers of modern India. The novel, though known, was based on romances and adventures of medieval patriarchs. Premchand brought it out of the world of dreamland and fantasy and introduced into it the living truth of human existence. He is the symbol of the most respectable and forceful trend in Urdu and Hindi fiction, and it is from his work that the Urdu short story branched off in different directions. Premchand appeared on the Urdu literary scene in the first decade of the twentieth century at a juncture when characters such as Scheherazade of *The Arabian Nights* and *Four Dervishes,* and Hatim Tai of the *Dāstāns,* viz., cyclic tales, lay in the background, with the princes and princesses of the *Maṣnawīs,* viz., verse narratives. In the foreground appeared Hamlet, Faust, Don Quixote and numerous characters of Tolstoy, Chekhov, Maupassant, and assorted Bengali writers, particularly Tagore and Sarat Chander Chatterjee. Premchand was an assimilating genius. His models were borrowed from the West but his subject-matter was typically Indian, and with him the Urdu fiction became a product of the soil.

At a time when his contemporaries, like Sajjad Hayder Yaldrum, Niaz Fatehpuri, Latifuddin Ahmad and Sultan Hyder Josh, were mostly entangled in the cobweb of romanticism, Premchand introduced Urdu short story to the realities of contemporary life. The dreamers and the aesthetes gave way to ordinary men and women engaged in the struggle for existence. Premchand did not present ideas, he presented *man*. Man to him was the destiny of the short story, its measure and its goal. Premchand was both a realist and an idealist, and the manner in which he blended the two is a tribute to his craftsmanship.

His first collection of short stories, *Soz-e-Watan* (Burning Love of Country, 1909) was confiscated and burned by the British government because of the patriotic zeal of the stories. Deeply influenced by the national movement for freedom, Premchand's fiction reads like a saga of India's national struggle against colonialism and provides a record of the socio-political history of that tumultuous period. Premchand's characters are drawn from all walks of life and from all classes, but he is at his best when portraying India's rural life, where he is unsurpassed in his depiction of tragedy and pathos. He showed a deep sympathy for the masses in their misery and poverty, for he saw beneath their squalor a certain dignity, worth and regard for humanity. His best fiction evokes the open air of the country-side, and it was here that Premchand encountered a toiling man who was "dark, semi-naked in loincloth and profusely sweating." He fell in love with that man, the eternal man, the peasant. That man in turn served as his source of inspiration and provided him with that sense of humanism which permeates his whole work and gives it a touch of the universal and the enduring. Premchand imparted to Urdu fiction an originality, a sympathetic treatment and a social and political awareness. His influences are deep and enduring, and a number of his contemporaties, from Sudarshan and Azam Kurevi to Afsar Meeruthi and Ali Abbas Husaini, reflected in their work Premchand's reformist and nationalistic zeal.

The thirties provided a turning point in the major trends of Urdu short story writing. Translations from Russian writers had already become common after the First World War. The decade was noted for its influx of Western influences, especially English and French, besides Russian. In 1931, the publication of an anthology of short stories, *Angāre* (Sparks), took the Urdu world by surprise. The stories, written by four newcomers, Sajjad Zaheer, Ahmed Ali, Rashid Jahan and Mahmood-uz-Zafar, were characterized by reformist politics and a spirit of rebellion against orthodoxy. Indirectly, however, the stories collectively introduced into Urdu fiction the latest trends in contemporary Western literature. With the publication of this anthology, a floodgate was opened to Marxian and Freudian influences and the imitation of James Joyce. A few years later, in 1935, the Marxist-inspired Progressive Writers' Movement was launched, and Premchand, who imbibed the spirit of socialism in his final years, presided over the Movement's first session shortly before his death in 1936. The Manifesto of the Progressive Writers provided the guide which was to be followed by most Urdu writers until after partition. Around this time the leading trio of Urdu short story writers—Saadat Hasan Manto, Rajinder Singh Bedi and Krishan Chander—came into prominence along with a host of other short story writers. Together they held sway over Urdu fiction for more than two decades, and some were active after the partition also.

The Urdu short story in the period after 1936 branched into two different lines: the sociological story, represented by Rajinder Singh Bedi, Krishan Chander and Ahmad Nadim Qasmi; and the psychological story, dominated by themes of sex, as best seen in the writings of Manto, Ismat Chughtai and Mumtaz Mufti. After Premchand, Saadat Hasan Manto, Krishan Chander and Rajinder Singh Bedi emerged as the best short story writers in Urdu. They were different from each other in the sense that Maupassant was different from Chekhov. Manto (1912-1955) dealt sardonically with middle class morality and conventions, with the ignoble in life, and particularly with the coarser aspects of sexual relations. He wrote exclusively about Indian urban life, usually focusing on degenerates, criminals and prostitutes. But whatever the theme, it was always told with clarity and simplicity in diction still unsurpassed in Urdu, and with an economy which gives only the essentials of character or situation heightened by sharp and vivid details. (See *'Bū'*, *'Dhuān'*, *'Hatak'*, *'Blouse'*, *'Kālī Shalwār'*, *'Ṭhanḍā Goshṭ'*).

Rajinder Singh Bedi (1915-1984), on the other hand, started with models provided mainly by Chekhov. He was more interested in the ordinary than in the unusual in human nature, and he presented his characters sympathetically and tenderly. Weaving his plots from commonplace events, his penetrating vision probes underlying relationships, which he presents with an ease and grace all his own. His portrayal of Indian domestic life and the Indian married woman is superb, and some of his characters, like Indu, Rano, and Lajwanti have become immortal in Urdu as the most realistic, sincere and sympathetic presentations of Indian womanhood.

Bedi does not idealize woman, but the suffering, enduring and tolerating nature of his characters imparts to them a touch of sanctity, a breath of greatness. The woman in Bedi's stories, whether a beloved, a wife, or a mother, is the suffering soul of creation, the all-pervasive spirit, the mother of the whole universe. Filled with a sense of abiding love, compassion and devotion, she undergoes hardship and pain in order to release joy and happiness in the male, the family, or even the universe.

In contrast, Manto was interested in the highly neurotic, the violent and grimy. In his stories we come across Saugandhi, Kulwant Kaur, or Mozelle, women pulsating with vibrant emotions, brimming with activity, aggrieved, assertive, even aggressive. Saugandhi, after being insulted by the wealthy *Seth,* wreaks vengeance on her friend Madho by disgracing him, and finally by going to bed with her mangy dog. Manto had tasted the poison of life and was deeply affected by it. He asserts that man is evil and beastly. But Bedi is too human to perceive only one side of life. In the manner of Chekhov he never fails to see a ray of sunlight and delicate beauty in a tragic situation. Most remarkable, however, is Bedi's simplicity in all its different manifestations. His stories have the simplest themes, but are permeated by an artistic quality of unfailing charm. His ability to create atmosphere and to delineate characters, and his realization of seemingly insignificant but psychologically important aspects of life made him the most noted short story writer of the post-Premchand period.

Despite the influence of Maupassant, the most widespread Western influence on the Urdu short story remains that of Chekhov. In fact, the influence of the great Russian runs like an undercurrent through the short stories of the forties and the fifties. Writers of the old guard, like Suhail Azimabadi, Hayat Ullah Ansari, Upendra Nath Ashk and Akhtar Orainvi; and of 'progressives' like Akhtar Husain Raipuri, Khwaja Ahmad Abbas, and Ahmed Nadim Qasmi; or of such 'non-progressives' as Mohammad Hasan Askari, Ghulam Abbas and Prem Nath Dar, were all in one way or another influenced by Chekhov.

Krishan Chander (1914-1977), one of the leading writers of the Progressive School, dedicated his art, "to show up the capitalist and the ruling classes in all their brutality and bestiality." (Sadiq, Mohammad, *Twentieth Century Urdu Literature*. 1947, p. 81.) And perhaps no other Urdu short story writer had a larger readership in India and Pakistan. Krishan Chander's stories are distinguished by fundamental humanism and abounding wit, as well as crisp rhetoric and suppressed poetry. A prolific writer, he produced about eighty volumes, which include more than a dozen novels. His work varies widely, ranging in scope from romantic, social and psychological themes to themes probing political, national and international problems. In fact, he writes about the whole gamut of contemporary problems and human relationship with a purpose—sometimes too obviously so. Art with him is a criticism of life and a vehicle for social uplift. Most of his work is spirited, with a tendency towards romanticism and formlessness. His weakness is that he is easily carried away by emotion and is frequently lacking in depth. According to Mohammad Sadiq, "he has never been able to outgrow his romanticism. It clings to him like an original sin." (Sadiq, *op. cit.*, p. 82.) Despite this penchant for romanticism, his stories usually have a foundation in fact, and his use of realistic detail within loosely spun plots generally gives his work an air of verisimilitude. He is significant for his combination of excellent storytelling, his idealistic approach and personal happy tone, a tone which reflects his own kindliness and good humour. The result is a pervasive charm, for he is not severe or objective like some, but tender and sympathetic with the misfortunes of humble people. What he lacks in technique and form, he supplies with his humanism and style, which is at once spontaneous, swift and sweeping, so that it often approaches the quality of a poem.

Ghulam Abbas and Mohammad Hassan Askari were the two other major short story writers of prepartition India. Two of Askari's famous stories, '*Harām Jādī*', and '*Chāe kī Pyālī*', were inspired by Chekhov's '*School Mistress*' and '*The Steppe*'. Ghulam Abbas, a painstaking craftsman, possessed a keen sense of character and wrote neatly trimmed stories as though seeking the closest possible connection between his characters and reality.

Ahmed Ali's earlier stories, show surrealistic influences, and his depiction of man as a puppet in a strange dreamlight world reminds the reader of Kafka. Aziz Ahmad (1913-1978), essentially a novelist, introduced into Urdu the fiction of ideas, perhaps inspired by Aldous Huxley. His story, '*Tasawwur-e-Shaikh*', is outstanding for its grasp of character and atmosphere. Freud's thought inspired many compositions by Ismat Chughtai, Mumtaz Mufti and a host of other writers. The themes of adolescence and sexual urge in the female have been effectively portrayed by Ismat, and Mumtaz Mufti's fascination with these themes is such that his early stories, with the exception of '*Āpā*', usually read like obviously constructed case studies. Ismat, aware of the concept of individuality in Indian society, never overlooks the Indianness of her characters while annexing psychoanalysis to her fiction. According to Al-e-Ahmad Suroor, "she has the mind of a rebel, the tongue of a woman and the sensibility of an artist." (*Tanqīdī Ishāre*, Lucknow, 1964, p. 42) Her lively style, robust language and realistic detail bring her characters to life. (See '*Chauthī kā Jorā*', '*Nanhī kī Nānī*', and '*Lihāf*'.)

In 1947, when the Indian subcontinent was divided, another stage began. With the reign of terror following the partition the imagination of writers was fired anew, and Urdu literature entered an era of depression, defeatism and outrage. The partition of India was perhaps the most important historical event to influence the development of Urdu fiction, for the concept of a common life and the compositeness of Indian culture, so deeply cherished by Urdu writers, received a severe setback. Writers suffered materially, for, with the country's partition their audience and readership were likewise divided. Furthermore, the partition, occasioned politically inspired communal hatred and mutual mistrust and brought widespread communal riots which rocked the whole of the subcontinent with bloodshed and arson. The loss of life and property was distressing, but the loss of certain cultural values was most devastating to sensitive writers, who for a number of years almost lost sight of the boon of freedom and the new opportunities brought by independence. This preoccupation with the subject of riots evoked a great number of riot stories in Urdu. The traditional romantic hero who, for a change, sometimes put on the face of an idealist or a sentimental revolutionary, now disappeared. He was replaced by the uprooted migrant, the abducted girl and the man with a guilty conscience.

Manto and Krishan Chander were more prolific than their contemporaries during this period, and it appeared that the tragic events of 1947 perfectly suited their individual styles—the former interested in the seamy side of sex and the latter in dramatizing humanism. Writing at tremendous speed and with

missionary zeal, they produced many stories which were limited
in scope and appeal. Manto's viewpoint was essentially cynical,
and many of his stories deteriorate into slapstick and contain
little artistic value. But being a master storyteller, Manto also
produced a few elaborately drawn stories, such as 'Khol Do',
'Thanḍā Gosht', 'Mozelle', and 'Tobā Tek Singh'—each with
meticulously conceived characters. The last is a snappy and
pungent satire on partition as seen through the eyes of a lunatic.
'Thanḍā Gosht' is a bitter portrayal of the mental pangs of a
rioter who carries off a young girl, rapes her only to discover
that she is dead, and is himself later killed by his own wife.
'Mozelle', however, differs in that it treats both the ignoble and
the noble. It is the story of a Bombay bohemian girl named
Mozelle who is Jewish by religion but who hates sectarianism.
Caring little for conventional morality, she leads a carefree
nonconformist life, but her heart is full of compassion and
sympathy for fellow human beings, and she goes to any extreme
to mitigate the misery of others. In the end she makes a bid to
save the life of a Sikh girl who is under attack by rioters in a
locality inhabited by Muslims. She succeeds in saving the girl but
is fatally injured herself. Mozelle is one of Manto's rare
characters who stands for positive values even to the extent of
laying down one's life to affirm these values.

Another notable riot story is 'Lājwantī', by Rajinder Singh
Bedi, perhaps the only one written by him on this theme. Sunder
Lal, Lajwanti's husband, is a social worker who helps restore
recovered females to their husbands and parents. His is a
suffering soul, as his wife, too, was abducted in the riots. Later,
when she is recovered and restored to him, he treats her very
sympathetically and tenderly, as if she were made of china and
would break at the slightest touch. (Lājwantī, lit., bashful, chaste,
is also the name of a flower—the touch-me-not, whose leaves
fold up when touched.) Sunder Lal avoids talking about her
immediate past lest it hurt her feelings, and he calls her a Devī
or goddess. On her part, Lajwanti wants him to accept her as a
weak, frail woman and to allow her to unburden herself to him of
all that has happened. Bedi very effectively portrays the suffering

of her soul. Lajwanti is restored to Sunder Lal, but her past, her real self, can never be restored.

Of Krishan Chander's riot stories, '*Ham Wahshī Hain*', '*Peshāwar Express*', '*Nayā Madrasa*', and '*Merā Bachcha*', are all notable for their pathos and moving narrative. In '*Merā Bachcha*,' Krishan Chander describes the Indian child as being subjected from birth to communal prejudices. '*Peshāwar Express*', is a story of a refugee train which runs through India and Pakistan, and through this journey Krishan Chander reveals both aspects of the grim tragedy.

Many writers on both sides of the border were concerned with communal peace and harmony, and most saw literature as a great synthesizing force. Some of the writers turned to allegory and expressionism to portray the upheaval of this era. Hayat Ullah Ansari's '*Shukr Guzār Ānkhen*', for example, is remarkable for the originality of approach. The main character possesses two selves, a bigoted one and a humane one. After murdering a bride at her request, he can never forget the grateful look in her eyes because she did not want to live without her dying husband. The tussle between the two selves is depicted grippingly. The story ends on a note of catharsis as the bigoted self is eventually obliterated by the humane self. Another new departure is seen in Prem Nath Dar's '*Ākh Thū*', a story which is expressionistic in technique. It relates a cannibalistic nightmare, wherein man eats the flesh of man. Interwoven in the plot are glimpses from our world, where beastly things are still done by man. The satire is effective in creating a sense of aversion and abhorrence at man's behaviour.

Frank and outspoken as these stories were, they served the purpose of exposing and displaying the emptiness of religious dogmatism and the hollowness of sectarian beliefs of the sub-continent .

Around 1950, when the riots had subsided and the two countries had settled down, riot stories sounded old and stale, and lacked purpose and appeal. Urdu fiction up to that time seemed to lend itself to the spirit of criticism which, as Albert Camus has remarked, "is born simultaneously with the spirit of rebellion and expresses on the aesthetic plane the same ambition." But the writers who wished to preserve the spirit of rebellion were discontented with the extreme difficulty of realizing their sentiments in fiction based on contemporary life. They knew something new, difficult and extremely hard to describe had happened to them. Yet they did not usually write about this happening *per se*. Freedom having been achieved, there was no point in writing patriotic or nationalistic stories. The appeal of the Freudian approach and the exploration of sexual fixations had also faded. The Progressive Writers' Movement, which had proved the source of inspiration during the previous two decades, declined in influence, and the writers were left without a banner to follow or a philosophy to guide them. This sense of vacuum in turn gave place to a feeling of nostalgia for a past which now appeared immensely rich and full of cultural values. This preoccupation with the past and its relationship with the present was more marked in Pakistan than in India. In the words of Aijaz Ahmad,

> The event of the partition of the subcontinent as in fact it occurred, meant a sudden violent break with ancestral homes and history for which the writer was not prepared, not emotionally. The price of the romance was a re-adjustment in the terms on which one lives with one's past and the memories of that past. The writer had now to choose a new, partly arbitrary, attitude towards his memories. Since the future was going to be so consciously different from the inherited past, the past had to be reconstructed, its meaning re-captured, so that one could again be reconciled with it. Nostalgia was a totally necessary and conscious creative act, perhaps the only one possible.
>
> ('Sense of History in the Modern Urdu Novel,' MS.)

Qurrat-ul-Ain Hyder, who had earlier come into prominence for her colourful, felicitous style and romantic themes now emerged as a trend-setter by writing on the cultural history of the composite life of north Indian Muslims and Hindus. Her ambitious and structurally complex novel, *Āg kā Daryā*, which deals with the quality and continuity of the cultural life in the subcontinent, became a phenomenal success. This novel brought the whole question of partition into focus once again. Later Qurrat-ul-Ain Hyder migrated back to India. Since then she has mainly written about the cultural personality of the two communities, and she has produced some of the best Urdu fiction of our time. Inspired as she is by a keen love for the beautiful in what is past and dying, she very ably succeeds in recreating and reliving that atmosphere. Her fiction, to borrow a term from E.M. Forster, is a study of "life in values" rather than "life in time". Employing the impressionistic technique and internal monologue, she depicts her men and women as existing in a bewitched twilight of recreated history, ultimately making the reader share with them a corner in that enchanted atmosphere. (See *'Jalā-Watan'*, *'Dālan Wālā'*, *'Housing Society'*.)

Intizar Husain, the most prominent of the short story writers of Pakistan, also wrote extensively about cultural change. Intizar is noted for his highly expressive prose, his exact diction, and for his mastery in creating atmosphere. Because he is in search of 'things that are lost', his stories, such as, *'Sānjh Bhaī Chaudes'*, *'Thandī Āg'*, *'Mahal Wāle'*, *'Majma'*, and *'Ākhrī Mom Battī'*, read like elegies on the fading culture of the Muslim nobility of Uttar Pradesh. Referring to the cultural revolution, he once said, "Of which property should I file my claim with the Government? I have left behind the Taj Mahal," and in *'Ākhrī Mom Battī'*, he laments the fate of a Shia mausoleum located in an area from which the Muslims have departed. Intizar Husain has also adapted the art of *Dāstān*, the classical cyclic tale, for telling present day stories. The best examples of this type are *'Zard Kutta'*, *'Ākhrī Ādmī'*, and *'Kāyā Kalap'*, which seem to have been influenced by Kafka in their elaborate symbolism and portrayal of animal characters.

Shaukat Siddiqui, too, has written about the changing social life of the Muslim migrants. Most of his characters, drawn from the noble families of North India, demonstrate his identification with those whose lives have become empty by the loss of the values they once cherished. *'Ajnabī'*, *'Patthar men Āg'*, *'Tāntiyā'*, and *'Nau-Chandī Jumerāt'* are remarkable for their profound, unsentimental and realistic depiction of cultural change. Likewise, Qazi Abdus Sattar is mainly concerned with the sad but inevitable fall of the landed aristocracy and the rise of common man in Uttar Pradesh. In his fiction, he attempts to preserve some of the cultural forms and ways of life of the nobility. He even goes to the extent of preseving the manner of speech, conduct, mode of dress, customs, ceremonials, and the layout of towns and villages of the pre-partition Uttar Pradesh.

In sharp contrast to the urbanists discussed above, ruralist and 'naturalist' writers such as Ahmad Nadim Qasmi, Balwant Singh, A. Hameed and Ashfaq Ahmad have made for themselves an important place in the Urdu short story. They are not many in number, however, and their writings scarcely constitute a trend. Ahmad Nadim Qasmi is one of the few pre-partition writers who braved all changes, kept up with his writing, and now commands more respect than before; and Imtiaz Ali Taj rightly called Qasmi the "Premchand of the Punjab." A versatile writer, he has written extensively both in prose and verse. He depicts rural life of the Panjab with all its romance and poverty, and touchingly captures the grandeur of nature in its contrast with the sad plight of the village dweller. "His interest in rural life sprang initially from his search for romance in the rustic, but later he began depicting rural life in all its beauty and misery, a fact which has tended to permeate his writing with a missionary zeal." (Ahmad, Jalaluddin *Pakistan Quarterly*, II, 2, p. 47. See *'Ātish-e-Gul*,' *'Sultan'*, *'Gandāsā'*.)

Balwant Singh's stories present the dynamic life of the virile Sikhs of the Punjab. Though he has drawn on the urban situation (see *'Sūrmā Singh'*, *'Jaggā'*, and *'Granthī'*), most of his characters breathe the open air of the country. They are unsophisticated farmers, workers, camel riders, and truck and taxi drivers. Untouched by industrialization, they appear disarmingly simple, sincere, straightforward and innocent. The Punjab of the Sikhs comes alive in the stories of Balwant Singh.

The styles of A. Hameed and Ashfaq Ahmad are different, but they both resemble the 'naturalists' in their love of romance and nature. Their stories reveal that there is much more to life than misery and woe; there is beauty and loveliness, they seem to say, which can be best appreciated when viewed against the background of natural scenery.

In the post-partition period, Ismat Chughtai's portrayal in her novels and short stories of the female in domestic setting influenced many women writers, Khadija Mastoor, Hajira Masroor, Shakila Akhtar and Jilani Bano emerging as the most prominent among them. Their stories, told from a woman's point of view, mainly deal with middle-class morality. The supressed feelings of women living in *purdah* have also been told effectively and candidly by these women writers. They make free use of domestic speech and the ladies' idiom in their stories, so much so that at times it becomes an end in itself, and as such detrimental to the development of the story. Khadija Mastoor, however, attends more to the craft and has a firmer grip on her characters than the others. She has also published a novel, *Āngan*.Though she too, works on the microcosm of a Muslim middle-class household, she far excels others in concentration, intensity of focus, and description of a social milieu. (See '*Khirman*', '*Dādā*'.)

Mumtaz Shirin (1924-1973) is different from the other women writers in the sense that her prose is more literary than colloquial, and the range and scope of her sympathies are much wider. She is both a critic and a short story writer, and she is at her best when dealing with human nature and the suffering of life. In '*Āīna*' the heightened ego of a young girl, on becoming aware of the pain of life, submerges before a benign, universal feeling, a feeling which brings about a change in her inner self. Her stories, '*Megh Malhār*' and '*Kaffāra*', are Kafkaesque in their treatment and symbolic content. The central figure of '*Kaffāra*' is a suffering mother who not only undergoes the pangs of creation but bears the sorrow of the death of her offspring, thus carrying an allusion to the suffering of the Virgin Mary for the Primeval Sin.

Another trend that found its beginning in the late fifties was the emphasis on the portrayal of the common man and normal life. In the stories of younger writers, the man in the street began receiving V.I.P. treatment. This is the point where a line can be drawn for the beginning of the new short story in Urdu; a short story which steers clear of socialistic and antisocialistic motivations. It is not a story of preconceived ideas based on class conflict; rather it is a free portrayal of the inner urges and problems of the common man. Its prime purpose is to depict daily life realistically and artistically and younger Indian writers such as Ram Lall, Devinder Isar, Iqbal Majeed, Sharvan Kumar Verma, Joginder Paul, Iqbal Mateen, Ghyas Ahmad Gaddi, Iwaz Saeed, and Ilyas Ahmad Gaddi, all show promise in their treatment of the themes of daily life; and Pakistani writers like Jamila Hashmi, Ghulam-us-Saqalain Naqvi, Sadiq Husain, Zamir-ud-Din, Farkhanda Lodhi, Raziya Fasih Ahmad and Muhammad Mansha Yaad do not take the ordinary in life as ordinary. The very ordinariness of life, ignored by the earlier writers, has now become deeply meaningful. All of these writers share a discontent with the cramping influences of political ideologies. Guided by their creative urge and inner experience, they have forced the older writers to pay heed to their protests against the cult of personality and affiliation with ideological groups. For they insist that life be viewed as a whole and not through the rigid formulae of political ideologies. Whereas the earlier stories mostly dealt with types—worker, cultivator, farmer, prostitute, criminal, freedom fighter, reformer, the new short story is interested in the character and nature of the individual. It is no longer necessary that the central character reach a culmination point in his life; instead, characterization has increasingly become more inward. According to the new writers, an individual is an individual first and last, and should be depicted as such.

Rajinder Singh Bedi, though an old-timer, insofar as his portrayal of normal day-to-day life is concerned, in fact represented this trend and in a sense dominated it. He was not a prolific writer, but whatever he produced in this difficult period is neatly trimmed and effective. In his story '*Apne Dukh Mujhe De Do,*' which is one of the best written in the post-riot period, he presents life in its totality. His method is again impersonal, but the realistic portrayal of domestic relationships is related with deep psychological understanding. The ebb and flow of Madan and Indu's household and their mundane pleasures and pains, hope and despair, suffering and gratification, are portrayed perceptively and artistically. Indu as a many-faceted character—daughter, wife. mother—is symbolic of a creative and benign woman, who must prevail in the end. This idea lends the story a metaphysical quality which has heightened its suggestiveness and charm. What S.S. Dulai said about another character of Bedi is equally true of Indu, that "her desire to bring her man around to give her 'her due' is deep and elemental. There is a largeness about it which is like the vastness of the earth and there is a softness in it like the gentle opening of the earth for the seed." (*Mahfil,* V. I & 2, p. 113). The combination of Freudian psychology with Indian tradition, however, is not always consistent, especially in the end, where Indu would have changed her personal beliefs and actions about love had she been told by Madan to do so. Yet the story derives much of its value from the insights it gives into the fullness of family life in India. Bedi made free use of mythology and symbolic technique in this story. This proved such a success that he later employed it on a much larger scale in his widely acclaimed novel, *Ek Chādar Mailī Sī*. The suggestive and symbolic technique of Bedi's later fiction brought it still closer to the new short story in Urdu.

The stories of the new writers are marked by certain characteristics which they share with literary movements in other parts of the world. They suffer from a vague sense of alienation and loss of faith, though some of the factors causing this feeling are not exactly the same as in the West. In India, the writer is faced with the problems of a nascent parliamentary democracy and a stagnant economy. The dreads of the last few decades for social justice in a welfare state, equality of opportunity and the closing of the gap between the haves and the have-nots have yet to be realized. The successive five-year plans have yet not been able to give relief to the poor. Millions still live virtually under the grim spectre of mass starvation. Corruption and nepotism are rampant, and there is widespread lack of enthusiasm for nobler causes. The individual feels like a cog in the inexorable wheel of a callously indifferent and inefficient bureaucracy.

More serious is the problem of the linguistic rights of Urdu. If the language in which a writer writes fails, he fails too. The new generation has come of age in this atmosphere of despondency, frustration and defeatism. James T. Farrell, commenting on the Indian literary scene, asked, "How critical should Indian writers be? Can they write with the fearless realism and desire for truth of a Zola, or some of the twentieth century American novelists? If they do, will they not be weakening their own countries?" (*The Illustrated Weekly of India*, Bombay, December 9, 1956). The observation which this question implies is hardly based on facts insofar as Urdu writers are concerned. Ram Lall, in his story '*OC*' (Officers' Coach), satirizes officialdom in the railways. Satish Batra's story, '*Chingārī*', criticizes the rise of a third-rate leadership in the country at the cost of worthier people and depicts objectively the mutual recriminations in the higher echelons of the ruling party in India. Qaiser Tamkeen's story, '*Un ko Khabar Hone Tak*', is a bitter portrayal of bureaucratic red-tapism. The story depicts a village woman whose husband died fighting armed bandits after which the government was gracious enough to announce a pension for her. For three years, the poor widow waited fo the pension, but she was told that the papers were being processed. Eventually, one hot summer afternoon, she collapsed in front of a government office. The government this time took more prompt action and right away announced a pension for her minor son, and thus a new file was opened. Still, this type of criticism is scant and sparse. The real problem involved is not that the writers are afraid of weakening their own country, but that there is a growing trend away from viewing man through society, and towards focusing on the inner individual. That is, there is a shift from socio-political concern to human existential awareness. The social passiveness or indifference noted in Urdu is of this nature, for the feeling is common that life is a drift over which one has little control. It was only in the late fifties and early sixties, when general disillusionment and despondency had already grown, that such existentialist literature started becoming popular among the new generation of Urdu writers.

Young Urdu writers, influenced by the works of Sartre and Camus and modern literary movements of the West, deliberately set out to write a new literature. They sincerely felt that their age was in many respects unprecedented and beyond all the conventions of past literature and art. To such writers, form was no more than an extension of content. It was not the storiness of the story that was important, but its atmosphere, its focus and concentration. Unnecessary details were squeezed out. Furthermore, it was no longer necessary, they felt, to maintain the conventional ordering of material in time and space. Stories employing broken narrative, intricate symbolism, uncommon or abstract syntax and expression became common. In the wake of this experimentation one trend clearly emerged—that of the symbolic and abstract story. This type of story was not entirely new in Urdu. Among the pre-partition writers, Krishan Chander's *'Ghālicha'* and *'Wahshī'* ; Mumtaz Shirin's *'Megh Malhār'*; and some stories of Ahmed Ali and Aziz Ahmad could be called somewhat symbolic in technique, but the symbolic and abstract story, caught on as a major trend only with the newcomers. Special among them on the Pakistan side are Anwar Sajjad *('Chaurāhā')*, Khalida Asghar *('Ek Būnd Lahū Kī')*, Ahmad Hamesh *('Makkhī')*, and Rashid Amjad *('Nārasāī kī Muthiyon men')*. The representative Indian writers include Balraj Manra

('*Composition Series*'), Surendra Prakash ('*Āp Bītī*', '*Dūsre Ādmī kā Drawing Room*', '*Rone kī Āwāz*'), Balraj Komal ('*Kūān*'), and Kumar Pashi ('*Zard Ghās Kā Samandar*'). They are thoughtful, challenging young men concerned with the degradation and uprootedness of modern man, and with their conviction that somehow the relation of the individual to his environment has been changed—and that there is no way of escape. The more sensitive among them feel that at whatever peril to their work and career, they must grapple with something new in contemporary experience, even if, hke everyone else, they find it extremely hard to say what this 'newness' is. Such writers recognize that the once-familiar social categories and bench marks have now become as uncertain and elusive as the moral imperatives of the nineteenth century seemed to writers of fifty years ago.

What these younger Urdu writers have in common with their counterparts in the west is an all-inclusive, emotionally mixed attitude towards the present—an attitude of hope and hatred, despair and love. These emotions are not as contradictory as they may appear. The new writers want to accept the present experience as it is, with its ugliness and its anti-poetic qualities, and transform it into an all-inclusive art. The present task of the writer, they insist, is to explore a chaotic multiplicity of meaning rather than to continue representing the surface of common experience.

At the same time there is an ongoing process of rediscovery of the Indian value system. The young writers' sudden interest in pre-historic cultures and in early Buddhism is as significant as their involvement in the existential void, though it is hard to say whether it is inspired by the west's artistic and intellectual interest in early India, or by the post-partition cultural revivalism in the subcontinent—or by both.

The young writers, like their counterparts in the west, detest the idea of material progress and view the results of industrialization as a catastrophe for human values. However, the industrialization of India is yet to be completed. India still lives in two worlds. The urban population, of course, is not unfamiliar with the stresses of jet and automobile culture, but a majority of the population in the countryside still lives steeped in ancient tradition. An intellectual tug-of-war rages between traditionalism and modernism, a conflict between orthodoxy and unorthodoxy that is in some ways unique to the Indian subcontinent. Nonetheless, the potentiality of destruction has become identical with the very concept of modern civilization, and is, above all else, the great unifying reality of the present age.

The changes seem to be of a basic nature, and one suspects that the guidelines of both social thought and literary conventions are being erased. Where, finally, does this leave us? There is, of course, no clear answer, for the emerging tendencies pointed out are still in a flux, still open to many pressures and possibilities. But it may not be out of place to say that the younger Urdu writers, as with their contemporaries in the other Indian languages, have begun to envisage that man may be on the threshold of enormous changes. Who knows whether Mir Taqi Mir's desire to behold the beauteous face of the beloved in the mirror of the moon may not finally be replaced by a fear of total annihilation? Thus the main question, as suggested by the younger generation, may no longer concern the conditions of existence but existence itself!

11

Rajinder Singh Bedi's Art: Metaphorical and Mythical Roots

1

FROM the point of view of style there are three traditions in the Urdu short story which deserve attention or are virile enough to perpetuate themselves for a long time—Premchand, Saadat Hasan Manto and Krishan Chander. Premchand's style was evolved from that grand tradition which was churned manna-like from the common man's down-to-earth everyday speech and generally known as *khaṛī bolī*. With minor changes Premchand's Urdu transformed itself into Hindi and vice versa. That is in a way its real strength. It would not be far from truth to say that even today the future of the common man's language rests on this tradition. So far as the linguistic style is concerned, after Premchand, scores of writers of Urdu fiction have followed in his footsteps and this tradition has shown no signs of waning or floundering. In Manto, we find a different aspect of the same grand tradition. Basically, it is the same style—only the rank greenery has been carefully mowed down and a nice lawn laid out and properly tended. The gold on which Premchand's alchemy of emotion and imagination had worked has attained greater refinement in Manto's literary crucible. There is an amazing smoothness and sophistication in Manto's diction, characteristic of a highly finished product. In Premchand, you find a basic ruggedness of language while in Manto it manifests itself in its most chiselled form, free from pedestrian unevenness or surfeit. In Manto, you don't find a single superfluous word. From that point of view, Manto's style is a high water mark of brevity. As against that, Krishan Chander is overgenerous in the use of words; in his prose you find an unimpeded flow of words, marked by adroitness and agility. His style conforms to all the embellishments of romanticism, like a bride decked in finery. But the effect of his magic does not last long. Soon it starts to create the effect of superficial gloss. The number of Krishan Chander's admirers has by no means diminished. But the fact remains that in the past many years the modern short story has rid itself of romantic influences and has started on a course bristling with new thinking. Of course, Manto's language which is free from exaggerated statement and pedestrian unevenness still commands attention and many writers of the present generation are under his influence. All the same, the present day life is so complex and demanding that simple language without any sort of artifice or obliquity cannot cope with it. No doubt, Manto's language can be highly suggestive but it cannot cast itself in the mould of modern expression which is replete with symbolism and metaphor. As we proceed we shall realise that the writers who have taken to the genre of the short story have through the use of metaphor, symbolism, allegory and parable, pulled the story out of its earlier simple edifice, almost giving it a new face.

Bedi started his literary career almost at the same time as Krishan Chander and Manto. But Krishan Chander because of his romantic flair and Manto because of his preoccupation with sex soon caught the reader's attention. From the very beginning Bedi must have realised that he could not write florid and picturesque prose like Krishan Chander nor deal with sex with the same uninhibited boldness as Manto. Whatever he wrote, he wrote with great care after weighing each word. Once Manto had a dig at him, "You think too much," he said to Bedi. "You think before you write. You think while you are writing and also after you have finished writing." To this Bedi retorted with his characteristic humour, "A Sikh may be lacking in many things but he is sure of himself in one thing: he is a good craftsman. Whatever he builds, he builds it to perfection, making sure every part of it rings true." The craft of writing and a sense of perfection had become second nature with Bedi from the very beginning. On account of his obsessive thinking what he lacked in spontaneity he more than made up by attention to artifice and by using the language creatively with its attendant graces.

In the foreword to his second volume of stories, *Grahan*, he wrote, "When something comes within the ken of my observation I do not try to describe it in its mundane, realistic details. I try to describe it as it emerges from my mind as a blend of imagination and reality."

The habit of finding the inner meaning in the outer reality gradually took Bedi into the realms of suggestion, symbolism, metaphor and allusion — in other words, the highly creative use of language. The signs of these early stirrings can easily be discerned in his first two collection of stories, *Dāna-o-Dām* and *Grahan*.

In the story, '*Rehmān ke Jūte*' (Rehman's Shoes), the fact of one shoe overriding the other is a portent of a journey in the offing. This journey can be from one place to another in the physical sense and also a journey to death in the spiritual sense. The old Rehman is going to another city to meet his married daughter and he dies on the way. In this manner Bedi culls out an inner meaning from a prevalent social belief or superstition.

In the same way, the story, '*Ighwā*' (Kidnapping), is symbolic of subduing Rai Saheb's daughter, Kanso. The Rai Saheb's house is under construction. Ali Ju, a handsome and strongly built Kashmiri labourer, is assigned the job of breaking the earth and boring a hole to drive in the pipe of the water tap. When asked by a fellow labourer he replies, "No tangible result till now. The ground is hard and stony. It'll require a lot of work." At the end of the story when Ali Ju succeeds in breaking the earth and the pipe hits the strata of underground water, the same night Kanso elopes with him.

But it is the story *'Grahan'* (Eclipse), in which Bedi has run the full gamut of a metaphor. Here for the first time he has blended a myth into a plot so as to transpose them into one another. In this story, we have the lunar eclipse and running parallel to it we have the earthly phenomenon of a similar nature happening to a woman; her fate too is under an eclipse. A man, out of evil design is out to tarnish her by making her the target of his lust. Holi is a poor helpless woman, completely at the mercy of her husband and his family. Her mother-in-law is the *Rahu* of the Hindu mythology while her husband is the *Ketu,* both preying upon the poor woman. Her husband is out to suck her blood and impose upon her a male's tyranny. But the tyranny of the society is far more cruel than the diabolical designs of the eclipse. Her attempt to escape from her in-laws' house in order to seek refuge with her parents is symbolic of her escape from the eclipse. While escaping from the *Ketu* of her in-laws' family she falls into the clutches of Kathu Ram, the shiphand of the coastal launch, who knows her from her childhood days back in her father's village. He takes her, an unsuspecting woman, to a room in the local *sarāe* (inn) on the plea of providing her night's shelter and forcibly tries to outrage her modesty. In this manner, this beautiful moon is ravished by *Ketu,* that is, tarnished by one eclipse and then by another. The significance of the story lies in the fact that here a myth has been used with such telling effect as to invest the story with a down-to-earth quality. In the finite we see the infinite and the outer mundane reality sparks off the vision of spiritual reality. In *'Grahan,'* Bedi has sown an acorn which in his stories written after Independence grows into a mighty oak, making the hall-mark of his fiction. In this context his story, *'Apne Dukh Mujhe De Do'* (Give Me Your Sorrows), and his novel, *Ek Chādar Mailī Sī* can be singled out for a special mention. To understand Bedi's virtuosity in the apt use of myth and metaphor which form the bedrock of his stories it is necessary to whisk the curtain of words apart and see the reality behind those words.

2

In the story, *'Apne Dukh Mujhe De Do,'* Indu, the female protagonist of the story, is, from the meaning of the word, also descriptive of the full moon which is the embodiment of beauty and love. It provides the sap of life to fruits and lends colour to flowers. It invigorates the blood and makes the soul more pervasive. Indu is also called *soma,* the divine manna of our ancient lore and the elixir of life without which life cannot exist. In this story, Indu is paired off with Madan which is another name of Kamadeva, the counterpart of the Greek Eros, the god of love. At one place, Bedi has also referred to Indu as *Rati* which has affinity with Kamadeva. In the Rig Veda Kamadeva has been regarded as the primal germ of mind, the basis of all creation. In the Greek pantheon, Eros and Cupid have also a similar connotation. It would appear as if the very names of the characters in the story are suggestive of the creative and destructive elements which restore an equilibrium in the creative process of the cosmos.

The basic idea of the story is the eternal and mysterious struggle between man and woman. Because Bedi's mind dwells more on woman than on man and he is fascinated by the feminine or the matriarchal element in the primeval beginnings of mankind (which will be discussed in some detail in *Ek Chādar Mailī Sī)* so evident in the eternal scheme of things, Bedi has given more importance to woman as against man. Madan is only a means, an instrument in the process of creation—a means in fact of testing genetic or sexual urges and instincts, something which makes the incomplete complete. All the same, the fact remains, that Indu is the subject, the cardinal factor that acts while Madan is the object, the one who is acted upon. Apart from the ingredient of love, Indu has other ingredients besides. She is a daughter and a wife and a mother too. But from the beginning till the end she is a mother or else a woman who stands for the whole creation and whose being is enmeshed in every particle of it, in its moon and the stars, who by becoming the earth has encompassed the whole sky within her arms with a vice-like grip. Time and again Bedi presents the woman of flesh and blood in terms of the archetypal image of woman.

> Madan's eyes and his Duhshasana-like arms had been for centuries denuding Draupadi of her clothes—Draupadi who in common parlance was known as wife. But through a mysterious source bolts upon bolts of cloth had been cascading down from the sky to cover up her nakedness. At last, tired, Duhshasana had collapsed on the ground while Draupadi was still standing there clad in the white garments of purity, looking like a goddess.

Madan is both the Pandavas and Kauravas. He is both Yudhishthira and Duryodhana, the one who protects and the one who denudes. In the man and woman relationship, apart from the pleasures of the flesh there is also spiritual bliss. Lord Krishna who gives yards and yards of cloth to woman to cover her nakedness in times of danger also acts as her shield to save her honour.

Alongwith the sincerity of love, the fuller confirmation of man's emotional attachment for woman becomes manifest when Madan becomes angry with Indu on discovering that she has become pregnant. He is overcome by the fear that she may die in child-birth.

> Nothing will happen to you, Indu. I can snatch you from the jaws of death.

This time it is Satyavan's and not Savitri's turn to be put on trial. But the irony of it is that Satyavan's turn never comes, nor will it ever come. Self-denial and self-sacrifice have only fallen to the lot of woman. Every time she has to wade through a river of blood and at the risk of her own annihilation she has to create a new being.

He was alone in the room along with Indu—Nand and Jasodha. And on the other side was Nandlal.

All seemed to be well with the world. Indu was looking on with an air of smug satisfaction. It appeared she had not only forgiven Madan's sins but of the entire mankind. As if elevated to the divine level of a *devī* (goddess) she was doling out the gift of forgiveness and compassion.

Now Indu was a mother, a mother to the whole world. She was Yasoda, who was to nurture Devaki's son, Krishna, that is the one who was to bring up Nandlal. By suffering herself she had to make others happy. That was why she had said to Madan on the wedding night, "Let me have your sorrows."
At that time . . .

Though the sky was clear of rain-laden clouds yet surprisingly it had started raining. The Ganga of her conjugal bliss was in spate. Flowing over its banks the river was flooding the entire terrain and the habitations around.

After a while, a beam of the heart started dripping . . .

A slow drizzle is more dangerous than a downpour. It is because falling from the sky, the raindrops percolate through the beam and start dripping over Indu and the child.

Bedi also made a metaphorical use of 'rain' and 'raindrops' in his novel, *Ek Chādar Mailī Sī*. Significantly, he presses these metaphors into service when the womb of the earth is gaping open and it is clamorous of rising up and embracing the sky in order to suck up its seed in the shape of 'water' and thus receive the debt the sky rightfully owes it.

In the novel as much as in the story, it is not a downpour but a soft, steady drizzle which percolates into the very fibre of the earth. Elsewhere we have already remarked that the other name of Indu or moon is *Soma* which is created from 'water' and is regarded as nectar and the elixir of life. There is a legend in the Vishnu Purana that Anasuya's son Soma was married to the 27 daughters of Rishi Daksha. But Soma loved Rohini only to the exclusion of the other sisters. Provoked by the other 26 daughters' jealousy, Daksha cursed Soma (the moon) that his beauty would not remain constant; it would keep waxing and waning. A woman's (Indu's) journey continues from its beginning to its ripeness and back. Sometimes she is a bud, then a flower and yet again a withered petal, which everytime it blossoms from a bud into a flower gives birth to a new bud. From light into darkness and back again from darkness into light. From existence to non-existence and back to existence. The life cycle goes on and on. Sometimes Indu is everything and at others nothing. Sometimes she is the full-moon night and at others complete darkness. In the last scene Madan is estranged from Indu. He is trying to go to another woman, someone in the bazaar, and Bedi rounds it off by saying, "Tonight instead of the full moon it was utter darkness".

But in love, from darkness to light, from refusal to consent, the journey is performed in one bound. In the twinkling of an eye Indu wearing a full-moon lustrous expression and holding Madan's hand transports him to a world where one can reach only after dying. Although this universal and pervasive feminine image has affinity with the Shivaite *Shakti* concept and Tantric convictions, yet the whole atmosphere of the story bristles with Vaishnavite overtones. Draupadi, Savitri, Sita are all Vaishnava concepts. Vaishnavite special *mantra: Om namo bhagavate vāsudevāya* has also been used to achieve certain effects. Here Vasudeva stands for Krishna who is regarded as Vasudeva's son and Vishnu's eighth *avatāra*. The child was also born on the Vijaya Dashmi day which, due to its association with Rama, is regarded as a Vaishnava festival. Perhaps through a mysterious inter-action of the conscious and unconscious mind Bedi wove these allusions into the weft and warp of his masterpiece story. Incidentally, as against *'Apne Dukh Mujhe De Do'*, the entire mythical atmosphere of *Ek Chādar Mailī Sī* evokes associations with Shaivism. Here too the woman forms the fulcrum around which the novel revolves. She is the epitome and the guardian angel of creation but there is a slight shift in the vision informing the novel and the story. In *'Apne Dukh Mujhe De Do'* Bedi is at pains to impress upon the reader that woman drinks hemlock (poison) of life to make the ambrosia of life available to man; she suffers in order to bring happiness in man's life. But in contrast to this, in *Ek Chādar Mailī Sī*, the problem in its glaring clarity is that of a woman trying to have an upper hand over man through the perpetuation of progeny. The woman thinks it is her rightful demand over man. In *'Apne Dukh Mujhe De Do'* Indu was now a Draupadi, now a Savitri and now Janak's daughter Sita. These are a woman's composite images, scintillating with love, sacrifice, respect and purity—all drawn from mythological traditions.

But in *Ek Chādar Mailī Sī*, Bedi views reality in its totality; now woman's positive and negative aspects exist cheek by jowl. The whole atmosphere of the novel is charged with violence and drenched in blood which are unmistakably associated with the cult of *Shaktī*, they overshadow the *tāntric* lore, blood sacrifices and such like practices which uphold murder as something sacrosanct. In the very beginning, a tell-tale hint is dropped in this direction: "This evening the disc of the sun was gruesomely blood-red as if in the abode of the sky an innocent person had been done to death."

The redness of the sun is used throughout as a metaphor denoting murder. Bedi has been careful not to use just any 'abode' but the abode in the sky which immediately invests it with metaphorical implications and brings to the fore the blood-curdling aspect of the whole narration having semantic associations with the *Shaktī* at the level of deep structure.

In the novel Kotla was the small village where pilgrims stayed. Under the shadow of Chaudhri's *havelī* (mansion) stood *Devī's* (the goddess') temple. According to the traditional belief, escaping from the crush and the rough and tumble of life the goddess had strayed into the village and had rested there for sometime. A temple had been raised over the place of her rest to commemorate the event. After a brief respite the goddess had hurried away towards Sialkot and had disappeared in the hills of Jammu and Kashmir.

The Devi has two aspects, positive and negative, or sublime and fierce. The sublime aspect is denoted by the image of Parvati, Uma or Gauri, signifying feminine beauty, love and affection while the fierce aspect is represented by Kali, Durga or Bhawani. She is depicted as dark-complexioned, having a terrifying visage, blood dripping from her mouth and hands. She stood triumphantly over *Rākshasa's* dead body which lay trampled under her feet. She is shown wearing a wild smile on her face. This allusion is used throughout to nail down the fact that those who abetted the crime of rape of the innocent young *yātrin* (pilgrim girl) will not escape ultimate punishment.

While dilating upon Mangal's and Rano's relationship, some critics have been tempted to draw a parallel with the Oedipus Complex of the western psychology. Quite likely, this image would have also titillated Bedi's mind. But we think Bedi did not set great store by Freud's theories of sex. He was more fascinated by ancient India's insight into sex. While creating his characters how could have Bedi escaped the vast and astounding influences of *Shaktī* according to which sometime she is a mother and sometime a life-partner? These influences must have been really pronounced for he had spent his childhood in a region of the Punjab where such concepts seemed to have held sway from prehistoric times.

There are more than one Bhairons, all of them in the image of the primeval man and all of them menacing and terrible. It is in conformity with such concepts that Shiva's consort, Devi, is also known as Bhairavi. In *Ek Chādar Mailī Sī*, Tiloka himself is one of those Bhairavas. He is fierce, highly volatile and given to violence. "He is going to kill me! *Hai* he'll kill me! Someone come and save me from this demon!" shouts Rano.

But instead of feeling contrite at the rumpus he had created, Tiloka was more obsessed with the thought of that pilgrim-girl and she had stayed in his mind all night. In the darkness of the night he was himself Meherban Das and Rano the pilgrim-girl. The other *Rākshasas* were Ghansham Das and the hermit, Bawa Haridas, who had conspired among themselves to ravish the pilgrim-girl who symbolised the Devi (the goddess). "But the mythical Devi was armed with the trident to fight off her ravishers. She hacked off Bhairava's head with one blow of the trident. But the innocent pilgrim-girl had only delicate rosy hands which she could only raise in supplication before her Bhairons. Her body was soft as water melon pulp which could not stand the onslaught of Meherban's knife. This was why the sun had turned deep crimson out of anger and had then disappeared somewhere in the sky, leaving the weak and young crescent moon to turn pale."

But the Devi can never be vanquished. She re-appears in the form of the pilgrim-girl's brother and sucks up Tiloka's blood.

> Squeezing his blood-drenched clothes he was rubbing the blood over his head... It appeared as if the Devi's soul had enterd his body. His face had turned hideous with the desire for vengeance and his eyes were spitting fire as he stood there glaring at Tiloka or Bhairon.

At the end of the novel the same young boy again appears in the garb of *Shakti* and saves Rano's elder daughter, Bari, from being sold off. He redeems her by marrying her.

It is worth mentioning here that although the cult of *Shakti* dominates the novel in a metaphysical sense yet after passing through the Dravidian matriarchal era (in which woman held the dominant position) the Indian cavalcade, as is known, passed through the patriarchal phase in which woman did not hold the same exalted position. From that time on she has been considered physically frail and socially too she has been holding an inferior status to man, specially in that class of society which is considered socially and economically backward.

Hence human suffering which is inherent in man and woman alike, has fallen to woman's lot in a larger measure. In our society, at the social level, a woman's dependence and deprivation stand in glaring contrast to what obtained in the olden times under the ancient Indian tradition. In Bedi's writings this contradiction in the man-woman relationship both in the social and spritual contexts has been brought out with emphatic candidness. That a woman's is a bleak ocean of woes and sorrows has again and again been dwelt upon in metaphorical terms with great understanding and compassion:

> O, God, may a daughter never be born even in an enemy's family. As she grows up a little, her parents wash their hands off by giving her away to her in-laws' house. If her in-laws don't like her or are annoyed with her, they drive her back to her parent's home. She is like a ball made of cloth. When it gets drenched in its own tears, it becomes so soggy that it loses the capacity even to keep rolling.

> Rano thought that when she had come to her in-laws' house she was at least assured of the prospects of getting food and clothes. But when the cruel God sent her daughter to her in-laws He did not even hold out the promise of food and clothes to her.

> Rano got up and turning back she looked at Jindan as if she wanted to say, 'So you are the mother who gives birth and bestows life? If it is true that you are mother to the world don't spurn me. Give me refuge. Take me under your wings. In this wide world I've no one else who can provide me shelter.'

> Rano looked in the direction of the young Chammu as if she was her childhood personified, her simplicity which could understand her woes. A childhood which was above the sins of omission and commission. Over-whelmed, Rano felt like hugging her to her heart and merge into her,

becoming one with her, never to return to this world where . . .

Heer said, "O, Jogi, (a wandering mendicant) what you say is far from truth, it is a lie. Does one ever go out to bring back an estranged lover? Does an estranged lover ever return to his beloved? My feet have turned sore and weary in search of my beloved. I have not come across anyone who could bring back the one who has gone away.

In the novel there are two occasions depicting a wedding. Once when Mangal is forcibly cornered to undergo the marriage rites and a second time when the pilgrim-girl's brother comes to marry Bari. In both places Bedi alludes to Shiva in an unpremeditated manner as it would seem.

It was a strange type of marriage party as if Shiva had come to claim Parvati. There was a *rudraksha* necklace round his neck and a snake curled round it. His mouth was stuffed with *dhatūrā* (thorn apple) and *bhang*. There was a cloth *langot* round his loins and a deer skin over his shoulder. He was carrying a trident in his hand. The members of the marriage party comprised monkeys, langoors, lions, tigers and elephants.

In the Puranas there is a reference to a long separation between Shiva and Parvati after their marriage and subsequent re-union. In the novel, due to the bizarre circumstances in which the marriage was solemnised, Mangal remains estranged from Rano. To draw Shiva towards Parvati and to disrupt Shiva's meditation Kamadeva and Rati were used as bait to distract his mind. In the novel, Salamatey acts as the counterpart to excite Mangal's carnal passion and to wean him away from Rano... But Rano, the Parvati of the house, half invisible and half visible like the eighth-day moon, blocks Mangal's way.

What was Rano trying to hide from him? There is something alluringly different from cosmetic unguents, puffs and powders, almond bark, *bindi* and other cosmetics. This has no relation with a woman's face nor with the womanly blandishments which she surreptitiously brings into play. When she has the effrontery of exposing her feminine being to the full, it dawns upon one why the eight day moon keeps half of itself hidden from view. Then gradually it casts off its *dupatta*, its *choli* (corset), its *angia* (brassiere): One day overwhelmed and dazed by its own passion it bursts forth and then squanders away its most cherished possession just as a full moon.

Utterly boozed, Mangal staggers forward and stops outside the door. Then finding the house plunged in darkness he retraces his steps. But while retreating he finds:

Rano was standing there. The moon in all its resplendent glory had waxed from half to full. Having attained its fullness, in its impatience, it had torn through the coverlets of the clouds and descended on earth.

Rano was standing before Mangal in tangible form which no wheat-eating male could resist. Between them hung a diaphanous curtain. And then her beauty took a langorous yawn, fifty-two weeks of the year, seven days of the week, eight *pahars* (parts) of the day. During this long time stretching into eternity there comes a moment when the moon leaps up with alacrity and devours the sun from head to foot in its penumbra of darkness.

After a grim and prolonged struggle it was in a way *Shakti's* triumph—a woman's triumph who had cast her man in her own mould. The vanquished sun, Mangal feeling shy at the advent of the night, peeped from behind the curtain of the moon and looked at the earth symbolised by Rano. He smiled at her. At this glorious moment of *Shakti's* triumph, Bedi has not overlooked the discord between a woman's inherent spiritual gracefulness and her social inequity.

Tonight in the abode of the sky, a helpless woman, defeated in her love, had at last pulled her torn and soiled sheet over her body and gone to sleep, disappointed and dejected.

In contrast, here is another wedding scene redolent of power and grandeur:

Rani had only to say yes and there would be a surfeit of conjugal happiness. And if she says no the doomsday would crash upon the same world in which man and animal, birds and reptiles, the earth and the sky will be faced with total annihilation. There will be no Noah left to Time and no soul left to God. The world will lose its resonance and light its brightness.

In the beginning, we had alluded to the fact that due to the shades of the Shiva cult the atmosphere of the novel is overcast with violence. After Tiloka's murder and the pilgrim girl's rape we are confronted with bloodcurdling scenes. When an unwilling Mangal was forcibly dragged to undergo marriage he was covered with blood. Similarly, on the wedding night, while struggling to snatch away the bottle of liquor from Mangal's hand, Rano hurts herself and blood spurts out from her head. Elsewhere in the novel, the tomato which had been left in the plate uneaten, reminded Mangal of Tiloka's dead body which was drenched in blood. On the wedding night he finds the same tomato resting on the cracked china plate – "a heart-shaped tomato cut into eight pieces." In the last chapter after Bari's marriage when Rano raises hands towards the temple she suddenly feels a hand stretching out in the dark from the pinnacle of the temple and then she sees a head hanging from its neck.

3

From the above discussion it is amply borne out that metaphor and mythical elements are of basic importance in Bedi's art. Quite often the inner structure of his stories is based on allusions drawn from the ancient Indian pantheon. But at the same time, it would be far from correct to infer that Bedi consciously raised the superstructure of his stories on these foundations. Evidently, there is something spontaneous about these stories for the structure evolves itself as if on its own taking a cue from these mythological allusions. In a manner of speaking, both go hand in hand, one taking its inspiration from the other. Bedi's creative process seems to be something like this: he tries to delve into the fathomless mysteries and secrets of life through the psychological build-up of his characters. He does not look at the natural disposition of man, his instincts, the carnal demands of his body, the spiritual urges of his soul at their superficial conscious level. On the other hand, he goes to their sub-conscious depths which have the ring of centuries behind them. In Bedi's writings an event is just not an isolated event but it is a link in an unbroken chain of numberless events, all carried forward in one sweep. Since in this creative process his journey is from the concrete to the abstract, from the event to the limitlessness of action, from the finite to the infinite or from the mundane to the metaphysical, he again and again resorts to the metaphor, symbolism, mythology and copious references to the Indian pantheon. In this respect Bedi's creative process is very different from Krishan Chander's and Manto's. Krishan Chander essentially remains at the surface. Manto has the penetrating eye to look behind the events. But Bedi is different from them inasmuch as, though his feet remain planted on *terra firma* his head soars in the sky. Bedi's style is complex and thought-provoking. His similes are not single or double but many-faceted and his characters are multi-dimensional whose one aspect is real and the other archetypal. It is evident that in his creative process, time and space have no bearing in the conventional sense. In his psychology one sees the shades of millennia of human thought. In this respect a moment stretches itself into centuries and a small house encompasses an entire universe. Bedi's men and women are not bound down to the present time but they represent the primeval men and women who have been undergoing human suffering since aeons and simultaneously enjoying the boon provided by this earth. Due to Bedi's multitudinal metaphors, the problems, loves, hates, joys and sorrows of his characters are not just their own as individuals but in them one can also see the sufferings of mankind and the feelings and emotions which have been the man's lot from time immemorial. These metaphysical overtones which lend his stories a kind of universality are the main characteristics of Bedi's art.

As we have explained earlier the metaphorical and mythical traces of Bedi's art can be discerned in his earlier stories. He has successfully used these literary devices in his earlier story, 'Grahan' (Eclipse). But at that time Bedi was not aware of the reach and power of his artistic virtuosity. After Independence the story, 'Lājwantī' must have firmly set him on this track although for all one knows his instinct and unconscious awareness might have played no mean part in it.

'Kokhjalī', the story which provides the title to one of his later volume of stories was published in 1949. But most of the stories included in this volume were written before Independence. But his style shows at its best in his story 'Apne Dukh Mujhe De Do.' After that Bedi seems to have come into his own; he had become fully conscious of his strength. Ek Chādar Mailī Sī was also written around the same time. After this novel there is no mistaking his forte as delineated in the effective use of myths and metaphors in his writings. Limitations of space preclude us from dilating on this theme any further and only passing references will be made to some of his other stories.

In the story 'Lājwantī', Bedi has drawn upon the episode of the washerman and the fate of Janak Dulari Sita in the Rāmāyaṇa to give significance to his story. In 'Jogiā' he has played upon a range of colours to create psychological effects. In *'Babbal'* to save the honour of the female character he has associated her name with Sita. Babbal, the small boy, is himself the naughty Lord Krishna who in a way saves Sita, the young girl from Darbari's lustful overtures. In *'Lambī Larkī'* (Too Tall For Marriage), one gets a cue to the meaning of the story from recitation of the significance of the 18th Chapter of the *Gītā* when the boat of granny's life finds its moorings immediately after the tall girl's marriage. In *'Hajjām Allahabad Ke'* (The Barbers of Allahabad), Lokpati, who does his business at the confluence of the mythical Saraswati has disfigured his clients through reckless tonsuring of their hair, the dig being at the present day political leadership and the bureaucracy. Perhaps this is Bedi's only story in which a metaphor runs its full gamut, lending it a symbolic colouring on the socio-political axis. *'Dīwālā'* (Bankruptcy) is the story of a *Bhābī* (brother's wife) and her brother-in law's (husband's brother's) sexual mores in which Bedi has raised some fundamental questions on the institution of marriage. The story's central character is a young man, Shital, who dabbles in fireworks. On the Gokulashtmi Day he not only breaks the ceremonial clay-pot in the role of Lord Krishna but also breaks the pot metaphorically, the obvious reference being to the woman who is enamoured of him. The mythological allusions in *'Eucalyptus'* are drawn from Christianity. Of Bedi's later stories, in *'Mithun'* we find erotic element and the concept of sexual unity as in the art of Khajuraho. In this, the male and the female aspects of sex are depicted as part of a total reality. The: concept of the twin stars as in Gemini also has its parallels in the Egyptian and Greek mythologies. But it was left to the Indian mind to find oneness in plurality. In his characteristic style, even is sexual absorption Bedi has culled the metaphysical aspect of universal creation which bears testimony to Bedi's unique way of looking at things.

It is often contended that Bedi gives undue importance to sex. As brought out in the above discussion, the tendency to lean upon the ancient Indian mythology was apparent in Bedi from the very beginning. But after Independence it became an integral part of his writing. For instance, one can't controvert the fact that in the collection, *Grahan*, seven stories which constitute half the number in this volume are centred round sex. If anything, the involvement with sex of course increased manifold after Independence for which his interest in the Indian mythology and the ancient tradition could have been responsible. Bedi was fully aware of the Indian mind's intellectual involvement with sex which is very different from Western sexual concepts. In India, these concepts are open and uninhibited, generally free from any taint of hypocrisy and cant. In the West the higher reaches of imagination which sees things in their exalted significance treat the physical aspect of sex as something taboo. But not so in the Indian mythology. No doubt, carnal pleasure and sensuality are its starting point. But this condition does not lead us to that kind of sensuality and crudity which are the characteristics of Western sensibility. Here the uninhibited depiction of the female form does not degenerate into that kind of obscenity with which our minds are so familiar. We have already alluded to Shiva Shakti and the Vishnu cult which form the important strands of Indian mythology. In both, sex plays an important role. Shiva Shakti tradition includes the concept of *linga* and *yoni*, the male and female sex organs. Krishna's *Rāslīlā* also revolves round sex and sublimates man-woman relationship, the only difference between the two perhaps being that Shiva Shakti has the indigenous roughness of the Dravidian mind whereas Krishna's *Rāslīlā* and the Sita and Rama relationships have the ethereal sophistication and refinement of the Aryan mind. Apart from these mythological accretions, Bedi's mind has also been informed by the other forms of fine art. In the old Indian art, sculpture and music the element of sex is far more pronounced than in similar art forms found in other civilisations. Here even the *rāgas* and *rāginīs* are assigned different male female images by which they are identified. Whether it is the stone sculpture of Khajuraho and Konark or the murals and images of Ajanta and Ellora, Bagh and Iravati, the erotic element in them has been depicted in a vivid, vibrant form. This expresses supreme joy and gay abandon which are a part of human nature and its cherished endowment. In the Indian tradition physical love is not seen apart from its spiritual aspect. The profane and sacred are not separate, they just form a single whole. For that matter, even obscenity has been shorn of its dross and vulgarity. Seen in this light, Bedi's writings come to assume a different significance:

> How lovely and loveable the world is—this world where God Himself has created man and asked the angels to bow before him. At last on a magnificent night she appears before her 'man'. The Veda *mantras* fall on her ears joined with the sound of the *Shāstras* whose message registers on her mind sometimes clearly, at others obliquely.

> It is she for whom the bridal songs are perfected and for whom passionate bricks are baked in kilns and for whom over the centuries the din of applause in the assemblage of people keeps increasing. The one who is going to be a future mother withdraws into herself like the earth which is going to be ravaged by the ploughman. He will come carrying a plough over his shoulder, its blade sharpened in a blazing furnace. A turban over his head, a plume flying over it, he resembles Raja Janak who will turn the sod of earth and break the buried clay pot from which will emerge the loving Sita and then one day 'he' will come to claim her hand in marriage, holding the sacred book in one hand, a goblet of wine in the other. In aeons gone by he has played with countless *gopīs* and danced with them. There is fear in his eyes and love and passion. He thinks this time he will have his way with the bright and beautiful maiden. He will have her again and again till he gets into a faint. Little does he realise that he is nothing but a straw in the fathomless ocean of life. Nothing more than an excuse for the perpetuation of life. To lend it mobility and then forget about it.

> — *'Lambī Laṛkī'*

Mohan had always seen a woman as something ephemeral,
an illusion. She is not inside what she looks from outside.
Good and bad, sinful or virtuous. It was an admixture, at
times beautiful, at others ugly. Again, a woman who looked
full-bodied in her clothes turned out to be thin when
stripped. And one who looked slim turned out to be full-
bodied and fleshy. What else is it if not *Māyā*? For
instance, a hefty and wholesome woman might turn out to
be a bore. It is futile to be afraid. And then to get
entangled with a bundle of bones yields far less gain than
what a wood-cutter derives by cutting down heaps of wood.
Māyā in fact is so fleeting as not to come within your
grasp and yet suddenly clutch your neck. If not woman
then what else is *Māyā*?

—'*Terminus se Pare*'

This kind of expression can touch erotic heights. It is well
known that many shades of eroticism are found in the traditional
ancient literature of the *Hitopadesha, Kathāsaritsāgara,
Shukasaptati* and thousands of fables and myths strewn in the
Puranas and elsewhere. The ancient literary tradition abounds in
the delineation of woman's nature and the secrets of physical
pleasure amounting to ecstasy. It is well-known that the classical
Indian tradition is marked by a typical candidness when it
comes to the question of sex. But the descriptions are neither
titillating nor arouse gross passion verging on lasciviousness.
The undercurrent is that of bliss generated by the male-female
union. Seen in that light, sex in Bedi belongs to the ancient
tradition. Passing through a maze of human relationships in
their varied forms he reaches the fathomless depths of the male-
female union. While unfolding the tangled strands of the
interaction of physical and spiritual bliss and while listening to
the throbs of the human heart, he sees man and woman so
united, becoming a part of the cosmic riddle.

4

Finally, a few words about Bedi's style in relation to the diction and language of the new story.

Lately, it has become common to eschew direct narration and use language at a purely imaginative level. This trend can be termed as a shift towards oblique expression which is opposed to all the traditional styles referred to in the beginning of this chapter. The styles of Premchand, Manto and Krishan Chander can be described as forming part of the tradition of direct expression. This is not to deny the fact that one does come across examples of symbolic expression in the older fiction writers. For instance, in Ahmed Ali's *'Maut se Pahle'* (Before Death), in Aziz Ahmed's *'Ibn-e-Sīnā aur Sadiyān'* (Ibn-e-Sina & Centuries) or in Krishan Chander's *'Ghālīcha'* (The Carpet). But such examples are few and far between whereas in the new fiction symbolism and allegorical expression have assumed the dimensions of a major trend. After Independence the writers among whom this trend of drifting away from direct narration has become more pronounced the name of Intizar Husain stands out conspicuously. In his stories and novels Intizar Husain distinguished himself by discovering the ingredients of symbolism and the like in the medieval fables and narratives. Intizar Husain's style can be called the extension or the offshoot of the style of the traditional fable or *Dāstān*, while Bedi's style has a mythological ring.

Among contemporary story writers there are some who in spite of favouring the style of direct expression in the bulk of their writing have also used the oblique or the allegorical style in some of their stories. In this context we have particularly Ram Lall and Joginder Paul in mind among others. We are referring to Ram Lall's *'Āngan'* (The Courtyard), Joginder Paul's *'Bāzyāft'* (Retrieval) and Iqbal Majeed's *'Peṭ kā Kechwā'* (The Earthworm in the Stomach). Apart from them, there are still some writers who attach great importance to literary embellishments such as purple patches, florid expression and similes coming thick and fast in their writings. It is an acknowledged fact that in creative writing simile is somewhat inferior to the metaphor. Simile is no doubt an accepted figure of speech and very much used in poetry, but it has serious limitations in terms of creative use, while a metaphor has no imaginative limitations. In the second place, in a simile, the subject and the object go hand in hand which makes it less compact and semantically less charged than the metaphor, resulting in unnecessary verbiage. Besides, the simile, unlike the metaphor, also takes away something of the suggestive element. In the Urdu short story a simile-laden prose is characteristic of Krishan Chander's style which gradually has been on the wane. It is in this context that the heritage of Bedi assumes great significance.

It is generally maintained that the language of the Urdu short story has now come closer to the language of poetry. By the language of poetry is not meant the florid language used by Krishan Chander and his followers. Their language is no doubt elegant but it is lacking in depth. In the short story of today, poetic language implies the language which uses such devices as symbolism, suggestion, metaphor, allegory and the like. It uses myths, motifs, beliefs, folklore in order to discover new ways of expression.

In the end the question inevitably arises that now that the practitioner of the short story form has thrown the traditional mode of expresssion overboard what sort of expression will take its place? What will be the language base on which the stylistic superstucture of the future short story will be raised? It is evident that Premchand's language has lagged behind in this literary journey. The question of Krishan Chander's language does not arise. That leaves Manto and of course Bedi in the field. As for Bedi, his style is so highly individualistic that it leaves no scope for any following or imitation. Not because the foundation of his language has been laid on myth and metaphor—for that matter these are the common property of every writer—but for the fact that Bedi's language is far removed from the mainstream. Thus by the process of elimination only Manto is left in the field as a sole contender. There is no doubt that being close to the basic Urdu, Manto's language will find wide acceptance and has in fact already gained in popularity more than others. In parenthesis, here one must draw a distinction between style and language. Style operates at two levels—the level of expression and the level of discourse. Where it is a question of the surface level Manto's language will surely pass muster. But when it comes to the question of the inner implication of discourse, it will have to resort to the tools of symbolism, the myth, the metaphor and allegory etc. In this one would not be able to get much help from Manto for obviously he is a writer of direct expression. Thus when it comes to finding one's depths via the myth and the metaphor Bedi will certainly serve as a beacon light.

allegory, for the result of a table

12

The 'New' Urdu Short Story: the Symbolic and Allegorical Devices and the Storiness

1

THE 'new' Urdu short story which made its beginning in the mid-fifties, and blossomed in the following two decades, was at the cross-roads in the eighties where it was bristling with uncomfortable and challenging questions. The reader was particularly anxious to know what direction the new Urdu story was going to take. The new story, in fact, as it was manifesting was more the result of a revolt and break from the past than merely an innovation in the sense of breaking new ground. The younger story writers were sensitive of new trends of thinking and the problems being raised by the new modes of expression, crystallizing in new styles of writing. A fire was raging in their hearts, sparked by acute anguish. As a result the new story was tossed on the high seas by the buffetings of sharp winds. Writers like Intizar Husain, Surendra Prakash, Anwar Sajjad, and others, changed the very complexion of the story. The main problem of the new story was the delineating of the changing concept of reality: Reality is not just what is apparent on the surface but is something which, beyond its form and shape is a renegade from the senses, and can only be realised not through the use of words as words, but through words as metaphors or symbols. Going by this, the story is not merely the handmaiden of conscious, logical relationships, but also takes into account the subconscious which plays a most significant role in the cognition of reality. To elaborate, the human relationships are not what they appear on the surface, and the concepts of time and space manifest themselves not in any logical manner, but as continuum in the flux of life. With this approach, the superficial romanticism of the old era, its hollow and empty sentimentalism, its loud, blatant effects and palpable designs and more so the exteriorisation of events came in for heavy onslaughts and were thrown by the wayside. The new story established its identity, through the manifestation of unalloyed reality and its new mode of expression which came to be regarded as its hallmark. For the new writers words were not just words. They were used as symbols and metaphors and stood for the subject, which could not be logically paraphrased. The very individuality of the individual was emphasised and in this lay his uniqueness. The writers grappled with the small joys and sorrows of life, and the basic truths and untruths, and the freedom of choice or the lack of it, which gave meaning to life. They knew what the anguish of the self meant. The story in its new form became a variegated mosaic of life.

A lot has been written in exhaustive detail on the new story. Nonetheless, in the last few years what has become a cause of deep concern is that after the seventies the scene that has emerged in relation to the new short story shows that many aspects have remained nebulous. The new generation, perhaps as a result of blind following or overemphasis on the symbolic or poetic use of language, has erroneously come to regard even belles-lettres and the personal essay also as story. There are many writers waiting at the cross-roads, speculating in which direction to go. The mix-up between the prose-poem and the new story has further added to the confusion. It is a matter of regret that literary criticism which could have played some role remained in the background and has not done its job.

In an earlier article[1], I was at some pains to point out that the symbolic story called for special type of creativity and was not story made easy for all writers. It is not that all writers should take to writing the symbolic story as a matter of course which betrays mob mentality. As a corollary, I maintained that it was not incumbent upon the common run of story writers who were not competent enough even to turn out an ordinary story, to inflict on their readers such symbolic stories which were absolutely unreadable. For that matter in the course of the last decade or so there has been a plethora of stories which even by stretching the imagination to its utmost cannot be termed as stories but in certain quarters were passed as such. It is feared that the spate of such so called symbolic stories which had as its proponents a mass of blind followers may seal the fate of the genuine new Urdu story.

2

In many quarters, the voice of this writer was deemed as a false cry. There was a lot of hue and cry, and it was contended that I was opposing the symbolic story because I wanted the Urdu short story to be put back in its old grooves. The sorrier part of it was that it was the antithesis of what I had actually said. Here I will be more concerned with the controversy that has raged around the symbolic and the allegorical story. Varis Alvi has particularly elaborated on this controversy. According to Varis Alvi, "an allegorical story represents an inferior kind of writing and it should be rejected outright."[2] He has been writing in this vein running down the use of allegorical devices and supporting the symbolic story for the past many years which has only made the confusion worse confounded.

To quote him:

Except for two or three stories all the others are allegorical and metaphorical written in the style now in vogue. I won't call an allegorical story a symbolic story because what they regard as 'symbolic story' is nothing but the mirage of an arid sandy waste in which their fount of creativity is drying up day by day.[3]

Salaam knows that what he is writing is allegory. He is also conscious of the fact that an allegory has to be rendered in simple, chaste, matter-of-fact style. You will no doubt come across a couple of stories which can be called symbolic but the bulk of them do not get out of the circle of allegory, and all the time move within this limit. This is indeed an inferior kind of art because in this kind of story the imagination cannot rise above the level of comparison and example whereas a realistic and symbolic story creates a reality which cannot be realised through any other mode.[4]

Such statements of Varis Alvi betray his being carried away by western influences. Had he set store by our cultural traditions and collective sensibility, he would not have rejected the allegorical element out of hand, as he has now done. He has ended by making another questionable statement:

When the writer fails to grapple successfully with reality and symbolism he resorts to allegory, *dāstān, kathā*, and fairy tales which show him an easy way out of his difficulties. Here imagination changes into fantasy. The discipline imposed by art and artistic sophistication are both sacrificed over primitive decadence and its inherent simplicity and lack of depth. This is the tragedy of the modern Urdu short story.[5]

It seems Varis Alvi is not aware of the fact that traditional stories are not merely the expression of simplicity. They in fact epitomise wisdom and profound human experience garnered over the centuries. It is however an altogether different fact that caught in the maelstrom of modernisation we turn a blind eye to the treasures hidden in these ancient pieces and ultimately our imagination gets so corroded that we lose the capacity to enjoy them. As regards the artistic sophistication, suffice it to say that deploying allegorical or metaphorical technique is neither finding an easy way out of difficulties, nor denying the discipline of art.

Something similar has been said by Baqar Mehdi:

> The new story is not competing with progressive story. In fact it is competing with the traditional tale and the *dāstān*-type story which mode is represented by Intizar Husain.

The same is the case with Varis Alvi. Otherwise be wouldn't have lumped together, the allegory, *dāstān, kathā* and fairy tales. At the same time he would not have regarded them as inferior to the symbolic and realistic stories. Before we can set up the points of discussion arising out of the above statements it must be clear that according to these critics there are three streams along which the new story flows—that is, the symbolic story, the realist story and the traditional story (which Varis Alvi has identified with allegory, *kathā* and *hikāyat*). The fun of it is that in spite if his rebellious proclivities Varis Alvi rates realist stories higher than the allegorical stories with the exception of the symbolic story. To discuss this point further let us first come to terms with the definition of allegory.

According to Harry Shaw it is:

> A method of representation in which a person, abstract idea,or event stands for itself and for something else. Allegory may be defined as extended metaphor. The term is often applied to a work of fiction in which the author intends characters and their action to be understood in terms other than their surface appearances and meanings. The most famous and the most obvious of such two-level narratives in English is Bunyan's *Pilgrim's Progress*. In Spenser's *Faerie Queene,* figures are actual characters and

also abstract qualities. Parts of Dante's *Divine Comedy* and Tennyson's *Idylls of the King* are also allegorical.[6]

From this it is evident that an allegory operates at two levels. A 'person, idea, or event' has its own individuality and also an extended meaning. Allegory is not primitive. It can be termed as primitive only in the sense in which abstract concept such as virtue, evil, fear, loyalty, love, etc., were personified for simple didactic ends. But the allegory has not been used only for that specific purpose. Roger Fowler has also called allegory an extended metaphor. He considers George Orwell's *1984* as an excellent example of allegory. Fowler has also hinted that if new criticism looks askance at allegory (as in the case of Varis Alvi), even so it is difficult to differentiate between allegory and symbolism at the face of it. In the words of Lorna Sage:

> The common distinction between allegory and symbolism falsifies the facts of literary experience . . . The clear-cut distinction between 'the music of ideas' (Richards on Eliot) and the 'dark conceit' of allegory is harder to make in practice than in theory: Yeats's *A Vision* systematises and expounds the mystery of his symbols much as Spenser did in *The Faerie Queene*. Cleanth Brooks in *The Well Wrought Urn* (1947) allegorises all the poems he explicates, so that they become 'parables about the nature of poetry', and Northrop Frye in *The Anatomy of Criticism* (1957) summed up this tendency by pointing out that all analysis was covert allegorizing.[7]

Lewis's viewpoint cannot also be ignored. According to him it is not necessary that there should be one-to-one relation between the inner and the surface meaning of a thing. Generally it is understood that in allegory mental concepts such as virtue, folly, wickedness, fear, love, etc., are delineated in concrete terms which create the relation of one to one. But it is not imperative, Sylvan Barnet has also come to the same conclusion:

There is an increasing tendency to blur the distinction between symbol and allegory, especially when the writer's invented word (usually associated with allegory) has no clear equations.[8]

It was not necessary for me to quote these sources. But Varis Alvi is so much steeped in western literature that he can't put a step forward without relying on it. Perhaps he may not relish Lorna Sage's views in which she gives allegory the place of structural symbolism instead of textural. In her words:

Allegory's distinctive feature is that it is a structural, rather than a textural symbolism: it is large-scale exposition in which problems are conceptualised and analysed into their constituent parts in order to be stated, if not solved. The typical plot is one in which the 'innocent'—Gulliver, Alice, the Lady in Milton's 'Comus', K. in Kafka's *The Castle*—is put through a series of experiences, which add up to an imaginative analysis of contemporary reality.[9]

Barnet has dwelt on the point that since symbolism harks to the higher world and the super real, it is deeply embedded in the subconscious. It also establishes relationship with the world of images and motifs which Carl Jung calls archetypes and which are abundantly available in myths and legends.

After this elaboration it is hardly necessary to point out that what Varis Alvi labelled three types of stories are actually not three but only two. In other words they are confined to the story of symbolism, and the straight realist story. Although the symbolic and allegorical, i.e., *Kathā, dāstān, hikāyat*-type, stories seem to strike separate notes, yet, in terms of metaphorical function, or in deep-structural meanings, they are not mutually exclusive, but are one. Since we cannot conceive symbolism as something apart from the sub-conscious, it cannot by the same token be separated from the mysteries of the sub-conscious some forms of which we come across in allegorical stories, *kathās, dāstāns, hikāyats*, etc. Hence the story of symbolism and the allegorical story are not two separate things, but are two stylistic expressions of the same creative process. The difference, as such, is that of the devices of expression, and not of mental processes. This thesis cannot be established unless it is tested in the crucible of some representative new stories.

3

In the first place it is necessary to put out of our way the wranglings relating to the *dāstān, kathā,* vis-a-vis the new Urdu story. Evidently we shall have to resort to Pakistan's foremost short story writer Intizar Husain's art in order to resolve this problem. Let us take one of his stories which was published under the title '*Nar Nārī.*'[10] It has three characters—the wife Madan Sundri, her husband Dhawal; and brother Gopi. Her husband and her brother immolate themselves in front of the Devi's (goddess's) temple. We find two dead bodies lying in the temple courtyard drenched in blood, the heads lying apart from the torsos. Madan Sundri wails and beats her breasts in lamentation. She recites hymns invoking the Devi, and is about to strike off her head with the same sword when the Devi is pleased with her. "Go and join their heads and bodies together," she tells Madan Sundri. "I've bequeathed new lives to your husband and brother." Madan Sundri almost swoons out of joy. In a hurry, she mistakenly joins her husband's head with her brother's torso and her brother's head to her husband's torso. She is about to rectify her mistake when both of them revive and the husband and the brother become a mix-up. Later on when she sleeps with her husband, his hands and body seem so unfamiliar to her. She is worried as to whose sister she is and whose wife. Her husband is also in a quandary. Is he the same person or someone else? This dual enigma runs through the entire story, generating tension and the main quest.

In the end, the mystery is sought to be resolved with the help of the parable of Usha and Prajapati.

Is it a symbolic or allegorical story? Who is Madan Sundri? Who is Dhawal? Evidently, no simple answer is possible to these questions. Or, for that matter, is it really a story? Ask any reader and he will say it *is* a story. It has characters and events and the story moves forward through the action and inter-action of events and characters. There is an allusion to the Devi (goddess) through whose boon their bodies are resurrected by joining their heads and torsos. The central theme of the story has the overtones of ancient myths and legends. Obviously, on account of non-real concepts the story cannot be called a realistic story. Nor does it personify the abstract concepts such as virtue, evil, fear, love, etc., and as such it does not conform to the traditional definition of an allegory either. It is not an allegory, nor is it a realistic story. Then what is it in its essence? Has the story writer written another story *a la Baitāl Pacchīsī*? And that is that! But all the same we have a legitimate right to pose a question. Apart from the narrative which is the surface structure of the story, are there other semantic relationships within the inner or deep structure of the story? After the joining of the heads and the torsos, it is Madan Sundri who first finds herself in a quandary. Tired after the day's work, when she lies down in bed by her husband's side, and falls into his ardent embrace, she suddenly realizes that something has gone wrong somewhere. She was so very familiar with her husband's body and previously when their bodies joined together in union she felt they had known each other for ages. They had known the mysterious curves of each other's bodies. When his hand knowingly travelled over her warm body her body would get electrified at the mere touch of his hand. But tonight it appeared as if these bodies were strangers. Was it the same body to which she used to cling at night? Now in spite of herself she wriggled out of Dhawal's clasp. "You are not you," she shouts in shock.

Dhawal's individuality at once becomes a stranger to her and she wonders "why had this person become so unfamiliar to her when she had been regarding him as her very own?"

If one carefully dwells on these lines, it becomes evident that the author is raising the question of the identity—the relationship through the ages, the merging of two bodies into each other and then falling apart as strangers. Do these denote that a metaphorical entity is evolving itself in Dhawal, whose individuality has suddenly gathered unknown contours? And one should not forget that this crisis of identity has arisen because a wrong head has been joined to a wrong torso. Dhawal lights the lamp and says to Madan Sundri, "Come to your senses, Madan. Just see if I'm not here. I ?" Madan Sundri looks abashed and says, "Yes you are you." But when he tries to possess her, she vehemently protests, "Dhawal, these are not your hands." And then she recalls the circumstances under which the mix-up had occurred.

Even those who have only a nodding acquaintance with Intizar Husain's art can easily understand the import of this structural framework. It is well-nigh impossible to paraphrase the elements which relate to the super-real. In other words, symbolism exists in a unique world of its own. The deciphering of a metaphor in the context of its semantic role lies in the fact that one can just sense its inner meaning without being able to lay his finger on it. Hence I can only hazard a suggestion that maybe the author is talking of some cultural personality in whom elemental and spiritual values merge into each other in evolving a new personality (as it has happened in the author's country). And yet that personality is so nebulous as to be unable to force its identity in the surroundings where it belongs. Characters conceived in this ancient manner can also have a contemporary symbolic connotation: the sundered heads which stand for migrant heads after passing through a horrible period of (post-partition) bloodshed and trauma are joined to new torsos—in other words, they find themselves on a new soil unfamiliar to them. With the synthesis in this manner a new cultural personality is expected to evolve which should be unitary. Madan Sundri, time and again, spurns Dhawal. But why? For that matter who is this Madan Sundri who keeps grovelling in quandaries? If the reader pays heed to the symbolic overtones as they emerge in the story he may be inclined to believe that Madan Sundri perhaps symbolises the society at large which has become unhinged and has become a victim of the crisis of idenity. Intizar Husain being an artist par excellence would not stop short by ending up the story just at this point. When the discussion between Madan Sundri and Dhawal comes to a head, the latter says in a decisive tone, "Oh, Madan, just as the Ganges is the most sacred river among rivers, and the Sumeru the most exalted among the mountains, in the same manner, the head is the superiormost part of the body. What are you so exercised over? A man is identified first and foremost by his head. Look at my head. Isn't it mine, to be sure?"

Here is not the writer trying to bring out the clash between the two points of view, the importance of the spiritual values (signified by head), or the importance of indigenous sociological values (signified by body, torso) in a culture. The new 'State' is a combination of both, but in a religious state, it is the super-structure which is emphasised again and again, but at the same time, the deep-structure too has its pulls and pressures, and unless a unified whole emerges, there is an on-going tussle between the super-structure and base of a culture. Needless to say, the setting up of a new 'State' (based on religion) and the resultant large scale migration has thrown up altogether new cultural questions which have yet to be resolved.

Madan Sundri is impressed by Dhawal's logic. The torso, she is led to believe belongs to the same head which rests upon it; she accepts it. But the matter gets complicated when Dhawal himself is assailed by doubts. He may unquestioningly abide by the mundane things of life. But culture makes its own demands. Dhawal looks at all the parts of his body, one by one and utters, "Hey Ram, is it me?" Then another wave of doubt assails him. "Is it really me?" He asks himself. "Or is it another person who has joined himself to me? Or that I have merged into someone else?" The more he muses over it the more he gets confused, "The whole of me is not me." Is not this a pointer towards the emergence of a new personality? Is not this indicative of the evolution of a new culture. We find that gradually Dhawal's trepidation increases. He was feeling guilty at heart; it was like a splinter of wood constantly racking the flesh. He was all the time labouring under the apprehension that it was someone else's body; he seemed to be at odds against his own being. The discerning reader who can grasp and appreciate the implications of symbolic expression, will see the deeper significance of the predicament of the characters involved. Any further elaboration of the implications of the story thus is redundant for the simple reason that a reader cannot miss the thrust of the story. To lend depth to Dhawal's symbolic character, Intizar Husain narrates a tale which assumes the character of a story within a story. This is a special feature of Intizar Husain's art and he generally uses this device to consolidate the underlying meanings of his work. Here Dhawal suddenly recalls the story of a princess who was in the bondage of a demon. Every morning this demon would hack off the head of the princess and placing it on a platter leave his den. In the evening the demon would return bellowing and join the head to the torso once again bringing the princess back to life. Dhawal would often think that though the princess was none too happy she had every reason to be pleased on one count: both the head and the torso belonged to her!

In conclusion Dhawal's anxiety mounts till it becomes an obsession with him. Alongwith Madan Sundri he goes to a *rishī* (sage) and tells him about his predicament. The *rishī* frowns at Dhawal and says, "You are indeed a fool that you should invite doubts about yourself. Why do you forget the supreme fact that you are a man and Madan Sundri is a woman? Go and do the job that is enjoined upon you!" The curtain lifts from before Dhawal's eyes. While passing through the woods he looks at Madan Sundri, just as aeons ago Prajapati had looked at Usha. Prajapati disports with her and she responds to his blandishments. "Go and have Madan Sundri. She is your property. Why have you got yourself involved in this rigmarole, forgetting that she *is* your preserve?" This is not just a man-woman relationship, but may allude to the relationship between the individual and the society also. In the same way, this relationship subsists between the man and earth, migrant and country, and citizen and state. In each case one is destined to be utilised or exploited, and the other must utilise or exploit.

There could be other semantic factors at work behind this structure. For instance, the phenomenon of migration denotes transplantation from one soil to another. A probe into the various manifestations of culture continues unabated. In culture itself there is the grafting of material and spiritual values. As for historical synthesis, the inter-action of forces in the different stages of man's evolution raises new questions leading to a process of adaptation and forming and re-forming patterns of culture.

In the context of this discussion, is there any justification in saying that such stories are 'primitive' stories, or they are lacking in symbolic import? Having said this, there is no need to overemphasise that in such stories symbolic elements are not super-imposed, rather they interact with allegorical elements to create the semantic structure. The sundering of the princess's head and the demons placing her head on a platter and then joining the same head to her torso in the evening are all allegorical devices. But the story is not just an allegory. An allegory and allegorical devices are not the same thing. Allegorical devices generate symbolic implications. Does not the above story demonstrate at every step that Dhawal and Madan Sundri are not merely allegorical characters? They have a universal symbolic import also. Certainly one can regard them as characters in a story and nothing more and enjoy them at the surface level. But they are something more than just surface characters. They are archetypes of man and woman who also point to something outside themselves; they serve as a cue for protagonists at another level of existence.

The above discussion leads to the conclusion that in such new stories the symbolic and the allegorical are not separate from each other. Further, that symbolism comes to us through the layers of the sub-conscious, and more often than not, the symbolic elements and the allegorical elements are fused together. Such stories may have the simplicity of the old traditional story, but they are not primitive, and the surface might be deceptive, or simply a requirement of artistic consideration as has been discussed above. To label such stories as primitive or brush them off as old-style allegorical stories is a mistake. In fact such stories are devices or offshoots of the symbolic story. At best they can be given the portmanto name of the 'symbolic-allegoric' story.

4

Let us now deal with a story by a short story writer from Islamabad whose credo is that 'I do not want to write a true story'. But he does not wish to write false stories either. He further adds, 'I want to write *afsāna* (imaginative short fiction)'. This implies that this writer differentiates between the realist story, non-realist story and *afsāna*. He also claims that 'I do not hang my creations on the pegs of theory.' But his characters are mostly drawn from the downtrodden and the under-privileged poor strata of society. They include Kodu *fakīr*, Alia barber, Sado carpenter, Shedo sweeperess, and the helpless Zenan who is so beautiful that she can spend hours together standing before the mirror to admire herself. She is a spirited woman— firebrand, surrounded by a raging fire, but she was bought for the price of a buffalo and an ass.

Three story collections of this writer have already seen the light of day—*Band Muṭṭhī men Jugnū* (Lahore 1975), *Maas aur Miṭṭī* (Islamabad 1980), and the latest collection, *Khalā andar Khalā* which appeared from Islamabad in 1983. This collection includes a story titled *'Tamāsha'* (a public performance spectacle, fun, show). It is rare to come across a story which shocks or sweeps us off our feet. *'Tamāsha'* is one such story. It may not be so shattering in the case of good verse but one has to struggle a lot with a good story— live vicariously its woes and travails, and forge unseen bonds with the story in which a pain flares up suddenly and overpowers you. We do not know whether Muhammad Mansha Yaad, the author has written this *afsāna* to evade writing a true or false story. Undoubtedly, this is a true story and not a false one either, and the style in which it has been written makes it an *afsāna* too. Let us have a quick look at the structure of the story:

1) A conjurer and his son *Jamūrā*, who acts as the conjurer's assistant, are seen travelling through a deserted land on foot in search of a promising locality for their performance.

2) While walking along the river bank they see a new locality across the river. But there is no bridge over the river, nor a boat near at hand to take them across the river.

3) They decide to swim across the river when the conjurer suddenly recalls a dream he had the previous night. It was a horrible dream and feels that the day is ominous for them and they must not get into the water.

4) They keep walking along the river bank and they see that the high minarets of the mosque across the river are moving with them. They also see a bridge in the distance.

5) They hear dogs barking and cows bellowing and come to the conclusion that a habitat must be somewhere nearby. They decide to spend the night in that locality. Refreshed by the night's sleep they would resume their journey in the morning.

6) But it is a strange locality. The father beats his drum and plays on his flute and people gather round them. But there are no men or women among them. Only children. And what strange children! Their hair is grey and their faces are wrinkled. There is no full-fledged man in the entire habitat.

7) The father first takes out three iron balls from his mouth. Then he shows some cups to the spectators which one by

one vanish from his hands. He shows many other tricks.
An empty glass suddenly fills with water. He turns the glass
upside down and the water does not fall out. He gets
himself stung by a snake, swallows a dagger and then
produces it from his stomach. The children do not clap,
nor do they express their appreciation in any other
manner. This had never happened before. The conjurer is
puzzled.

8)   The conjurer announces that he is going to perform his
master trick. He would cut his boy *Jamūrā's* throat with a
knife and after having killed him in this manner he would
bring the boy back to life, in one piece. This
announcement is greeted with loud clapping by the
children. The conjurer is surprised because the spectators
generally do not relish this trick and often dissuade him
from performing it. Asking his son to lie prostrate on the
ground he covers him with a sheet of cloth and goes to
work on him with his knife. The spectators clap loudly and
throw coins at the conjurer to express their appreciation.
In a jiffy the crowd melts away and the *maidān* becomes
empty. The father calls out to his son but the son does not
respond. Feeling apprehensive, the father removes the
sheet from the boy's body. He finds that the boy is lying
dead, drenched in blood. His neck has been cut.

Each of the steps enumerated above gains in meaning from
the preceding one, having a potential scope to give a twist to the
story. The writer could turn the story in a different direction at
every step. For instance, the conjurer and his son *Jamūrā* are
out on a journey, to travel being the antithesis of home. The
more they walk towards the unknown locality, the farther it
recedes from them. They could have crossed the bridge and
entered the locality. But if the author had allowed this to
happen, the element of mystery would have disappeared and the
grotesque leading to sinister possibilities would have also faded.
Again, the place where they end up is a strange habitat of

pygmies, all of whom appear to have aged before time. The same thing could have been shown the other way round, but in that case the impact of the story would have been diluted. In this manner one can seek the opposite of each action with immense possibilities of providing cutting edges to developments and giving them different meanings. In the end, the conjurer's performance could have led to some other result but in that case would the reader have got the same shock and left with a frightening question?

The story has a regular plot. The events take place in logical sequence. There is movement in the story and unity of effect. There are three clear-cut characters in the story—the conjurer, the *Jamūrā*, and the spectators, and the characters are in consonance with the events and in conformity with the dialogue. The story builds up to a climax and moves towards a definite end. Is it then a conventional story? Going by the structure of the story and the phases through which it passes no sensible reader would dare say that it is a conventional story. Well, if it is not a conventional story, can it claim to be a symbolic story? Or, is it an allegorical story? Or in the words of Munsha Yaad, is it simply an *afsāna* and neither a true story nor a false story? The plain fact is that these questions do not admit of a facile answer, nor preclude answers to them. The problem, however, becomes a bit difficult because, regretfully, in some quarters strait-jacketed classifications, admitting of no flexibility in placing a story in its rightful place, are made. However, a redeeming feature is that in our above discussion, it has been made out amply that in Urdu fiction, the symbolic and the allegorical stories do not stand apart from each other as is often maintained in certain quarters. Without going into greater details, we would only touch upon a few points in the interest of clarification.

Having studied the structure let us consider some other elements of the story.

They duly see a locality across the river but the snag is that there is no bridge over the river nor a boat within sight. After some hesitation the father says, "Have a heart, son. With Allah's

name on our lips we shall take the plunge" Then he suddenly
remembers the previous night's dream and he changes his
mind.

"What dream are you talking of, *Abbā*? "
"It was a horrible dream, son."
"Horrible in what way, *Abbā*? "
"Son, I saw that I was facing a big crowd of spectators. I was
standing there, a snake curled round my neck. The
children were clapping gleefully and throwing coins on the
sheet spread on the ground. Suddenly the snake which I
had nurtured like a son dug its fangs into my neck,
injecting all its venom in my body."
"What happened next, *Abbā*? "

The old man explained that darkness descended before his
eyes: Gathering my strength which was ebbing away fast, I called
you to come to my rescue. Then my own scream pulled me out
of my sleep. I found it was midnight, the moon had disappeared
and the dogs were howling in the dark. I saw you lying curled up
due to cold. I covered you with a sheet in the same manner as I
cover you in a *tamāsha* before proceeding to cut your throat
and then bringing you back to life. But in the stillness of the
eerie night, the act of covering your body seemed very ominous,
and after that sleep deserted me.

Is this dream not the central allegorical episode around
which the story has been woven? The manner in which the
allegorical treatment has deepened the semantic dimensions of
the story, could any other way have been possible? In the first
place, there is this horrendous atmosphere in which the story
unfolds itself. In the second place, the story is rendered more
gruesome because of the son's murder at the hands of the father.
The father had nurtured the poisonous snake with the same
affection that he had lavished on his son and yet it had dug its
fangs into his skin. Here it is the son that kills his father while in
the story it is a transformation inasmuch as it is the father that
kills his progeny. In the second part of the dream, namely, "in

that eerie part of the night I found the act of covering my son with a bedsheet very ominous" forebodes the tragic end of the story. However, the end of the story is indeed startling and unexpected too.

Besides the dream, there are many other allegorical ingredients in the story. For instance, father and son keep walking along the river bank and along with them the minarets of the mosque also keep moving. The morning merges into the afternoon but the distance from the bridge does not diminish. By the same token, when they reach the locality they do not find any grown-up man there; there are children only, and although they appear to have aged, they are still children, etc.

As it is, it is a three-tiered story in terms of events all of which are allegorical. But on the basis of these factors can one say that the story is only allegorical and nothing more? It would however be unfair to come to a finality without considering many other semantic dimensions of the story.

Who is this old man and who is this son? Are they just the conjurer and his *jamūrā*, or are they a part of that mysterious *tamāsha* (spectacle) that unfolds itself everyday before our eyes? And what kind of journey is it? After covering the long journey into the darkness of the night, by sunrise they reach the bank of the river. Is it the life's journey? Does this darkness represent the past which we leave behind in the limbo of time? Does the sunrise stand for the immediate present in which we are walking along the river of time? The father and son, being segments of the past and the present mankind respectively, are striving to cross the river. But has one ever succeeded in crossing the river of time? Man is lost in quest of those unknown habitats but the more he travels, the more mystifying these become. The morning changes into noon and the noon descends into the evening but the mysteries of life always elude us. The moment they are resolved they again come thick and fast upon us.

"Jamūre, is it not rather strange that the bridge keeps moving ahead of us all the time?"

"And the locality too, *Abbā*. The minarets too are moving
abreast of us?"

"Isn't it rather strange, *Jamūre?*"

"Yes, very strange, *Abbā*."

"There is some mystery behind it, son."

"*Abbā*, we play tricks on the people every day. I think they
are playing tricks on us today."

The son is subservient to his father. Generally they put their
heads together in regaling the public. But now both have
reached a stage of time where a cruel joke is going to be played
on them. They get tired and weary of the long journey. Their feet
become sore with walking and their lips get chapped. The old
man suddenly stops and says,

"Stop, son. Perhaps we are not fated to reach the locality
across the river."

"Then what's the way out, *Abbā?*"

"Let's turn back, son."

"No, *Abbā* our destination is the locality across the river."

It is evident that the son is more enthusiastic than the father
in quest of his goal. The new generation is more arduous and
demanding than the old in pursuit of its objective. Otherwise it is
a travesty of facts to call it new. That the new generation is
considered to be more brainy and daring we get a proof of it
from the many dialogues between the father and the son.

The relationship between the father and the son is that of the
provider and the provided. It is also of the protector and the
'concept' to be protected, i.e., the 'new system' or the 'new
society' and the ruler or the guiding hand. Perhaps this is the
aspect which serves as the pivotal point of the story.

It has already been pointed out that the story is surrounded
by an aura of mystery. On reaching that eerie locality the old
man suddenly stops and his eyes are glued to a plum tree. The
boy picks up a clod of earth and hurls it at the tree bringing
down a plum of which he takes one bite and then throws it away.

"May God have mercy on us," the father says, "some mystery surrounds the plum tree."

The son raises his head and looks at the sky. The father says, "I see swallows in the sky, son."

"Yes, *Abbā*, a whole flock of them."

"They must be flying away in search of food."

"Who knows they may be in search of something else."

"What else, son?"

"Elephants, *Abbā*."

"No, son, these are not that kind of swallows. These are the ones which ride on elephant's backs and chirp."

"Let's go away from here, *Abbā*. Somehow I don't like the place."

This has an allusion to the Holy Book. The swallows here don't symbolise goodness, virtue or the benediction of God. They are caught in a web of mystery. It is not the right place to be in for the father and the son. We must not forget that the title of the story is *Tamāsha* which loosely means a spectacle. It could have an ironic or sarcastic ring. The locality in which the father and son find themselves seems to be a haunted place. Has the present day society (maybe of the author or otherwise) been caught in some such situation where the society itself is busy massacring its own cherished values or setting at nought its own system and order? Otherwise the father would not have said in such a gloomy tone, "Son, my hands have become sore with beating the drum and my inside is drained by constantly blowing on the flute."

By the time we reach this point don't we begin to feel that the old man could be the symbol of our times who is reeling under a crisis of values? His arms have become stiff with ceaselessly beating the drum and his breathing has become strained by playing on the flute. But nobody seems to be concerned about it. It is because the people have lost their sense of values and the era in which they are living seems to have lost its meaning. Whether it is a spectacle involving the balls, or of multiplying them, making two into four, or of emptying a full glass, or vice versa or of swallowing a burning cigarette—nothing ever leaves

an imprint on the viewers' minds. It is just a spectacle which
goes on and on and nothing more. Every value has become
empty and devoid of meaning. The spectators standing around
are raw and immature. In that locality, you "do not come across
a man of normal stature." The society in short has become
denuded of the real values of life and its people have lost the
urge and the dignity to stake their all for values they should have
cherished most. These values can be material, i.e., mundane, as
well as spiritual or simply political. In this age 'the children'
don't allow anyone to exist: they just tick them off. Who are these
'children'? They are the mentally immature people who have
kept terror-stricken people under their heels and have cut the
'big ones' to size. The last item of the performance is cutting the
boy's neck after making him to lie down on the ground. We find
the boy lying drenched in blood and his head sundered from
his body. The father has butchered his son, maybe, the society
its cherished leader, or an ideal, or a system, say *democracy,*
which lies murdered, and what a 'fun' for the 'people' who have
all disappeared after the *tamāsha*!

Taking it universally, in the same manner, is not man
butchering his own values? Isn't society also doing the same?
Hasn't mankind lost its inner self? Hasn't man become
homeless and is now wandering about like a rootless nomad?

Above we have placed all the three aspects of the story—
traditional, symbolic and allegorical to enable the reader to
decide the category, if at all a category has to be fixed, in which
the story can be placed.

Even a perfunctory study of the story's structure will show that
it is not a traditional story. From a closer interpretation of the
story it would appear that the author has also pressed the
element of allegory into service. A further interpretation would
force the view that the story is out and out a symbolic one, and
the allegoric element is also a part of the symbolic structure.
Besides, one may read the story at its literal level and derive
some pleasure from it. But the pleasure is enhanced and the
story shows itself in its full stature when we take into account its
symbolic overtones as well. Of course, in the interest of brevity,

we have dwelt on those aspects only which we thought were semantically more loaded than others.

To repeat again, the symbolic and allegorical elements in a story cannot be considered apart from each other. I would not even for a moment maintain that the two cannot stand apart in their own right. Certainly they can and one can substantiate this by quoting chapter and verse. I only maintain that in the new Urdu short story the symbolic and the allegorical elements very frequently merge into each other, which is all for the good for it lends strength to the story structurally and otherwise, more so to its symbolic import. To deny this fact tantamounts to diluting or even negating the creative impulse or sensitivity of the new Urdu story. The fact is that whatever the structure of the story or its style, it is imperative that it must have impact and be able not only to sustain the reader's interest but also give him pleasure. Catharsis which is the true measure of good literature is equally relevant to the genre of the story whether ancient or modern. Whether the story is symbolic or allegorical or a hybrid of both, whether it is based on realism, whether it has high emotional content or deals more with the subconscious than the conscious, it is necessary that it should illumine our minds with new experience of life. It must have the power to grip our hearts and minds. It should make us wonder and induce us to brood, ruminate and think. It should open up new vistas of life before us. This is the hall-mark, nay the quintessence or the kernel of a story. It is the sacred duty of the story writer to preserve and invigorate this precious element and guard it against any onslaughts.

5

After this discusion it may not be out of place to see how the younger Urdu story writers in India are dealing with the new story at the creative level. In this context I would like to take the example of a story, 'Anjām-e-Kār'[11] by the Bombay writer, Salaam Bin Razzaaq.

When I first read this story, I expected that if not the modern critics at least some of the progressives would lift the curtain thereby revealing its semantic associations. The story has all the ingredients which generally appeal a progressive critics's heart— the law, the police, the wine-bibber, the notorious joints, social tyranny and high-handedness, the poor have-nots reeling under the tyrants' heel, etc. Salaam's collection received rave reviews, but in essence it hardly made any difference in his literary status. The praise had come on the basis of theme and content and not overall assessment.

Salaam prepared the structure of this story with great care. A clerk, that is, a white collar worker, has settled down in a slum with his newly-wedded wife. One evening when the clerk returns from his office he finds a cronie of Shamu *Dādā* who runs an illicit liquor shop in the slum and is considered the overlord of the area, hiding bottles of hooch in the gutter in front of the clerk's shanty. When the clerk objects, the fellow, a notorious hoodlum of the locality, takes away the bottles but soon returns with Shamu Dada. The young clerk tries to convince these hoodlums of the justness of his request. But Shamu Dada is furious, taking the clerk's request as an act of defiance which he would not tolerate. He threatens the clerk by flourishing a knife in his face. But the situation is saved just in time when the clerk's wife rushes out and pushes her husband back into the shanty. The young man is convinced that Shamu Dada is selling illicit liquor in contravention of the law, and the law would bring the man to book for that. Considering the fact that law is on his side, in spite of his wife's caution, he stealthily goes to the police station to lodge a report. The constable and the havildar at the police station take no notice of him. But he is not the one to give up so easily. Undeterred, he appears before the police inspector. "I know you have had a raw deal," the inspector tells him. "I can send two or three constables with you. But how is it going to help you? The fellow will obtain a bail and you have to live in their midst." "But Sir, the law . . . " the clerk reminds him. "Forget about the law," the inspector says. "I know the law as much as you know it. The police can certainly take action on your report but it cannot give you any guarantee for your security round the clock. You're a simple inexperienced man," the inspector further adds. "You will do well to leave the place if you take my advice. But if you want to live where you are now living then learn to be chummy with these goondas." The clerk is stunned. He had come to the police station with high hopes but he only met with humiliation. He quietly walks out of the police station. As he enters his *mohalla* he finds that Shamu Dada's liquor joint is humming with activity as before. The liquor glasses tinkle and the revellers utter profanities as they booze. Instead of going home, the clerk proceeds towards Shamu's liquor joint. The goondas are surprised to see him there. Shamu emerges in his usual *banyān* and *lungī*. People think that the young clerk is out to create trouble and expect that things would soon come to a head. Pulling up his *lungī,* Shamu asks in a harsh voice, "You! what do you want?" The young man replies in a calm, gentle voice, "A *pāo* (quarter) of *mausambī* (country liquor) and a bottle of soda!"

Evidently, it is a realistic story. But is it really so? Before coming to grips with this question it is necessary to draw attention to some basic facts. The effectiveness of Salaam's style also shows in depicting the nervousness of the clerk's wife when confronted with the unsavoury situation created by the goondas. On one side the goondas are ready to fly at the clerk's throat and on the other side there is the husband's faith in the long arm of the law. The wife persistently keeps reminding her husband to change the place and live elsewhere while he keeps his ears glued to the hullabaloo raised by the hoodlums in the lane outside his house. In very short cameos the writer gives graphic descriptions of the water receptacles ranged in front of the public tap, the queue before the public lavatory, the woes of Zulaikha who keeps borrowing *āṭṭā* from her neighbours and the street brawls every Sunday. All these add up to show effectively the sordid picture of slum-living.

The surface-level reading yields the meaning that even if man wants to fight evil he is forced to connive at it. In the present state of maladministration the police has to compromise with evil by joining hands with the goondas. If the story had ended just at this point, it would have still made acceptable reading. But the story goes further. Although we spit fire against injustice and inequity and also ourselves become victims to this violently chaotic state of affairs, yet we fail to see the far-reaching, injurious effects of this situation which silently corrodes the fabric of our social life. Although it is not a symbolic story and is apparently a realistic story, yet if it had been written thirty years ago, it would have sunk into the morass of palpable motive colouring the story, and the writer would have raised storms of protest at every step and excited the reader's pity. At the same time he would have come out with a heavy dose of advice in a loud and blatant fashion. But today's story writer, even if he does not profess to be a writer of a symbolic story, is fully conscious of the non-creative aspects of the so-called 'realistic' story, specially its cloying sentimentality masquerading as romance which embraces the entire society. If the writer has been able to grasp the artistic and literary aspects of the story, then one may freely assume that the new story has a 'new' realistic dimension too. It is true that the new trends discernible in the short story and its spirit of rebelliousness have in no small measure contributed to the restoration of its health and literary prestige. Now one is prone to look askance at those who adopt uncreative and non-literary stances and only take into consideration a story's subject and its material to the exclusion of everything else. Modernism has been a many-faceted entity. Movements come and go, trends set in and depart. But the receding floods fertilise many new fields which yield new crops. Among the new writers we have those with leftist leanings, there are radicals who are anti-establishment in their political, social and moral stances, and there are still others who draw their inspiration from our ancient culture and religious founts. The new story can also be a story of comment and also a free-wheeling instrument of non-commitment. Just as one cannot legitimately judge the merit of a story on the basis of its subject and material, in the same manner non-commitment or commitment cannot be the sole criterion for judging the beauty of a story. Whether a story is symbolic or realistic, in our opinion the real question is whether we can only read it at its single-layered or superficial level, or it lends itself to a reading yielding meaning at its many-tiered inner depths. As we have explained earlier it calls for a creative attitude and metaphorical ingenuity. A very meaningful symbol in the hands of an ordinary writer can boomerang as a meaningless puzzle. On the other hand, even if there is no conscious use of symbol in a realistic story, in the hands of a competent writer, adept in the use of narrative and other literary devices, the story can on its own give symbolic sparks.

There are such instances galore in the story '*Anjām-e-Kār*' itself. At least it can safely be said that here the question is not that of the importance of the law, and of compromise with evil. A psychological aspect of it can also be that evil corrodes the human mind in *slow* degrees. In our beings we have good and evil existing cheek by jowl. The young man in the story connives at evil time and again. "It did not matter much to me so long as the dirt existed in the lane but now it has come to my very doorstep and this is a challenge enough for any decent man." At another point in the story the wife tells him, "Better turn a blind eye to it. Let him keep the bottles where he wants to. You lose nothing by it." But the young man's fight against evil continues. He goes to the police station, the citadel of law and order, and faces humiliation at every step. A stage comes when his resistance weakens and then ultimately vanishes.

The story takes yet another psychological turn. Its strand runs through the entire story in the character of the young clerk. He is an ordinary man of modest means. He wants to live in peace, keeping clear of any trouble. He sends away Shamu Dada's crony by using placatory means. But when Shamu comes bang outside his door he still tries to keep his cool. He wants to avoid trouble. But Shamu's man plants the liquor bottles in the gutter right outside his door. He feels outraged but does not give expression to his feelings. "Do your worst!" Shamu cries. "You, *sālā!* Your mother's . . . .! One slap and you will start grovelling in dust. I fuck your law!" The knife comes out menacingly. But the young man must not run away. He would lose face in the eyes of his neighbours. It would be his moral and physical death. Just then with great presence of mind his wife pulls him into the house. Perhaps he knows his mind for later on he says, "Perhaps my sub-conscious was also seeking refuge in this manner. Humiliation, anger, fear . . . . I was in such a terrible state of mind." Now he is left with a powerful desire to seek revenge which eludes him even at the police station. Getting into the liquor joint on his way back home does not denote compromise with evil. Nor does it signify retreat of virtue against evil. Perhaps this is revenge of a kind.

Thirdly, there could be a finer touch of irony in the whole situation. Under the circumstance, perhaps the only way to take his revenge was to assert that he could have his way with his tormentors; this would give him a feeling of triumph. He accordingly enters the liquor joint and orders for a "*pāo ser mausambī* and a bottle of soda." In utter surprise, the end of Shamu's *lungī* slips out of his hand. The following sentences in the story are not devoid of significance: "For an instant—even it was only for an instant—I found Shamu looking so helpless. It gave me such a feeling of satisfaction on seeing those goons reeling in helplessness." The last sentence only goes to accentuate the irony.

> For a few seconds no one spoke. Using that arrested moment to full effect I further added, "And a plate of fried liver!"

It is evident that after passing through a stage of annihilation the character in the story passes through a stage of self-assertion in order to retrieve what had been unwittingly destroyed.

Fourthly, the story can also have an existential slant of which we discern signs in many places. The story in fact, throws one such hint at the very start:

> In the evening when returning home from the office I could not imagine that there was trouble in the offing, that I would be up against such heavy odds as would shatter me

completely. If I wanted to, I could have easily averted the crisis. But a man cannot have his way in everything. There are certain things far beyond a man's reach which he cannot mould according to his sweet will. Maybe it is such unpredictable things that are given the appelation of accident. However, to cut the matter short, I found myself in the stranglehold of circumstance and I could see no way of extricating myself from this dire situation.

This undercurrent of inevitability runs through the entire story. The wife knew that her husband was only a petty clerk and none too well-off. Yet like any housewife, she could not dispel the longing for a good house from her mind. She was very unhappy in those slummy surroundings but worry or unhappiness cannot resolve any problems. When the clerk heard the knife clicking open:

Suddenly ants crawled over my body from head to toe. In spite of my best efforts the situation had gone out of my control. For a moment my entire body shook with fear. I was encountering such situation for the first time in my life.

He does not want to live in that hovel but he has to. He does not want to fight but the situation of fight builds up despite himself. He wants to save himself from a situation that would make him feel so helpless but is forced into such a situation. He wants to keep his cool and yet anger gets the better of him. He can't stand the sight of Shamu's liquor joint but the live charcoals in the *seekh kabāb* oven blaze in his heart. A police station is the last place in the world which he would ever care to visit but circumstances force him to visit it. When he emerges from the police station broken in spirit due to the tug-of-war that has been going on in his mind between tyranny and liberation, he whines: "No, I don't want to register any complaint." His mind had gone vacant. The wave of stench rising from the gutter greets him. Ultimately he is sucked up by the inevitability of existence. Thus despite a framework of realism there are many semantic dimensions that can be discussed. Admittedly, it is not a symbolic story but nobody can dispute its different readings and depth of meaning.

6

Things have not been that complex. But when a discussion takes a serious turn even simple things sometimes come in for explanation. By now it has become clear that the narrative story which runs the full gamut of the metaphorical, allegorical types and the *Katbā, Qissa,* myths and legends is not very different from the symbolic story. We should weed out the idea from our heads that only the symbolic story can be termed as the new story. Even the realistic story, if it does not skim over the events superficially but delves deep into the inner meaning of things, and reads as a 'multiple text', cannot be exiled from the domain of the new story. The fact is that in creative writing the 'signified' is simply not amenable to any definition. When the 'signifier' is used at the surface level then there may be the relationship of one to one between the word and the meaning. But when it is used beyond the visual to signify the super-real or the other, then the metaphor is evoked. Symbol is, as is known, an extended form of metaphorical application. It should be marked that we have borrowed the concept of the symbol from the West. Hence if very few symbolic stories have been written we must ponder why it is so despite so much talk about the symbol. Like the blood in our veins, the allegorical elements connected with simile and metaphor, have seeped into Urdu language in various forms. And then metaphors themselves have scores of kinds and manifestations. In fiction, this very metaphorical expression can be discerned, overtly or covertly in allegorical writings such as the *katbā* and the *hikāyat* literature and the fables. Is it by sheer accident that down the centuries these modes of writings whether in folk tales or in sophisticated forms of fiction have been catering to our aesthetic sensibilities? As regards their impact on

our lives in general, they have sharpened our insights and added
to our pleasure by becoming constant means of entertainment. It
is not necessary to remind about the stories of the *Panchatantra*
whose original version has been lost in the limbo of time. The
Purnabhadra Jain's version dating back to the 2nd century A.D.
has left its influence over the entire world of fiction. Somadeva's
Kathāsaritsāgara which covers many volumes and Narayana's
Hitopadesha cannot be regarded apart from the stories of the
Panchatantra. The same is true of the thousands of stories from
the *Purānas*. In Naushervan Adil's times the *Panchatantra* was
translated into Pahlavi in the sixth century A.D. and by the ninth
century its Arabic version, *Kalīlah-o-Dimnah* was known all
over the Islamic world. It was through the Islamic influence that
the bulk of these stories were made available in most of the
European languages. Whether they are fables of *Bidpai*, tales of
Alf-Lailah (The Arabian Nights) or the *hikāyats* from *Gulistān*,
in all of them the Indian influence has been predominant,
followed by the Greek and Islamic influence, though to a lesser
extent. The same is true of the *Jātaka* stories dating back to the
fifth century B.C. and centred round Lord Buddha. We must also
not forget Rumi's *Masnavī-e-Ma'navī's* tales which gained
currency in the thirteenth century A.D.

In short, culled from many countries of the eastern world
these have become a part of early world literature. They have
created a strange cultural effect and provided a creative stimulus.
But curiously enough in this vast range of literature there was no
concept of the 'pure symbol' as such, which came down to us
only a few decades ago from the West. No doubt in our age-long
tradition of fiction the allegorical strains have manifested
themselves in various forms in which legend and myth, allegory,
kathā, and *hikāyat*, have remained in the vanguard, and no
wonder that they consciously or unconsciously come to the
rescue of the new writer who is constantly in search of new
modes of expression.

Nobody would claim that the new story can discharge its
responsibility by repeating these old stories, masquerading as
new with touch-up changes required by the spirit of the times.

Nonetheless, if the new writers can draw upon the vast treasure of the past to evolve new metaphorical and allegorical insights, as has been demonstrated by quoting the example of Intizar Husain's *Nar Nārī*, why should they invite the ire of the detractors of the new story? And why should they swear by 'pure symbolism'? However, what requires a forceful assertion is that in Urdu fiction the real need is that the metaphoric element should function in its true form coupled with a comprehensive awareness of the many-tiered semantic fusion with the story which the writer would evolve in his own light. It is not of much consequence as to by what devices these effects are achieved. It should by and large be left to the writer's creative talent and literary virtuosity as to how or at what level he uses these devices.

It is encouraging that through writers such as Surendra Prakash and Intizar Husain, the new Urdu short story has found a way to link the present with the cultural past. One is reminded here of what Claude Levi-Strauss once said, "This is a tremendous force, we in the West have lost this extraordinary sense of genealogy. We have no anchor points left." If the new Urdu short story is in search of these anchor points, and has located some, the effort need not be decried, rather it calls for a critical reconsideration and reinterpretation.

In the end it would bear stressing that the story, as a genre has some generic characterstics which make their own demands. It would not be to our advantage to get caught in the quicksands of symbolism and ignore those characteristics, which we would be doing at our own cost. It would only make our writing jejune and even nonsensical, though seemingly it may masquerade as good writing, which indeed is no matter for pride. Tomes have been written in eulogising the story as art form. But it cannot be overlooked that as a literary genre the story has an 'elemental' characteristic which can be called as its 'kernel' or the 'storiness'. This core must always be there from which the super-structure of the story is raised. The innumerable centuries had gone into the making of *kathās*, and *hikāyats*, and preserving and safeguarding this 'kernel'. To ride roughshod over it amounts to annihilating collectively our literary self. Perhaps it is due to the deep-rooted sub-conscious drives of our aesthetic urge that the new Urdu story is not so much symbolic as it is allegorical. And although allegorical, it is still not devoid of metaphorical and symbolic overtones. But whether symbolic, or allegorical, or realist if it is not shorn of the generic 'kernel' and does not fail to present new levels of consciousness, and at the same time does not steer clear from problems of the times, and evokes semantic layeredness, it is certainly the new story. And in such a new story the flame of revolt keeps burning.

Notes

1. *'Nayā Afsāna, Riwāyat se Inhirāf aur Muqallidīn ke liye Lamba-e-Fikriya'* in *Urdu Afsāna, Riwāyat aur Masāil*, Delhi 1981, pp. 734-43.

2. Quarterly *Jawāz*, Malegaon (Nasik), May 1983.

3. *Ibid.*, p. 28.

4. *Ibid.*, pp. 28-29.

5. *Ibid.*, p. 33.

6. *Dictonary of Literary Terms*, Toronto 1972, p. 10.

7. Roger Fowler, ed., *Modern Critical Terms*, London 1973, p. 6.

8. *Literary Terms*, Boston 1960, p. 6.

9. *Modern Critical Terms*, op.cit., p. 5.

10. Quarterly *Shab-Khoon*, Allahabad, March-April 1982.

11. *Nangī Dopahar kā Sipāhī*, Bombay 1977.

13

Krishan Chander:
an Impression

IN the long course of the Urdu short story Krishan Chander's
(1914-1977) is a venerable name which will challenge us with a
host of perennial questions. Among his contemporaries, Saadat
Hasan Manto's and Rajinder Singh Bedi's are two other very
important names. As a writer, Manto was a highly controversial
figure and had even come under a cloud. But gradually he came
back into his own and is regarded as a great writer by any
reckoning. In the beginning, Manto and Krishan Chander held
supreme in the field of Urdu fiction with Bedi lagging far behind,
having only two volumes of short stories to his name. But after
Independence and till 1979-1980, Bedi's development as a writer
of fiction continued unabated and achieved remarkable
proportions. Taking into account the artistic aspect of the genre,
Manto and Bedi are regarded as superior to Krishan Chander. It
is also a fact that Krishan Chander's best literary output reached
its height before the period of 1955-1960, and thereafter the
graph of his writing had stopped going up but instead started
steeply tapering down. Nevertheless, Krishan Chander remained
Krishan Chander. After Premchand, his name counts among the

first three great Urdu short story writers. From the point of view of art, he lacks some of the qualities which are so highly pronounced in Manto and Bedi. Still Krishan Chander can hold his ground even though his detractors had openly started picking holes in his stories while he was still living and that streak of criticism has continued to this day. But despite that, nobody can take away from Krishan Chander his significance, or deny his contribution to Urdu Literature. Perhaps no other contemporary short story writer in Urdu enjoyed a larger readership. The typical features of his stories are fundamental humanism and abounding wit, as well as charm of style and suppressed poetry.

Born in 1914, Krishan Chander spent the greater part of his early life in Kashmir, where the beauty of nature left a permanent mark on his aesthetic sensibility. He was educated at Forman Christian College, Lahore, where he completed his master's degree in English. for a number of years he wrote for the Ambala *Tribune*, and the weekly *Northern Review*, and then became attached to the All India Radio. But, dissatisfied with government service, he moved to Bombay, where he continued to write for the movies till his death in 1977.

A prolific writer, he produced more than eighty volumes, which include more than thirty collections of short stories and more than twenty novels.[1] The themes of his work are as varied as can be—romantic, social, psychological, political, national, international. In fact, he covered the whole gamut of contemporary problems and human relationships. He was influenced by Marxism and wrote with a purpose, sometimes too obviously so. Art with him was a criticism of life and a vehicle for social uplift. Most of his work is spirited, with a tendency towards romanticizing and formlessness. His readers were pleased by his racy idealism, sentimentalism and sincere exhortation. His stories usually have a foundation in fact and, in addition, his choice of realistic detail within loosely spun plots gives his work an air of verisimilitude. He is significant for his combination of storytelling, idealistic approach and a personal, happy tone. The tone reflects his own kindliness and good humour. He can be called a 'charmer'. Like some, he is not severe or objective, but tender and sympathetic towards the misfortunes of humble people. What he lacks in technique and form, he makes up by his humanism and style. His style is at once spontaneous, charged, swift and sweeping, and often approaches the qualities of poetry in prose.

Perhaps because of his early experiences in Kashmir, perhaps because of his sympathetic treatment of people, in his early stories Krishan Chander displays a remarkable ability to deepen the effect of his portrayals of oppressed people by setting them within a framework of exceptional natural beauty. A superb painter of scene, from his very first collection, *Tilism-e-Khayāl* (The Magic of Thought), he was unequalled in Urdu for his ability to contrast effectively and painfully human cruelty with the lush scenery of the mountains, rivers, lakes, fields and villages of Kashmir. As might be expected in some of these stories he depicted the natural scene at such length that he seems to have forsaken progressive principles and overlooked the harsh realities of life by taking refuge in nature.

Almost as an antidote to the kind of romantic excess into which his depiction of nature led him, in some other stories Krishan Chander adopted a satirical tone. Among stories of this kind are '*Ghālīcha*', (Carpet), '*Mahālakshmī kā Pul*', (The Bridge of Mahalakshmi), '*Kālū Bhangī*', (Kalu the Sweeper); '*Brahmaputra*' (Brahmaputra), and '*Anna Dātā*', (Food Giver). '*Anna Dātā*', especially, a story of the Bengal famine told in three parts from three different points of view, was, because of the sharpness of its satire, the intensity of its feeling and the courage of its theme, extremely influential.

Krishan Chander did a tremendous amount of writing, on varied subjects, in different contexts, in different styles and at many intellectual levels. In his language there was a flow and a mellifluousness which is the divine gift of only a chosen few. His poetic bent of mind, his romantic streak, his love of nature, his mellowness, his humanity and deep urge for the alleviation of suffering are ingredients which add up to create an altogether new world of which even if some parts are demolished, the parts that remain would still bear testimony to his great qualities as a writer. His sense of beauty, depth of feeling, high aspirations, the dynamic forces of creativity will still come through, chaste and whole, when tested in the crucible of time.

It is difficult to run through the full gamut of Krishan Chander's writings in one sweep. Even so, if his writings are appraised on a selective basis, a many-faceted personality will emerge which is unique in many ways. The quintessence of Krishan Chander's writing is his love of beauty in all its manifestations. Love of nature being so basic dominated the early phase of his writing. The flow of his prose and its sheer poetry are an expression of his love of beauty. In his story '*In a Boat over the Jehlum*' and in other short story masterpieces there are characters such as Aangi, Buggi, Gomti, Shaama which heighten the intensity of beauty and in which sadness and beauty vie with each other bringing out the inequities of life. In these stories one finds the sweetness of romance blunted by the sharp edge of sorrow. In those days, Krishan Chander had broken new ground and had given Urdu literature a new kind of story which had an abiding influence on those who came after him. Even a most discerning critic like Muhammad Hasan Askari who was so drastic in his judgments had given Krishan Chander's story '*Zindagī ke Mor par*' (At the Turning of Life) a pride of place attained by few other stories. In the early morning Prakash Chand goes out into fields for a walk-cum-bath. He listens to the sound of the water-wheel and is enraptured by it. In this meaningless sound he feels an undefined joy and closes his eyes to savour it. The source unknown, the destination of his journey of life, unattainable while bathing with closed eyes, he keeps watching the peasant sitting behind the bullocks who go round and round doing their allotted stint... Maybe some people may see in this story the grinding wheel of society elevated to a metaphor which revolves round our moribund customs and rites and which has made man its plaything. But here one feels Krishan Chander is actually listening to the music of the spheres in the sound produced by the water-wheel. At one stroke he rises above the institution of marriage and breaks his shackles from society as such. He is thinking of the order and the system of things where man and his world become inconsequential. He is astounded at the dance of the universe, its orderliness and everlastingness. His imagination almost freezes with horror at the immensity of the whole thing. At the same time he draws solace and comfort from it. There is a sense of hidden revolt in his chain of thoughts. There is a sense of defeat but it is not lacking in courage and comes with a sense of relief. One finds a great versatility in Krishan Chander's best known stories. They have overtones of naked romance and stark realism, both of them vying with each other.

With his story *'Balcony'* (At the Hotel Firdaus) Krishan Chander's art takes a new turn. Romance no longer exists at a personal level. It becomes idealized—something worthy of being emulated. It is Beethoven's symphony and also the harbinger of a new spring, replete with a sense of exhilaration. In his literary journey where *'Balcony'* stands as a milestone, the other stories such as *'Garjan kī Ek Shaam'*, *'Ṭūṭe hue Taare'*, *'Nashe kī Maut'*, *'Purāne Khuda'* are left far behind. A time comes when the artist in Krishan Chander finds himself face to face with the horrors of the partition of India. The same sense of stern social realism found its expression in *'The Peshawar Express'*, and it took in its sweep such stories as *'Ham Vahshī Hain'*, *'Teen Ghunḍe'*, *'Lāl Bāgh'* and *'Dūsrī Maut'*.

After Independence, Krishan Chander turned out stories at breathless pace. In 1947 and 1948 five volumes of his stories were published under the titles, *Ham Wahshī Hain, Ek Girjā Ek Khandak, Ajantā Se Aage, Samundar Door Hai,* and *Teen Ghunḍe*. One more strand of his fiction writing revolves round his novels *Shikast* and *Jab Khet Jāge*. There was a time when these novels were immensely popular. *Shikast* (Defeat) dealing with the failure of love in a class and status-conscious society, expounds its theme through two parallel love affairs, that of Vanti, the daughter of a woman of doubtful reputation, and Shyam, a college student with revolutionary ideas, and that of the half-*brāhmin,* half-*chamār* Chandra and Mohan Singh, a Rajput youth. Although marred by Shyam's excessively long speeches, in which the author's voice is clearly discernible, this novel amply demonstrates not only Krishan Chander's charming writing style but also his ability to portray the injurious effects on human freedom of both poverty and the restraints imposed by the caste system.

Written immediately after Independence, *Jab Khet Jāge* (When the Fields Awoke) deals with the problems of the Telengana peasants and especially with their attempts to retain land given to them as a result of reforms in the land tenure system. The novel focusses on the young peasant leader Raghu Rao who is about to be hanged as the novel opens. Depicting Raghu Rao's memories during his last night in prison, the novel provides a moving portrayal of the economic difficulties of peasants, of Raghu Rao's fleeting love affair with a tribal woman, of his various activities within the peasants' movement and of the confrontation with the government that led to his execution. Although the novel is marred both in its plot and its development of theme, nevertheless it accurately reflects Krishan Chander's socialist convictions, and is considered by many his best novel.

There are many aspects to Krishan Chander's art. He wrote on varied subjects, tried new experiments and adopted various techniques. He also wrote a new-fangled story such as '*Surāeli Tasweer*' and a plotless story such as '*The Carpet*'. As for his stories, '*Kālū Bhangī*' and '*Do Farlāng Lambī Sarak*', they are of such high order that any anthology would readily give them pride of place. '*Kālū Bhangī*' is the story of a nondescript, colourless, sweeper working in a hospital. Krishan Chander has laid bare the sordid aspects of this poor scavenger who leads such a pedestrian life and yet beauty shines through these gloomy details. In '*Do Farlāng Lambī Sarak*' the road itself is elevated to the level of a living character. The story assumes the garb of an allegory in which Krishan Chander goes one step further and perceives the society metaphorically. '*Brahmaputra*', '*Pānī kā Darakht*', '*But Jāgte Hain*', '*Phool Surkh Hain*' and '*Mahālakshmī kā Pul*' are stories which can be clubbed together in the same category, and leave an indelible imprint on the mind.

In Krishan Chander's stories we have sublime peaks and low valleys. But these valleys are not just flat terrains. They have lakes and fountains and meandering streams which look like streaks of silver.

It is a matter of regret that Krishan Chander's extreme idealism often flawed his art. His emotions often degenerate into the maudlin, and the tendency to skim over the surface of things made him to drift towards bellicose subjects. Despite that his sense of beauty is so overwhelming and his humanity so permeating that even in his weaker moments Krishan Chander's writings never pall or become pedestrian. He can always be recognised among a host of writers as someone distinctly apart from others. Among the makers of the Urdu fiction his name will always command respect.

Note

1. Some of the important collections of short stories and novels of Krishan Chander are the following:

    1. *Tilism-e-Khayāl*, Lahore 1938;
    2. *Nazzāre*, Lahore 1940;
    3. *Shikast*, Delhi 1940;
    4. *Zindagī ke Mor par*, Lahore 1943;
    5. *Purāne Khudā*, Lahore 1944;
    6. *Anna-Dātā*, Delhi 1945;
    7. *Ham Vahshī Hain*, Bombay 1947;
    8. *Ek Girjā Ek Khandaq*, Bombay 1948;
    9. *Ajantā se Aage*, Bombay 1948;
    10. *Jab Khet Jāge*, Bombay 1952;
    11. *Toofān kī Kalian*, Delhi 1954;
    12. *Kitāb kā Kafan*, Delhi 1956;
    13. *Ek Gadhe kī Sarguzasht*, Delhi 1957;
    14. *Merī Yādon ke Chinār*, Delhi 1962;

15. *Dādar Pul ke Bacche,* Delhi 1965;
16. *Dil kisī kā Dost Nahīn,* Delhi 1966.

Krishan Chander has been widely translated into many Indian and foreign languages. Some of the well-known English translations are: *I Cannot Die,* tr. of the novel, *Anna-Dātā,* by Khwaja Ahmad Abbas, Poona 1945; *Flame and Flower,* fifteen short stories tr. by the author, Bombay 1951; *Virgin and the Well,* eight short stories tr. by the author, Dehra Dun 1968; *Seven Faces of London,* novel tr. by L. Hayat Bouman, New Delhi 1968; *The Dreamer,* eleven short stories tr. by Jai Ratan, Delhi 1970; *Mr. Ass Comes to Town, Ek Gadhe kī Sarguzasht,* novel tr. by Helen Bouman, Delhi 1968; *A Thousand Lovers, Ek Aurat Hazār Dīwāne,* novel tr. by Jai Ratan, Delhi 1971; *Krishan Chander: Selected Short Stories,* ed. by Gopi Chand Narang, and tr. by Jai Ratan, New Delhi 1990.

14

The Three Language Formula and Urdu

INDIA is a multi-lingual country with scores of regional and tribal languages; and a democratic system of education has to provide for the instruction and adoption of these languages as media of instruction, while at the same time it must strive for the eventual development of a *lingua franca* which may serve as the common national language of the country. To meet this complex linguistic situation the three language formula was accepted by the Government of India as the national policy base for prescribing languages to be studied at different stages of school education.

The graduated three language formula as recommended by the Education Commission of 1964-66 consisted of the following:

(1) The mother tongue or the regional language;
(2) The official language of the Union or the associate official language of the Union so long as it exists; and
(3) A modern Indian or foreign language not covered under (1) and (2) and other than used as the medium of instruction.

The three language formula alongwith most of the recommendations of the Education Commission was accepted by the state governments, yet there has been a vast difference in the acceptance and implementation of these instructions by the States and the Union Territories with regard to the number of languages prescribed to be taught in the schools. There are differences as to the status of the mother tongue vis-a-vis the State language; and also of modern languages vis-a-vis classical and foreign languages. There are also differences about the stages at which the different languages should be introduced and for how long they should be taught.

Furthermore, it is not only the States or the Union Territories, but also the educational organisations and societies which have been interpreting the three language formula differently. The present language instructional scene in the country, if not chaotic, certainly does not present a cohesive picture either. It, therefore, calls for a serious reconsideration of the problem in the light of the experience gained during the last two decades.

There cannot be any denying the fact that the acceptance of the three language formula, whatever the variations in its implementation and interpretation, has created a widespread realisation that the linguistic structure of India, both formally and functionally is peculiar and a special solution has to be provided to meet the situation. Consequently the general opposition to the notion of a 'heavy language load' in the school curriculum has melted away, and it is now generally accepted that the acquisition of three to four languages at the lower primary, higher primary, and secondary stages is practicable, and imperative for the Indian school system.

Nevertheless, the uneven application and different interpretations of the three language formula have led to certain problems some of which are quite formidable in nature. One of these is the provision of the instruction of the mother tongue and the adoption of the mother tongue as the medium of instruction in areas where the mother tongue is not the State language. There are various situations of this type, the two main being where the mother tongue of a linguistic group is related to the State language or, secondly, where the mother tongue is not related to the State language.

One glaring example of relegating the mother tongue to the background is the policy adopted by Kendriya Vidyalaya Sangathan. The general practice in these Central Schools is to teach the three languages, Hindi, English and Sanskrit, though they allow the teaching of regional language as an additional language where a prescribed number of students opt for it. Obviously, this calls for a review. As pointed out earlier, there are linguistic groups and sub-groups in the States whose mother tongue is different from the regional languages of the States.

To say the least, any educational system that does not provide for the teaching of the mother tongue as first language (L1), and the imparting of primary education through the medium of the mother tongue cannot be termed sound. Therefore, any restructuring of the programme of language instruction in the curriculum of schools has to be based on the assumption that a provision will have to be made for the teaching of the mother tongue and also the adoption of the mother tongue as a medium of instruction, at least at the initial level, in situations where a mother tongue is not a State official language. A recent investigation conducted by the Central Institute of Indian Languages, Mysore, revealed that in order to get full advantage of the mother tongue medium a global attempt has to be made for improvements of conditions at all levels including those of methods, materials and media of teaching.

The other major problem is the provision of the classical languages like Sanskrit in the three language formula vis-a-vis modern Indian languages. While the importance of the study of a classical language and of the special claim that Sanskrit has on the national system of education cannot be denied, the provision of Sanskrit or any classical language should not be made either at the cost of minority languages in a given State situation, or at the cost of modern Indian languages different from the State language, thereby eliminating the scope of a North-South linguistic interaction in the Indian school system which was originally intended by the framers of the three language formula.

The Education Commission Report in its para 8.48, *Study of Classical Languages*, states clearly: "In our opinion, this formula has to be restricted to the modern Indian languages only . . . Under the circumstances, classical languages can be provided in the school curriculum on an *optional* basis only. This may be done from Class VIII onwards." These recommendations, so far as practice goes, have been flouted by a large number of States and educational institutions, obviously, at the cost of the mother tongues or the modern Indian languages.

Any revision of the framework concerning the place of languages in the curriculum of schools has also to take into account the projected implementation of the national language policy which aims at a gradual switch over from English to modern Indian languages in every sphere of the national life and a planned bi-lingualism, (or tri-lingualism), with a few major constitutionally recognised languages as second (or third) languages. Still, educational considerations do necessitate the adoption of certain non-literary and unrecognized languages for teaching and learning purposes, but as these languages will not be of general use outside the linguistic groups to which they belong, after a certain stage their teaching will fade out.

According to the 1971 Census there were more than 800 languages in India, while the NCERT survey of 1973 lists as many as 368 mother tongues out of which 57 languages, Indian as well as foreign, modern as well as classical, were being studied and used as media of instruction in the different States and Union Territories. Any new instructional policy concerning languages has to take these facts into consideration. Since the matter is quite problematic, one way of approaching it could be through viewing this in terms of linguistic situations obtaining in different regions of the country. Some major situations could be the following:

Situation 1: Where mother tongue L1 is the same as the State language, and the student can learn Hindi as L2, and English as L3.

Situation 2: Where mother tongue L1 is the same as the State language, and the student opts for English as L2 and Hindi as L3.

Situation 3: Where mother tongue L1 is Hindi, and the student opts for English as L2 and Sanskrit as L3.

Situation 4: Where mother tongue L1 is Hindi, and the student opts for Sanskrit as L2 and English as L3.

Situation 5: Where mother tongue L1 is English, and the student opts for the State language as L2 and Hindi as L3.

Situation 6: Where the mother tongue L1 is English, and the student opts for Hindi as L2 and the State language as L3.

Situation 7: Where the mother tongue L1 is a minority language different from the State language, and the student starts with mother tongue as L1, opts for the State language as L2, Hindi as L3 and may learn English as L4.

Situation 8: Where the mother tongue L1 is a minority language different from the State language, and the student starts with mother tongue as L1, opts for the State language as L2, English as L3, and has to learn Hindi as L4.

The adoption of either L1, L2, L3 or L4 as medium of instruction will generate further linguistic situations on the lines mentioned above. The mother tongue, if it is a non-recognised, non-literary language, or a tribal language, of course, will fade out after the primary or early primary stage, and the State language or Hindi or English will take over the position of the medium of instruction. As it appears, the three language formula may have to accommodate the teaching of a fourth, optional language, especially in regions where a language other than the State language is spoken by a substantial number of speakers, or where a minority language is strongly identified with ethnic or cultural groups.

This situation could be satisfactorily met by the provision of the option of a fourth language at the secondary stage, which translated into practical terms may mean the provision of Sanskrit, or Arabic, or a language from the South in the Hindi speaking states, and the provision of Sanskrit, Arabic, English, (or any other Indian language not covered earlier) in the non-Hindi speaking areas.

Finally, a fresh look is also called for at the stage where different languages are to be introduced in the school. In this regard, the recommendations made by the Education Commission have been the following:

1. Lower Primary Stage (Classes I–IV). The mother tongue or the regional language.

2. Higher Primary Stage (Classes V–VII) Two languages, (i) the mother tongue or the regional language, (ii) Hindi or English, (iii) Hindi, English or the regional language may be studied on optional basis.

3. Lower Secondary Stage (Classes VIII–X).

Three languages. In non-Hindi speaking areas, these languages will normally be (i) the mother tongue or the regional language, (ii) Hindi at a higher or lower level, and (iii) English at a higher or lower level. In Hindi speaking areas they will normally be (i) the mother tongue or the regional language, (ii) English or Hindi if English has already been taken as mother tongue, and (iii) modern Indian language other than Hindi, preferably a South Indian language.

The basic drawback of the above framework is the bracketing of the mother tongue in an is/or relationship with the regional language. It has been argued that introducing a child to a second language at a very early age will require the provision of many more qualified teachers for millions of children in our primary schools. This perhaps may not be as formidable a task as it appears to be, since given the bi-lingualism obtaining in any area in India, it may not be that impracticable to impart a second language instruction at the lower primary stage.

There perhaps has been a long-standing line of argument supporting this view. A note of dissent included in the Languages Section of the Education Commission Report (Section 8.41) given by Kumari S. Panandikar perhaps calls for a serious reconsideration in the light of the present experience. She observed:

> "In my opinion, a study of three languages should be obligatory not only at the lower secondary stage as recommended by the majority of the members of the Commission, but at a stage lower, that is at the higher primary stage, and these three languages, should be the mother tongue, Hindi and English in the non-Hindi speaking areas, and the mother tongue, a modern Indian language and English in the Hindi speaking areas."

Keeping in view the fact that the introduction of a second language at the lower primary stage certainly does not constitute a 'mythical language load' of a child, we would like to suggest that the introduction of a second language at the level of Class III, i.e., the *lower primary stage,* may be given serious consideration, and if adopted, this may meet the exigencies of the complex linguistic situation prevailing in our multi-lingual society. At this stage it may appear to be a drastic suggestion, but given the enormity of the problem, and scores of unlisted mother tongues clamouring for teaching status, this perhaps is the only way out. It may not catch the fancy of our educationists right away, but the present writer is convinced that one day if a solution to this vexed problem is to be found, it will have to be in the direction outlined above. The suggested framework will, therefore, be the following:

I. Lower Primary Stage

Classes I–IV

(i) Mother Tongue (From Class I)
(ii) State Official Language *if different* from the mother tongue or Hindi or any modern Indian language (From Class III)

II Higher Primary Stage

(Classes V – VII)

(i) State Official Language
(ii) Hindi in non-Hindi areas or any modern Indian language other than English in Hindi areas.
(iii) English (introduction of L3 English if Hindi was provided at lower primary stage, or Hindi if English was provided at lower primary stage as mother tongue)

III Lower Secondary Stage

(Classes VIII–X)

Non-Hindi Speaking areas:

(i) The State Official Language
(ii) Hindi, or English
(iii) English, or Hindi

Hindi Speaking areas:

(i) Hindi
(ii) A modern Indian language other than Hindi and English
(iii) English

Note: 1. Arrangement for teaching of classical languages such as Sanskrit should be made as optional subjects of study at the higher primary stage and/or lower secondary stage.

2. For students who profess a classical language such as Sanskrit as their mother tongue, provision may be made to offer it as L1 from primary stage if such students are in a sizeable number.

In the light of this framework, a speaker of Dogri, Konkani, or a tribal language (which is not recognised as State Official Language) may start with his mother tongue as L1 and learn Kashmiri, or Marathi, or Assamese, being the State's Official Language respectively as L2 at the primary stage; and choosing this as L1 from the higher primary stage, may proceed with the study of Hindi as L2 and of English as L3 in the later school career.

Similarly, the above proposal can also meet the requirement of the Urdu minority in the Hindi belt. An Urdu speaker may get started with Urdu as L1, offer Hindi as L2, and may later take up English as L3. For Hindi speakers the revised formula provides for teaching of Sanskrit in its own right, and not at the cost of modern languages, i.e., a Hindi speaker may study Hindi as L1, Sanskrit as L2 and English as L3. The teaching of classical language to students who do not have the opportunity to take it at an earlier stage, however, will have to be provided on an additional optional basis as a 'subject of study' at the secondary stage.

Similarly, for a speaker of one State Official Language receiving education in an area where another Official Language is spoken,(e.g., L1 mother tongue Tamil, L2 State Official Language Kannada, and L3 Hindi), the provision of English, if need be, may be made on the same basis as outlined above as an optional additional language.

All other inter-related problems, such as the teaching of languages as skills, or as subjects of study, or their adoption as media of instructions, as also the problems concerning the preparation of text-books, and the training of language teachers, all these will have to be reconsidered in the light of adoption of the new framework concerning the place of language in the school curriculum.

15

Development and Use of Writing System Across Cultures: the Case of Arabo-Persian Urdu Orthographical Model

THE Urdu language, alongwith Hindi, is widely spoken in India and Pakistan, and is generally understood throughout South-Asia, and also in Sheikhdoms of the Persian Gulf. The Urdu language uses a writing system which is different from its Indo-Aryan origin, and which originated for the Semitic group of languages and was developed for Arabic. The following study will discuss the problems of adoption of a Semitic orthographical model for an Indo-Aryan speech; how far each has reacted to the constraints of the other; and how far it has accepted the cross-cultural challenges to the spread of reading and writing.

1

The Semitic writing systems are known to be the oldest in the world; most scholars agree that Egypt was the place of origin.

The Greek word 'alphabet' itself is derived from the name of the first two letters, *alpha* and *beta*, which are of Semitic origin. The Greek alphabet is thought to be derived from a Canaanitish variety of North Semitic script, which came to the Greeks through the Phoenicians. The Greek names for its letters, *alpha, beta, gamma, delta,* etc., demonstrate their origin by corresponding closely with the Semitic names (cf. the Hebrew, *aleph, beth, gimel, daleth*[1] and the Arabic, *alif, bā, jīm, dāl* etc.). The Greek, Latin and many European scripts followed this pattern and were related, however distantly to the earlier Semitic-Phoenician characters.

The Arabic writing developed from a form of Aramaic used by the Nabataeans, an Arabian people. The oldest record of it now extant is a stele from Tema in north-west Arabia, dating from the fifth century B.C. or perhaps earlier. The graffiti on the rocks of Mt. Sinai carry the record of the development of this alphabet down to the third century A.D.[2] In the early Islamic period two types of Arabic writing existed: the *Kufic* and the *Naskhī*. Annemarie Schimmel is of the view that from the very beginning, the two different types of writing seemed to have existed side by side. A cursive forerunner of the later so-called *Naskhī* style was found on papyri and was, therefore used for correspondence, perhaps because it was easy to write. For copying the Holy Book, however, *Kufic* was used.[3]

The Arabic alphabet was mainly consonantal with only three long vowels, and with a total of twenty-eight characters. The order was the following:

ابجل ا (alif)   ب (ba)   ج (jim)   د (dal)
1   2   3   4

هوز ء (ha)   و (waw)   ز (za)
5   6   7

حطى ح (ha)   ط (ta)   ى (ya)
8   9   10

کلمن ک (kaf) 20	ل (lam) 30	م (mim) 40	ن (nun) 50
سعفص س (sin) 60	ع ('ain) 70	ون (fa) 80	ص (sad) 90
قرشت ق (qaf) 100	ر (ra) 200	ش (śin) 300	ت (ta) 400
نخنث ث (tha) 500	خ (kha) 600	ذ (dhal) 700	
ضظغ ض (dad) 800	ظ (za) 900	غ (ghain) 1000	

The last six characters were not contained in the earlier Semitic
and Phoenician scripts, but were added later in the Arabic
model.

The Quran played a central role in the development of
Arabic script. Once the need to record the Quran was
recognized, writing shot into prominence in a relatively short
time. Since the quality of the script had to be worthy of the
divine revelation, the early growth of writing was marked by an
"astonishing calligraphic development, transforming the Arabic
script into an artistic medium that best reflected the Arab genius
and attracted their best artistic talent."[4] Among all arts
calligraphy can be considered as the most typical expression of
the Islamic spirit. Annemarie Schimmel has observed that the
Quran itself "stressed several times the importance of writing; for
example in the earliest Sura, 96/3-4, God is described as the
Almighty Who 'taught man with the Pen'. The idea of writing is
found everywhere in the Holy Book."[5] With the advent of Islam,
Arabic writing spread to many countries in the Middle East, and
eventually to Iran, Afghanistan and India. The *Kufic* script had
specific proportional measurements and a pronounced
angularity and squareness, with short vertical strokes and

extended horizontal lines. Beginning with the second half of the eighth century, it attained a pre-eminence which endured for more than three hundred years, and became, by common consent, the sole hieratic script of the Arabic speaking people. However, the absence of diacritical marks often caused difficulties in deciphering since a rather large number of Arabic letters appeared exactly alike without diacritical marks. In course of time *Kufic* script was discontinued except for formal purposes. *Naskhī* dominated, in fact being the parent of all later cursive writing.[6]

The present arrangement of letters   دزرز   خج   ابتث in place of letters   ابجل   هوز   حطى   was of a later development first introduced by lexicographers.[7] The same original twenty-eight characters were rearranged in view of their visual similarity for ease of learning and writing. This arrangement has since gained currency and is fully established. (cf. Chart of Arabic Alphabet).

Later, when the Iranians adopted Arabic script for their language, they added four characters by modifying the phonetically proximate characters of Arabic to signify those phonemes which did not exist in Arabic. These were پ (for p), چ (for č), ژ (for ž), and گ (for g).[8] These were called '*bā-e-fārsī*', '*jīm-e-fārsī*', '*zā-e-fārsī*', and '*kāf-e-fārsī*' respectively signifying the modified characters of Arabic.

Changing under the impact of the Iranian aesthetic demands of line, shape and workmanship, Arabic writing blossomed, developing new styles; during the Umayyad period, six cursive styles were developed, generally known as "*al-Aqlām al-Sittah* or *Shish Qalam* (the six pens)."[9] These were *Naskhī* (script), *Thuluth* (one-third), *Muhaqqaq* (established), *Rayhānī* (basil-like), *Riqā‘* (notes) and *Tawqī‘* (signing). In the course of a few centuries they were further enriched by the evolution of yet another four cursive styles, i.e., *Ghubār* (dust-like), *Tūmār* (heaped up), *Ta‘līq* (hanging), and *Nasta‘liq* (elegant).[10] These, in turn, were followed by still finer varieties such as *Shikastah* (broken), *Dīvānī* (court), *Jalī* (prominent), *Gulzār* (rose-garden), *Tughrā* (imperial signet). Each of these styles is reflective in its own way of the ethnic and cultural personality of the people associated with it, but the intricacies and distinguishing features of each are calligraphic and, therefore, are outside the scope of this study.

Our interest was with the emergence of *Ta'līq* and *Nasta'līq* in Iran during the Safavid period. Though these scripts never gained great favour with the Arabs, in course of time they became the native styles of Iran and some of the neighbouring countries. Compared to *Ta'līq*, the *Nasta'līq* was a lighter, more elegant style, and though the Turks remained for a long time faithful to the *Ta'līq* script,[11] the Indians preferred the *Nasta'līq* (a compound of the names of *Naskh* and *Ta'līq*). Eventually *Nasta'līq* became the most popular style of writing in the vast regions stretching from the western parts of Iran to the eastern parts of North India. This emergence of *Nasta'līq* and its rise to the status of the Persian national script is attributed to the Persian calligrapher Mir Ali Sultan al-Tabrizi (*d.* 1416).[12]

The Islamic-Hindu encounter on the Indian sub-continent brought new challenges and promoted a synthetic model based on the Arabo-Persian system. The Arabesque already evolved in the Islamic countries for decorating mosques and minarets reached a new high in the architectural monuments of the Mughals. For centuries *Nasta'līq* has been the major writing system in India, and it exists simultaneously with *Devanāgarī*, *Kaithī*, *Laṇḍā*, and many other Aryan and Dravidian indigenous models prevalent in India for numerous local languages. Though some modified varieties of *Naskhī* were used for some languages, especially Sindhi, for many others *Nasta'līq* was the most popular script. Urdu played a central role in this respect, and languages like the Punjabi and Kashmiri adopted *Nasta'līq* under the influence of Urdu.[13] In fact, through Urdu *Nasta'līq* has been fully established in India and Pakistan, and the discussion that follows concerns *Nasta'līq*. Muhammad Hamidullah is of the opinion that more than one hundred languages of the world are written in the Arabic script.[14] Though the case may have been overstated, it is a fact that many languages of India and Pakistan have adopted this script, and Urdu is the most prominent of them.

2

The adoption of the Arabic script for the Urdu language posed many problems. After the advent of Islam in North India in the 11th century, the Urdu language developed over a long period of time as a linguistic *modus vivendi* between Muslims and Hindus. Urdu as a Modern Indo-Aryan language has its base in the western *apabhransas*, while at the same time it borrowed freely from Arabic and Persian especially at the morphological level. The Arabo-Persian naturalised element is the distinguishing mark of Urdu. The Indian sub-continent is an area of such great linguistic diversity that almost all of its languages, Indo-Aryan or Dravidian, depending on the nature of the contact, received the impact of Arabic and Persian. Sindhi, Saraiki, Punjabi, Kashmiri and many other related languages received these influences. But compared to these languages which are confined to their particular regions, the Urdu language was destined to play a larger role as the inter-regional, inter-communal speech of the whole of the sub-continent. While maintaining a delicate balance between the Indo-Aryan base and the Arabo-Persian superstructure, Urdu grew steadily as a language of interaction between the newcomers and the local inhabitants from the eleventh through the fifteenth centuries, and attained the status of a literary language first in the Deccan in the fifteenth century. Beginning with the seventeenth century Urdu started flourishing alongside Persian in North India, and eventually replaced it after the fall of the Mughals in the middle of the nineteenth century. Because of its association with the medieval mystical movements as well as with the socio-religious reform movement, known as the *Bhakti* movement, the Urdu language emerged through medieval times as the functional speech of the millions of people throughout the length and breadth of India. The same position is occupied by Hindi. Both Hindi and Urdu share the same dialectal base, and by and large have a common grammar, yet both are independent languages in their own right. Hindi uses the *Devanāgarī* script and has a preponderance of Sanskritic borrowings; Urdu uses the Arabo-Persian script and achieves a fusion between the Sanskritic and Arabo-Persian elements. The common core between the two languages written in both scripts is generally referred to as Hindustani, and this has been serving as the *lingua franca* of the peoples of the sub-continent for speech and literacy over the last many centuries.

The problems of the adoption of the Arabo-Persian model which was an alien script for the Indo-Aryan Urdu language were unique and varied; most of them were faced as part of the processes of naturalisation that take place between two contact languages over long periods of history. One of the major problems was in the category of stop sounds, since the Semitic model was somewhat deficient in this respect. This was solved in part earlier, in the Persian language by the addition of symbols for the labial p, palatal č, and velar g (ﭖ ﭺ ﮒ) sounds, since Persian, itself a language of Indo-Iranian stock, possessed these sounds. In Urdu these letters were adopted *en masse* from Persian along with the Persian spirant ž ژ . The main challenge in this category, however, was presented by features of retroflexion and aspiration, which neither Arabic nor Persian possessed. The Urdu language, like Hindi, has three retroflex sounds, two in the stop category, i.e., ṭ ﭦ , and ḍ ڈ , and one in the flap category, i.e., ṛ ڑ . (Hindi has an additional retroflex ṇ ण which is changed to simple n, in common speech.) Different systems were tried for showing retroflexion in the adopted Arabo-Persian orthographical model at different stages of time. As is known, the similar consonantal letters of the Arabo-Persian model are differentiated by placement of one, two or three dots above, below or within the body of the letter. To begin with, in Urdu the retroflexion was indicated by placing four dots on the letters representing the closest simple sounds. The earliest manuscripts of the fourteenth and the fifteenth centuries written in both *Naskhī* and *Nasta'līq* display the use of this device, ﺖ ﺩ ﺭ . But since the placement of four dots was cumbersome and time-consuming, it was later changed by placement of a bar above two dots, e.g., ڗ ڗ ڗ. But even this did not suit the quick movements of the hand, and eventually by the eighteenth century the dots were replaced by a small *toe* mark ٮ placed over the letters, ٹ ڈ ڑ which in the course of time became standardized as a mark of retroflexion in Urdu.

Aspiration was another feature that posed a challenge. The Arabo-Persian model was deficient in this respect too, because neither Arabic nor Persian possessed this feature, whereas aspiration of the complete set of stop sounds has been a distingushing mark of Indo-Aryan speeches. Urdu possesses all the twenty stop sounds, simple as well as their aspirated counterparts. Partial aspiration was also met in the spirant, lateral and nasal categories, and in the flap category aspiration was as common as it was with the stops. Since the borrowed orthographical model lacked any mark for aspiration, the earliest Urdu manuscripts show that in the beginning the aspiration was simply deleted, and aspirated sounds were written as simple sounds. Later the letter *hāe havvaz* ہ was used after the simple letters, such as جہ کہ سہ بہی تہا, but this created confusion because the aspirated stops and the spirant h caused problems of syllable boundary. In the course of time, therefore, the *hāe-do-čashmī* was introduced as the mark of aspiration. Though Urdu, unlike Hindi and Sindhi, did not provide ten independent letters indicative of aspirated sounds, the use of *hāe-do-čashmī* with stop letters, e.g., بھ. بھ. تھ دھ کھ گھ served the purpose. It was economical and has since been standardized.[15]

Another aspect was the provision of adequate letters for the vocalic system of Urdu which is similar to that of Hindi. The Semitic model was mainly consonantal with only three letters for vocalics, e.g., ا و ی. Later Arabic diacritical marks were added to denote the long and short distinctions, e.g., *kasrah*, *fathah*, and *zammah*, but neither Arabic nor Persian had the mid-front /e/ and the mid-back /o/. Since *Alif* is the only pure vocalic letter, all vowel sounds initially are written with the *Alif;*

the ٵ , and ک which stand for /ō/ and /ī/, have a double orthographical function since initially they also occur for semi-vowels /w/ and /y/. The same letters ٯ , and ک were given the still additional responsibility of representing the mid-front /e/ and mid-back /o/ , e.g., ے and ٯ , of course with the help of differentiating diacritical marks of *kasrah* and *zammah*, but these marks were seldom used in general writing. Similarly, the diphthongs /ai/ and /au/ were indicated by the same letters ے and ٯ , by placing the diacritical mark *fathah* on the preceding letter. Thus the vocalic orthographical system of Urdu was an important expansion on the earlier Semitic model, and while based on three basic letters and three diacritical marks, it functioned for the ten vowel sounds. Though marked by economy of effort, and also of space, because it assumes mother tongue acquaintance on the part of the reader, it is somewhat complicated, and creates problems of reading and pronouncing in multi-lingual societies where Urdu is prevalent.

Nasalization is another Indo-Aryan feature which functions significantly at all levels in the Urdu language. This challenge was met by a simple deletion device: dropping the medial dot in the nasal consonantal letter finally. Medially, nasalization of vocalics is not indicated, and is made out by the native speaker from the context, or is marked with a small raised crescent diacritic, ں .

Yet another interesting aspect is the influence of the borrowed orthographical models on the phonology of the recipient languages. The main area of impact was on the spirant category in which both Arabic and Persian are richer than the Indo-Aryan speeches. Urdu in this category naturalised four sounds from the Arabic, e.g., ث ز ح خ , and one from Persian, i.e., ژ . The only other influence is in the stop category, i.e., the uvular ق which came from the Arabic, like the other five sounds, via Persian. Apart from these six letters whose sounds are the distinguishing phonological marks of Urdu amongst all the Indo-Aryan tongues, there is yet another interesting area of influence where some letters of the Arabo-Persian orthography have been accepted which in Urdu have no distinct sounds of their own. This occurred because of the heavy lexical borrowings which necessitated the *en masse* adoption of the Arabo-Persian orthography. In this process while Urdu got six such sounds which were new to the Modern Indo-Aryan, it also had to retain letters which in Urdu did not represent any distinct sounds. They stayed on because of thousands of loans in which they occurred, and have been in common usage, e.g., the fricatives ذ ث ه غ , the phyrangeal ح (ḥ) and the 'emphatics' ص ض ط ظ (ṣ ẓ ṭ ḍ). Though each of these letters represents a distinct sound ṣ ẓ ṭ ḍ in Arabic, in Urdu these were approximated phonologically to the nearest related sound, e.g., ث and ص to س (s); ح to ہ (h); ذ ض and ظ to ز (z); and ط to ت (t). (cf. Chart of Urdu Alphabet). These letters, therefore, form two sets of duplicators, one set of triplicators, and one set of quadruplicators, the knowledge of which is essential in Urdu because they carry a lot of lexical weight and are frequently used. The case of the letter ع a phyrangeal stop ('), and the mark *Hamzah* ء , the glottal catch (ʔ) is different in the sense that both of these have almost lost their consonantal character in Urdu, and instead, are used as vocalic markers. ع is a phyrangeal consonantal, and *Hamzah* is a glottal catch in Arabic, but ع in Urdu functions as a vowel, and is approximated to *Alif.* It occurs for any of the ten Urdu vowels, except for purposes of prosody; whereas *Hamzah* has no phonological function whatsoever in Urdu, and occurs only as an orthographical marker for diphthongs or for conjunct vowels.[16]

The Urdu writing system, therefore, is unique in the sense that it represents three phonological layers, i.e., the indigenous layer of the Indo-Aryan, and the borrowed layers of the Semitic and the Indo-Iranian, and all of these have been moulded into a single phonological system in Urdu. As discussed above, since the borrowed Semitic model was deficient in retroflexion, aspiration, nasalization and vocalics, the Urdu system added three retroflexes, eleven aspirates, and four vocalics, a total of eighteen sounds thus enlarging the borrowed model by about one half. Conversely, the influences worked in the other direction, too. Urdu accepted six new consonantals, and retained seven such consonantal letters which though they had lost their distinct sounds, were lexically functional, thus enlarging Urdu's own phonological-orthographical base by about one-third. All these adaptations and changes give the Urdu language its distinguishing character of moulding the three systems into a single whole, and making it fully functional. The role of the duplicators and triplicators, and the deficiency of vocalic letters, though, create problems of irregular spellings and make learning difficult, yet at the same time, the system is marked by economy of effort and space. It is fully functional, and is used widely in India and Pakistan, not only for mass media, administration, education, and literature, but also for the spread of literacy amongst millions of people.

The figures concerning the spread of Urdu in India and Pakistan are as follows:

India

Status of language	One of the sixteen national languages of the country
Population (1979)	643,896,000[17]
Growth rate	2% per annum
Mother tongue speakers	28,600,428
Male	14,925,238
Female	13,675,190[18]

Provinces	
Uttar Pradesh	9,273,000
Bihar	4,993,000
Maharashtra	3,662,000
Andhra Pradesh	3,300,000
Karnataka	2,600,000
Madhya Pradesh	988,275
Bengal	950,300

Tamil Nadu	759,600
Rajasthan	651,000
Gujarat	581,500[19]

Literacy (based on censuses from the last thirty years)

Census	Number of literate persons per 1,000 persons	Number of literate males per 1,000 males	Number of literate females per 1,000 females
1971	293	395	184
1961	240	344	130
1951	167	249	79

Literacy rate
39.5 per cent (male literacy)

30 per cent (adult literacy)[20]

Pakistan

Status of language	National language of the country
Population (1979)	78,527,000
Growth rate	2.9 per cent per annum
Literacy rate	21 per cent (adults)[21]

3

The adoption of the Arabo-Persian writing model has yet another interesting aspect to it: the symbolism of letters which is widely known in India and Pakistan. Each of the twenty-eight original letters has its numerical value, according to the order of the old Semitic alphabet, i.e., ابجد هوز حطی , and to combine the letters meaningfully in order to count with them to give the date of birth, or death or an important event is quite common (for numerical values of letters see pages 222–223). The early Islamic mysticism knew these correspondences, but it was especially in the Indo-Persian areas that the art of producing a chronogram by quoting a meaningful word or a hemistitch has been practised with incredible skill. In many cases, the reader can understand the date of the completion of a book or a monument from the numerical value of its name. This practice still exists in India and Pakistan.

Annemarie Schimmel has discussed how the letters themselves form an important part of the symbolic language in mystical and profane poetry and prose, and some of them are charged with religious qualities:[22]

> *Alif*, the first letter, a straight line, numerical value 1, is the *chiffre* for the graceful slim stature of the beloved but at the same time, and much more, the symbol of *Allah*, the One God, free from every worldy quality, the Absolute Unity. The poets often claim that they have learnt only the *Alif* which is better than the whole alphabet: to know God's uniqueness and unity is more important than to know the manifold things visible in the world. Besides, in religious languages, the *mīm* ﻣ, a small round ring or almost dot, numerical value 40, is the abbreviation of Muhammad, recipient of the Divine word; the wordplay of the *Ḥadīth Qudsī* (Divine revelation outside the Qur'an: "I am *Aḥmad without mīm*", namely *Aḥad*, "One") is commonplace with the mystics, hinting at the difference of only one *mīm* between *Aḥmad*/Muhammad and *Aḥad*/One. The numerical value of 40 of the *mīm* being considered to allude to the 40 degrees of emanations which lie between God and man . . . The *bā* ﺏ, second letter of the alphabet, with which the *basmala* begins and which forms, thus, the beginning of the Qur'an, is considered the first manifestation of Divine wisdom, the coming into the world of the Absolute; and in its dot all the mysteries of creation are contained . . . Many letters, like *dāl* ﺩ , *jīm*

ح , lām ل , qāf ق ,have been compared to the curls or tresses of beloved, the *nūn* ن to a curl with a mole, the *sīn* س to his teeth, the *sād* ص or *'ain* ع to his almond-shaped eyes . . . *'Ain* ع again plays an important role in Shia piety as the letter of Ali the friend of God. As to the *he* ﮦ which has been likened by poets sometimes to the weeping eyes . . . The *lām-alif* لا , essentially ligature, has often symbolized close union for good or bad purposes. To write 11 instead of *Huwa*, 'He', is as common as to abbreviate the *basmala* according to its numerical value (= 786).

The writing commands a great respect in the Urdu milieu not only among the literate, but even more so among the illiterate masses. A piece of paper on which something is scribed is handled carefully because one is afraid of stepping on or otherwise soiling a religious saying or the Divine name.[23]

The Urdu language is one of the finest by-products of the Indo-Muslim culture serving millions of people in India, Pakistan, and the Sheikhdoms of the Persian Gulf. Aesthetically it is an attractive speech, and the tremendous popularity it enjoys might have something to do with its enriched three-tier phonological system with an Indo-Aryan base and a Semitic and Iranian super-structure. Basically Prakritic, and having naturalised much of the Arabo-Persian lexicon, the Urdu language possesses features of retroflexion, aspiration and nasalization for which the original Semitic orthographical models had to be enlarged. The influences worked in the other direction too, and in turn the Urdu phonology was enriched by many new sounds, some letters had to be changed to their nearest sounds or altogether merged. Urdu thus promoted a synthetic model presenting a blend of the Semitic consonantal and Prakritic vocalic systems. Presently, in its standardized form which is used in India, and Pakistan where Urdu is the national language, this synthetic model is fully functional for millions of people for everyday communication, writing, and for literary expression.

Table 1 : Arabic Alphabet

Sign	Name	Equivalent	Sign	Name	Equivalent
ا	alif	'(*)	ض	dād	d
ب	bā	b	ط	tā	t
ت	tā	t	ظ	zā	z
ث	thā	th	ع	'an	'(+)
ج	jīm	j	غ	ghain	gh
ح	hā	h	ف	fā	f
خ	khā	kh	ق	qāf	q
د	dāl	d	ک	kāf	k
ذ	dhāl	dh	ل	lām	l
ر	rā	r	م	mīm	m
ز	zā	z	ن	nūn	n
س	sīn	s	ه	hā	h
ش	shīn	sh	و	wāw	w
ص	sād	s	ي	yā	y

* A glottal stop when used as a sign of vowel length; represented by a macron when used as a sign of vowel length.

+ A pharyngeal sound.

Table 2 : Urdu Alphabet

Sign	Name	Equivalent	Sign	Name	Equivalent
ا	alif	ā(a)	ص	ṣuad	ṣ
ب	be	b	ض	ẓuad	ẓ
پ	pe	p	ط	ṭoe	ṭ
ت	te	t	ظ	ẓoe	ẓ
ٹ	ṭe	ṭ	ع	'ain	'(*)
ث	ṣe	ṣ	غ	ghain	gh
ج	jīm	j	ف	fe	f
چ	če	č	ق	qāf	q
ح	he	ḥ	ک	kāf	k
خ	khe	x(kh)	گ	gāf	g
د	dāl	d	ل	lām	l
ڈ	ḍāl	ḍ	م	mīm	m
ذ	zāl	z	ن	nūn	n
ر	re	r	و	wāo	o(ū, au)
ڑ	ṛe	ṛ	ہ	he	h
ز	ze	z	ھ	hāe do čašmī	aspiration
ژ	že	ž	٬	hamzah	conjunct-vowel marker
س	sin	s	ی	chōṭī ye	ī
ش	šin	š (sh)	ے	baṛī ye	e (ai)

Notes

1. B.F.C. Atkinson in *Encyclopaedia Britannica*, p. 663.

2. Joshua Whatmough in *Encyclopaedia Britannica*, p. 668.

3. Annemarie Schimmel, *Islamic Calligraphy*, p. 4.

4. Y.H. Safadi, *Islamic Calligraphy*, p. 7.

5. *Ibid.*, p. 1.

6. Schimmel, *Islamic Calligraphy*, p. 5.

7. Muhammad Hamidullah, *Urdū Daira-e-Ma'ārif-e-Islāmiya*, p. 962.

8. *Ibid.*, p. 964.

9. Safadi, *Islamic Calligraphy*, p. 17.

10. Schimmel, *Islamic Calligraphy*, pp. 7-9; Muhammad Is-haq Siddiqi, *Fann-e-Tahrīr kī Tārīkh*, pp. 245-261.

11. Schimmel, *Islamic Calligraphy*, p. 5.

12. Ihteramuddin Ahmad Shaghil Usmani, *Sahīfa-e-Khush-Nawīsān*, pp. 45-49.

13. Hamidullah, *Urdū Daira-e-Ma'ārif-e-Islāmiya*, p. 964.

14. *Ibid.*, p. 967.

15. Gopi Chand Narang, *Imlā Nāmah*, pp. 13-22.

16. *Ibid.*, pp. 63-69.

17. *Third World*, Section on India.

18. R.C. Nigam, *Census of India 1971*, Monograph 10, p. 252.

19. *Ibid.*, p. 333.

20. D. Natarajan, *Census of India 1971*, Monograph 9, p. ii, v.

21. *Third World*, Section on Pakistan.

22. Schimmel, *Islamic Calligraphy*, pp. 12-14.

23. *Ibid.*, p. 14.

Works Cited

Muhammad Hamidullah, "Khatt", in *Urdu Dāira-e-Ma'ārif-e-Islāmiyah*, Punjab University Lahore, Vol. 8, 1973, pp. 960-967.

Gopi Chand Narang, ed., *Imlā Nāmah*, (Recommendations for standardisation of Urdu script), New Delhi 1974; 2nd ed. 1990.

D. Natarajan, ed., *Census of India 1971*, Extracts from the All India Census Reports on Literacy, Monograph No. 9, New Delhi 1972.

R.C. Nigam, *Census of India 1971*, Language Handbook on Mother Tongues in Census, Monograph No. 10, New Delhi 1972.

Y.H. Safadi, *Islamic Calligraphy*, London 1978.

Annemarie Schimmel, *Islamic Calligraphy*, (in the series: Iconography of Religions), Leiden 1970.

Ihteramuddin Ahmad Shaghil Usmani, *Sahīfa-e-Khush-Nawīsān*, Aligarh 1963.

Muhammad Is-haq Siddiqi, *Fann-e-Tahrīr kī Tārīkh*, Aligarh 1962.

Third World 1982, South Publications, London 1981.

B.F.C. Atkinson, Joshua Whatmough, "Alphabet" in *Encyclopaedia Britannica*, Chicago 1970, Vol. I, pp. 662-669.

Index